"A beautiful book. A dialogical exploration of the human condition drawing on science, philosophy, psychology, poetry, art, spirituality – which is to say, open, un-dogmatic, and resourceful. One feels appreciation of life's depths and surfaces, one's own life and life of the Other. The writing is down to earth, personal and accessible, drawing on a rich background of human struggle, backslides and growth. We are born all life long and the Work of the Other furthers contact with the Work of Being."

Michael Eigen, *author of* The Challenge of Being Human, The Sensitive Self, The Psychoanalytic Mystic *and* Contact with the Depths.

"This book is an intriguing journey in search of our basic experience of otherness in its various manifestations. There is a beautiful variance of voices that come together in a space of mutual enhancement. The concepts of dialogue and of trueness are dealt with in a unique fashion, in which the writers actively follow each other in the here and now. They thus inspire a hope that we as therapists and as human beings can rediscover our natural urge and curiosity for relations, for opening to the unknown, for co-creating."

Ofra Eshel, *faculty, training and supervising analyst, Israel Psychoanalytic Society and Institute, and honorary member of the New Center for Psychoanalysis, Los Angeles; author of* The Emergence of Analytic Oneness: Into the Heart of Psychoanalysis

"We can no more change our heartfelt commitments by talking to ourselves, than by defensively reiterating them in divisive dispute. But conversing with trusted others can. Glimpsing ourselves reflected in their caring eyes, enables the kind of potentially transformative self- distancing we can never achieve alone. *Relational Conversations* explores this epitome of relational psychology with uncanny insight, first by taking the psychotherapeutic dialogical interaction between analyst and patient as paradigmatic of true otherness, and by reflecting on it in a series of truly transformative non-Socratic dialogues."

Menachem Fisch, *professor emeritus of history and philosophy of science, director of the Center for Religious and Interreligious Studies at Tel Aviv University, and author of* The View from Within: Normativity and the Limits of Self-Criticism; Creatively Undecided: Toward a History and Philosophy of Scientific Agency; Dialogues of Reason: Science, Politics, Religion *and other books*

Relational Conversations on Meeting and Becoming

The Birth of a True Other

Demonstrating a relational, dialogic way of thinking and writing, this book offers an innovative perspective on the human potential for intersubjective engagement and on the nature of true encounter.

The authors engage in creative, associative dialogues and trialogues inspired by psychoanalysis and Buddhism, poetry and religion, theory and case studies, academic and free styles of writing – each enriching the other. Reflecting on the essence of relating, they convey a flow between inner, private reveries and shared ones, and between individual expressions of thought and evolvements of newly born thirds. Through this interdisciplinary, experimental setting, the authors explore the possibility to reach truths and meanings that each individual would not have achieved on their own.

Offering new concepts and formulations that may nourish psychotherapists' thought and be usefully implemented in their practice, this book presents a pressingly unique and essential viewpoint for psychoanalysts and psychoanalytic psychotherapists in training and in practice.

Michal Barnea-Astrog is a writer, senior Hakomi trainer and therapist in private practice. She teaches seminars on the dialogue between psychoanalysis and Buddhism and is the founder and head of the Three-Year Hakomi Training in Israel. She is the author of *Carved by Experience: Vipassana, Psychoanalysis and the Mind Investigating Itself* (Karnac, 2017), *Psychoanalytic and Buddhist Reflections on Gentleness: Sensitivity, Fear and the Drive Towards Truth* (Routledge, 2019), and the novels *Migration* (Pardess, 2021) and *The Coming Years* (Shta'yim, 2022).

Mitchel Becker is a clinical psychologist in private practice. He teaches courses on the work of Wilfred Bion at the Psychotherapy Programs of Bar Ilan University. Mitchel's articles have been published in many psychoanalytic journals. He has written chapters in *The Comprehensive Handbook of Psychotherapy Integration* (eds. Stricker & Gold, Springer, 1993) and in *The Spiritual Psyche in Psychotherapy* (eds. Pearson & Marllo, Routledge, 2021).

RELATIONAL PERSPECTIVES BOOK SERIES

ADRIENNE HARRIS, STEVEN KUCHUCK & EYAL ROZMARIN
Series Editors

STEPHEN MITCHELL
Founding Editor

LEWIS ARON
Editor Emeritus

The Relational Perspectives Book Series (RPBS) publishes books that grow out of or contribute to the relational tradition in contemporary psychoanalysis. The term *relational psychoanalysis* was first used by Greenberg and Mitchell[1] to bridge the traditions of interpersonal relations, as developed within interpersonal psychoanalysis and object relations, as developed within contemporary British theory. But, under the seminal work of the late Stephen A. Mitchell, the term *relational psychoanalysis* grew and began to accrue to itself many other influences and developments. Various tributaries—interpersonal psychoanalysis, object relations theory, self psychology, empirical infancy research, feminism, queer theory, sociocultural studies and elements of contemporary Freudian and Kleinian thought—flow into this tradition, which understands relational configurations between self and others, both real and fantasied, as the primary subject of psychoanalytic investigation.

We refer to the relational tradition, rather than to a relational school, to highlight that we are identifying a trend, a tendency within contemporary psychoanalysis, not a more formally organized or coherent school or system of beliefs. Our use of the term *relational* signifies a dimension of theory and practice that has become salient across the wide spectrum of contemporary psychoanalysis. Now under the editorial supervision of Adrienne Harris, Steven Kuchuck and Eyal Rozmarin, the Relational Perspectives Book Series originated in 1990 under the editorial eye of the late Stephen A. Mitchell. Mitchell was the most prolific and influential of the originators of the relational tradition. Committed to dialogue among psychoanalysts, he abhorred the authoritarianism that dictated adherence to a rigid set of beliefs or technical restrictions. He championed open discussion, comparative and integrative approaches, and promoted new voices across the generations. Mitchell was later joined by the late Lewis Aron, also a visionary and influential writer, teacher and leading thinker in relational psychoanalysis.

Included in the Relational Perspectives Book Series are authors and works that come from within the relational tradition, those that extend and develop that tradition, and works that critique relational approaches or compare and contrast them with alternative points of view. The series includes our most distinguished senior psychoanalysts, along with younger contributors who bring fresh vision. Our aim is to enable a deepening of relational thinking while reaching across disciplinary and social boundaries in order to foster an inclusive and international literature.

A full list of titles in this series is available at https://www.routledge.com/Relational-Perspectives-Book-Series/book-series/LEARPBS.

1 Greenberg, J. & Mitchell, S. (1983). *Object relations in psychoanalytic theory.* Cambridge, MA: Harvard University Press.

Relational Conversations on Meeting and Becoming

The Birth of a True Other

Edited by Michal Barnea-Astrog
and Mitchel Becker

Routledge
Taylor & Francis Group

LONDON AND NEW YORK

Cover image: Michal Helfman, untitled.

First published 2023
by Routledge
4 Park Square, Milton Park, Abingdon, Oxon OX14 4RN

and by Routledge
605 Third Avenue, New York, NY 10158

Routledge is an imprint of the Taylor & Francis Group, an informa business

British Library Cataloguing-in-Publication Data
A catalogue record for this book is available from the British Library

Library of Congress Cataloging-in-Publication Data
Names: Barnea-Astrog, Michal, editor. | Becker, Mitchel, 1957- editor.
Title: Relational conversations on meeting and becoming : the birth of a
    true other / edited by Michal Barnea-Astrog and Mitchel Becker.
Description: Milton Park, Abingdon, Oxon ; New York, NY : Routledge,
    2023. | Includes bibliographical references and index.
Identifiers: LCCN 2022028255 (print) | LCCN 2022028256 (ebook) |
    ISBN 9781032351407 (hardback) | ISBN 9781032351414 (paperback) |
    ISBN 9781003325499 (ebook)
Subjects: LCSH: Psychoanalysis. | Dialogue analysis. | Other (Philosophy)
Classification: LCC BF175.4.P45 R45 2023 (print) | LCC BF175.4.P45
    (ebook) | DDC 150.19/5—dc23/eng/20220629
LC record available at https://lccn.loc.gov/2022028255
LC ebook record available at https://lccn.loc.gov/2022028256

Every effort has been made to contact copyright-holders. Please advise the publisher of any errors or omissions, and these will be corrected in subsequent editions.

ISBN: 978-1-032-35140-7 (hbk)
ISBN: 978-1-032-35141-4 (pbk)
ISBN: 978-1-003-32549-9 (ebk)

DOI: 10.4324/9781003325499

Typeset in Times New Roman
by KnowledgeWorks Global Ltd.

To all those who seek true dialogue

Contents

Acknowledgements

We are in deep gratitude to our many teachers, colleagues, students and patients, who have entered into dialogue with us and have afforded us to cultivate a capacity and place to ponder.

We want to thank the Relational Perspectives Book Series' Editors, Adrien Harris, Steven Kuchuck and Eyal Rozmarin, for supporting our book. We express our immense appreciation and wonder to our co-writers, who inspired us to create beyond what we could have ever created alone.

Finally, we thank with love those friends and family, who offer us shelter from the storm.

Contributors

Hagit Aharoni is a training and supervising psychoanalyst and faculty member of the Israel Psychoanalytic Society. She is a faculty member of the Israel Winnicott Center, where she is also head of "Sha'atnez": A platform for multi-disciplinary thinking. She is the author of several interdisciplinary publications related to the interface between psychoanalysis and literature. She is the co-editor and translator into Hebrew of a number of psychoanalytic books, including works by Bion, Ogden and Tustin. She works in private practice in Tel Aviv.

Michal Barnea-Astrog is a writer, senior Hakomi trainer and therapist in private practice. She teaches seminars on the dialogue between psychoanalysis and Buddhism and is the founder and head of the Three-Year Hakomi Training in Israel. She is the author of *Carved by Experience: Vipassana, Psychoanalysis, and the Mind Investigating Itself* (Karnac, 2017), *Psychoanalytic and Buddhist Reflections on Gentleness: Sensitivity, Fear, and the Drive Towards Truth* (Routledge, 2019), and the novels (published in Hebrew) *Migration* (Pardess, 2021) and *The Coming Years* (Shta'yim, 2022).

Mitchel Becker is a clinical psychologist in private practice. He teaches courses on the work of Wilfred Bion at the Psychotherapy Programs of Bar Ilan University. Mitchel's articles have been published in many psychoanalytic journals. He has written chapters in *The Comprehensive Handbook of Psychotherapy Integration* (eds. Stricker & Gold, Springer, 1993) and in *The Spiritual Psyche in Psychotherapy* (eds. Pearson & Marllo, Routledge, 2021).

Irene Bleier Lewenhoff is a poet, born and raised in Uruguay and living in Israel. She has published six poetry books: three in Spanish (published in Uruguay) – *Ustedes* (Ediciones Imaginarias, 1996), *Identidad* (Trilce, 2000) and *Algunas sombras arboles* (Yauguru, 2009) – and three in Hebrew (all published in Israel by Pardes) – *Mother Tongue* (2012), *Broken Language* (2015) and *End of Shift* (2019). Irene's poems have been published, among others, in *Helicon Poetry Periodical* (2011, 2019) and in *A Sea of Voices: Women Poets in Israel* (edited by Marjorie Agosin, Sherman Asher Pub. Santa Fe, 2008). She is also a senior certified nurse, specializing in Group Therapy, Risk Management and improving Quality of Medical Practice.

Hilit Brodsky-Erel is a training and supervising psychoanalyst at the Israeli Psychoanalytic Society, a faculty member and head of The Program for Psychoanalytic Psychotherapy at the school of Social Work of Bar Ilan University, and a lecturer in the Program of Psychotherapy at the Faculty of Medicine, Tel Aviv University. She is recipient of the Hayman Prize of the International Psychoanalytic Association and of the Psychoanalytic Training Today Award of the IPA. Dr. Brodsky is the editor of *Criss-Cross: On Art, Culture and Psychoanalysis* (Resling, 2020).

Paul R. Fleischman was chief resident in psychiatry at Yale University, practised psychiatry for thirty-five years, and has been honoured by the American Psychiatry Association with the Oskar Pfister Award for being "… an outstanding contributor to the humanistic and spiritual side of psychiatric and medical issues." He is the author of numerous popular and professional articles and books, including, *The Healing Spirit: Religious Issues in Psychotherapy; Cultivating Inner Peace; Karma and Chaos: Collected and New Essays on Vipassana Meditation; and Wonder: When and Why the World Appears Radiant*. He has given over one hundred and fifty talks at universities and other venues in the United States and around the world including Harvard, Yale, MIT, Tufts, Chicago, Stanford, Google and many others.

Rina Lazar is a clinical psychologist in private practice in Tel Aviv. She is a senior teacher and supervisor in the Core Program – the Relational Track, and the Ph.D. Studies in Psychoanalysis and its Interfaces, in the Program of Psychotherapy at the Faculty of Medicine, Tel Aviv University. She is a member of the International Association of Relational Psychoanalysis and Psychotherapy

(IARPP) and the first chairperson of the Israeli chapter of the IARPP. Rina is the editor of *Talking about Evil* (Routledge, 2017) and co-editor of *Desire and The Blind Spot* (Hakibutz Hameuchad, 2005, 2007). She has published papers in various psychoanalytic journals on topics such as psychoanalysis versus psychotherapy; repetition compulsion; subject, subjectivity and intersubjectivity; hatred; the dead mother; intimacy; mourning and melancholy; sacrifice and abuse.

Clara Mucci is a full professor of Dynamic Psychology at the University of Bergamo, Italy, and a psychoanalyst in private practice (trained at SIPP, Società Italiana Psicoterapia Psicoanalitica). She served as a full professor of English Literature and Shakespearean Drama until 2012. Clara is a member of SIPP, IARPP and APA (Division 39), and supervisor and trainer at SIPeP-Sandor Ferenczi. Professor Mucci is the author of various monographs on Shakespeare and psychoanalytic theory. Her major publications in English are *Beyond Individual and Collective Trauma* (Karnac, 2013; Routledge, 2017), *Borderline Bodies: Affect Regulation Therapy for Personality Disorders* (Norton, 2018), and *Resilience and Survival: Understanding and Healing Intergenerational Trauma* (Confer, 2022). She is the co-editor, with G. Craparo, of *Unrepressed Unconscious, Implicit Memory and Clinical Work* (Karnac, 2017). She lectures extensively in Europe and in the US and is a teacher and supervisor in several training schools of psychoanalysis and psychotherapy, in Italy, England and the US.

Yorai Sella is a clinical psychologist, a humanistic psychotherapist and a member of the Tel Aviv Institute for Contemporary Psychoanalysis. He founded Maga School of Zen-Shiatsu and co-directs Dmut Institute for Presence and Vitality Psychotherapy. He teaches in the Self Psychology post-graduate track at the Faculty of Medicine, Tel Aviv University. He is a member of the conceptual-development committee of the Integrative Psychiatry service, Ha'emek Hospital and a founding-member of The Israeli Association for Interdisciplinary Psychotherapy. Dr. Sella has published fiction, poetry and professional publications, including *From Dualism to Oneness in Psychoanalysis: a Zen Perspective on the Mind-Body Question* (Routledge, 2018). He has been practising Tai-Chi and martial arts for the past 35 years and is a student of Zen-Buddhism.

Foreword

In every living moment, an encounter takes place: body and mind meet the elements of reality, inner and outer, material and mental, hidden or overt. This is an encounter between the absorbing and the absorbed, and the psyche relates to it in ways that reflect its unique characteristics, inclinations, history of experiences and motivational investments. The features and contents of these encounters and the manner in which the psyche relates to them are the substances and cement creating and evolving one's world. The meeting of psyches is the meeting of worlds.

A meeting of worlds means transformation has occurred, an incessant change. What was shall never return. It may become frozen in time, or exiled and lost in space, or be preserved or develop and grow – but either way, the contact has made its mark and left its effect.

What makes the encounter fertile? What makes a dialogue growth enhancing? When or under what conditions does the meeting bring us closer to ourselves and to the other, and when does it create distance, disconnect and alienate? When does the meeting take us beyond self-hood and beyond the duality of an I and a You, and when does it cause us to constrict our sense of self, disengage from the other and create a confrontational or violent stance towards the other and towards experience?

In this book, we invited a few writers to creatively meet these questions through associative dialogues and trialogues. Curious to explore both contents and modes of relating, we encouraged a flow between inner, private reveries and shared ones, between predetermined courses and states of spontaneity and improvisation, and between individual expressions of thought and evolvements of creative thirds, emerging from both conversants and belonging to neither. We found ourselves, with each text and co-writer, engaged in unexpected communications: communications that take place in heart and mind, filter to the written page, and from there reach and touch the other in their new shape.

In each part of the book, every text is an open-ended, open-handed stream of thought, inviting the next one to follow it. Through this experimental setting we explore – in real time and in hindsight reflection – the capacity to truly meet. We examine the encounter's qualities, its enhancers and inhibiters, and its influence on the sense of self and sense of reality, on the relation and on the co-created.

Our Story

It has been about three years since we, Michal and Mitchel, met to discuss the possibility of writing together. A mutual friend, Boaz Shalgi, was the matchmaker. We both shared a penchant for seeing how different orientations interact and create an exciting dialectic. The dialectics of Buddhism and psychoanalysis, as well as that of experiential psychotherapy and psychoanalytic thought for Michal; and the dialectics of Judaism and psychoanalysis, of self-psychology, object relations and relational psychoanalysis, as well as a dialectic method of psychotherapy integrating psychoanalysis with cognitive-behavioural and family therapy for Mitchel – were subject matters of our investigation and writing for years prior to our encounter.

Our discussion went from the personal to the universal as we shared stories to see if there would be a valuable place of meeting between us. Suddenly it became clear that we were both, in genuinely different ways, deeply interested in the experience of relation, and particularly in the nature of encounter and dialogue – both in the therapeutic context and beyond it.

Michal was looking for a partner for "dialogic writing," a kind of writing where one person's text evokes in the other thoughts, feelings, ideas and experiences that inspire him to write a new text that he wouldn't have written otherwise. She wanted to engage in a responsive, mutually generative way of writing – as a means for relation and for creation, and as an experiment in surrendering to taking in the other's voice and words, letting them move things around and following whatever new words they bring along. Mitchel was long engaged in an exploration of the relational turn that relational psychoanalysis brought to psychoanalysis. He was investigating what he called the "True Other," a sort of complementary counterpart of Winnicott's True Self as well as a descendent of Bion's O or absolute truth. This term he began to revere and to formulate some 10 years ago, in a paper he wrote for the 2011 International Association for Relational Psychoanalysis and Psychotherapy conference in Madrid (Becker, In Press), and which, in the course of co-writing this book (how appropriate!) he fully defined for the first time.

We wondered how our writing can reflect on dialogue in a manner that would bring its essence to life. Thus was formed our idea of constructing a book that will allow us to dialogically write about dialogue: a relational way of writing about relation. In the format we imagined, the act of conversing would reflect and hopefully reveal the unique process of dialogue. Of course, patient and therapist are always attempting to create dialogue. But now, in addition, we sought to see how therapists, thinkers and poets create and grow from dialogue in the communicative mode of writing. It took some time to form. It took some time before we were able to clearly communicate to ourselves and to others what we are actually trying to do. Gradually, while conversing and writing, we allowed the full structure and unique qualities of this book to emerge on their own.

Within the vast world of relation, there are many dichotomous conceptualizations: subject-object vs. subject-subject, part-objects vs. whole-objects, complementarity vs. intersubjectivity, and monadic vs. dyadic. We began to see our personal preferences as possessing difference as well as sameness. Michal's language, born of a dialectic between Buddhist and psychoanalytic traditions, as well as the experiential approach of the Refined Hakomi Method to human experience and to human relations, often speaks of self-referential, projective modes of attention and perception vs. non-fixated, fluid modes, which depart the self as an overpowering focal point. Mitchel's language, drawn from a deep respect for integrating theories and traditions and viewing the dialectic as a source of endless change and movement, speaks in the Buberian terms of I-It and I-You. Here are a few words about each of these views, and how they interact to form a living, breathing, arms-reaching fabric, through our continuous dialogue.

The Fabric of Perspectives: Voices Interact

A meeting moment, in Michal's language, necessarily occurs in present time. But one meeting moment follows the next: the moments of feeling or thought conception, emerging from the mists of the unknown and gathering into a definable content; the moments of articulation; the moments of re-reading, re-writing, reflecting; the moments when the eyes of the other meet the text, leading to reflecting and responding; the moments when the other's response touch us and leave its effects.

As therapists, writers and teachers – and as human beings aspiring to thoughtful and ethical existence – we're always committed to looking inward, and to looking back and ahead: we look inwards to examine our own experiences at the moments of meeting, our own reactions and motivations; we look back at what was done and how it came to be, examining our apparent or hidden part in it; and we look ahead with the intention to navigate our course of action in routs that may lead to meaningful, beneficial, worthy destinations. So we are dedicated to past-to-future self-reflection; but at the same time, we are dedicated to the selfless flow of moment-to-moment becoming. We do our best, again and again, to relinquish memory, desire and the urgent need to grasp, to control and even to understand. How do these two movements coincide, then?

Imagine a sort of an asymmetric star-like course of mental activity, where the attentional investment is located within the sense of self, and from there it goes out to meet any external or internal object, any "other" – someone's figure, someone's gaze, voice, words or state; any bodily experience, idea, past memory or thought of the future; any other event in space and time, in fact – and once it has met it, goes immediately back to the old self-port. It returns different than it was at the moment of departure, of course. It cannot evade the influence of the meeting, the effect of the touch of whatever was met. Yet it prefers returning than moving on: it feels safer in the supposedly familiar self-sense. It adheres to it. It keeps getting sucked back. Yes, so and so happened, but now I'm back home. And from there I'll go out again – a split of a second from now, and tomorrow, and the day after – to meet the next occurrences. This is the mondain, conventional manner of relating, which Freud (1901b), in a sense, has captured so beautifully in the phrase "continuous current of 'personal reference'," and described in the following words:

> It is as if I were obliged to compare everything I hear about other people with myself; as if my personal complexes were put on the alert whenever another person is brought to my notice. This cannot possibly be an individual peculiarity of my own: it must rather contain an indication of the way in which we understand 'something other than ourself' in general.

(pp. 24–25)

In this normal manner of relating, then, the self and the self's inclinations are a sort of magnetic reference point (Barnea-Astrog, 2017) against which everything is examined and to which everything returns.

Now imagine another course of mental activity that isn't compelled to constantly go back. It meets, it feels, it senses, it is aware of experience. It is affected and recreated. Then it goes out to the next moment of meeting from the new place in which it had found itself, moving along with whatever it brings. It follows what is, what becomes, without clinging to what was and to what was actually or falsely known. It rides the waves of experience and of encounter with much commitment to truth and to knowledge, to scrupulous self-reflection – but with no "memory and desire," without holding on.

Of course, this intimately non-grasping following movement is not our default mode, and achieving it is not obvious at all. It requires sufficient trust, curiosity and freedom. It requires them at the same time as it generates them. It takes us into new territories, to unexpected acquaintances, forms of relatedness and communication, experiences and states. The line goes on, there's a continuity; but it is the continuity of flow and linkage, not of solidity and adherence.

In this mode, which is of course temporary, comes and goes – one doesn't go back because one accepts the fact that the self of the past and the other of the past and the meeting moment of the past are not there anymore to come back to. One also does not contract in anxiety nor collapse in despair in the face of the loss that occurs every moment – since there's enough hunger for reality, enough capacity to love, enough F in O.

In parallel to Michal's above-mentioned relational dialectic, Mitchel has written on the dialectic between the monadic and intersubjective modes of being (Becker & Shalgi, 2006), on the capacity to play (Becker & Shalgi 2005), to imagine, to dream and to engage in reverie and in projective identification. As it evolved, Mitchel's work became a synthesis of Winnicott's ideas about the True Self and the use of an object, Bion's concepts of linking and O, and Buber's dialectic of I-IT and I-You. In constructing a composite view of their thinking, relating is seen as alternating between an interaction with an object, a thing and a non-vital "beta" substance – and a form of encounter in which the link is one of passion, vitality and truth, where a transcendental becoming transpires.

Buber (1923) writes:

> Whoever says You does not have something for his object. For wherever there is something there is also another something; every It borders on other Its; It is only by virtue on bordering on others. But where You is said there is no something. You has no borders. Whoever says You does not have something; he has nothing. But he stands in relation.
>
> (p. 55)

Psychoanalytic literature has always honoured the dictum "know thyself" and the sense that there is a True Self. Becoming aware of that True Self was always a crucial aspect of therapy and certainly an incredible challenge to achieve. For Mitchel, a natural outgrowth of Relational Psychoanalysis is the understanding that the existence of a True Self meant that there also exists a True Other. The first chapter of this book attempts to describe the phenomenon of True Other. For now, we will suffice by saying that in line with Buber's nearly mystical vision of the I-You encounter, the apprehending of a True Other is a frighteningly difficult mission. Discovering the other is most assuredly a long and arduous journey – a journey which, in a sense, will never be complete.

And yet, not meeting a True Other, in Mitchel's language, would be tantamount to someone's passing by the burning bush and taking no notice. The most basic and meaningful truths are infinite and are always present and potentially available to be encountered by the psyche. Our capacity to contain and digest the truth of relation is determined to a large extent by our capacity to bear frustration, pain, disappointment and hurt. We therefore consistently and significantly miss the smile, the *hineni* (the biblical "here am I" in the face of truth, of G-d), and the unmediated aesthetic experiences in our lives. The event is most assuredly mechanically registered, as in the form of undigested beta material; but the psyche takes in no nourishment. Is this not everyone's quiet tragedy, and they know not why they sense themselves empty and alone?

The further we got in our joint journey, the more we discovered how our different perceptions of experience are mutually enhancing. The "magnetic self-reference point" that Michal discusses leads to, in Mitchel's language, a missing out on life due to an incapacity to take in a truth in one's world – a missing of the burning bush. The self maintains the status quo by clinging to the magnetic field, which is the crystallized self-representation and what about the other?

Gradually, it became almost tangible to us that an other is the crucial element to make a transcendence of the fixated self-reference point a possibility. The eyes of the other are the road map of one's self, and the True Other is one's companion on the many roads to true knowledge of one's own nature and interconnectedness with the world. In that meeting with a True Other, there may also be a co-existent, constant verbal and non-verbal "commenting," approving or disapproving. But that is not of importance. What is paramount is a loving relation and an actual learning experience, which afford the couple an innate freedom to take the real and passionate path of growth. This growth is a direct expression of the I-You relation; and the I-You relation entails a fluid state of following, of openness to spontaneous becoming, of no narcissistic desire nor grasping for understanding, of surrender to the relation as it unfolds.

We humans who struggle with the issues of intimacy, dependence and vulnerability are fully aware of the many hindrances presented by our social world to those who seek a place in which to flourish together. Our world seems to be an endless attack on sincerity, authenticity, true love and intimacy. Sometimes the conditions seem to be utterly adversarial to the I-You encounter.

In this book, we invite you to ponder the meaning of a true encounter with one's self and with an other. We have no desire to tie down this encounter to a definitory essence, but rather, a wish to be able to "name it" when it arrives, and perhaps sense the intimately transcendental moment. You are welcome to follow the different lines of thought, voices, tones and hues offered by the writers. To go and return in a star-like self-reference guided movement, or, whenever possible, to leave it behind for a while and move along. You are welcome to dwell in the spaces, use the suggested links, protest any lack and create your own. We offer our deep gratitude for true otherness in its many forms.

Chapters Outline

Mitchel opens the **first dialogue** of this book by describing the two separate and very different processes of Adam and Eve's creation. These two creations, he suggests, are two typologies of the human's experience of being; and when considered together, they form an existential dialectic between a need for mastery and a need to learn, between certainty and uncertainty, between a wish to cope and to order and a seeking the unknown, and between a being innately social and essentially lonely.

Mitchel portrays the story of creation as representing the human's search for dialogue between these inherently contradictory aspects of human existence and its expression in relationships. This crucial dialogue takes place on the Sabbath, a metaphorical day of rest or a Winnicottian transitional space, where the dialectics of our existence become alive. From this position, the concept True Other is drawn and defined. Our most basic need for and fear of love is then described.

In her dialogue with Mitchel's paper, Rina examines our supposedly most intimate relation – the one between our bodies, our language and ourselves. Rina sees this complex partnership as a relation between "intimate strangers" and explores it through the experience of illness and that of the transgender patient. She sees these themes as cardinal to motherhood in large and to our "mothering" (caringminding) our bodies in particular. Eve's trespassing God's place (what she calls creationism) is, in this view, a central pole in our dealing with our bodies as a strange intimate other in times of disease and in the process of transforming our gender. Themes of confrontation, creation and protest are inevitable ingredients of these life events, where our bodies are sensed as either a "primeval matter," as "the clay in the potter's hand" (Jeremiah, 18:6), or as a "finished product," a datum, a kind of "dead end." The theme of God is then conceptualized as the Place[1] humans construct while looking for our psychic home on earth – the one that would fit our body, soul and heart.

Mitchel, in response to Rina, continues their tumultuous search for the other by exploring the issues of me-ness as originally conceived by Sullivan, Good-me, Bad-me and Not-me. These Me's are senses of self as co-created between the self and significant others. We seek the Other in order to nourish our soul, and yet both I and You are limited to how much otherness each soul can bear. These limitations stem from the profound fears of Not-me, of shame, of too-muchness and of total abandonment. Mitchel ends this chapter with the wished-for joy of sensing with no shame the eyes of a True Other as they see all of our Me's.

In our **first "associative trialogue"**, a poet is invited to meet her quest for you-ness as a writer. Irene delves into the basic essence of her writing, of her desire and need to write and be heard. She ponders the meaning of her attempting to touch the reader. She contemplates the dialectic between a seeking of truth and the fear of a defensive falseness. How does her search become beyond the self? How do our many fears conquer the creative spirit? Irene expresses her love and deep respect of "the word" as the representative of our humanity.

Michal and Mitchel each find themselves responding by contemplating the meanings of pining for an essential, true and perhaps primitive link. Michal suggests that the familiar, habitual and automatic are actually an unknown disguised as known. She offers a vignette to show how this can be handled therapeutically with sympathetic curiosity rather than suspicion. She journeys through her own poetic voice and the voices of Wilfred Bion, Hanna Arendt and Virginia Woolf, adding the Buddhist concept of Kamma – creative actions of body, speech and mind – to describe her view of how the word is tied to vast and timeless meanings brought to conscious and unconscious currents of human experience, creating mental space in and between minds, while traversing it at the same time.

Mitchel differentiates moments of true dialogue, when truth touches two at the same shared moment, from interactions based on deep suspicion of the other, in which the experience is one of mis-representation, coercion and being taken hostage. He uses Toni Morrison's The Bluest Eye and Erich Fromm's The Art of Loving to further his conceptualizations of love and hate. True otherness and the accompanying freedom are seen as the opposite phenomenon of hate, emptiness and mutual impoverishment.

Irene closes the trialogue with further reflections on the relation between fear, love and truth-seeking. She reverts to the language of poetry, in which literary defamiliarization acts to crush the obvious, as a way for allowing oneself to be cast into the unknown, to con-tact fear and to engage in a true dialogue. She takes inspiration from Lewis Carroll and his Alice, as well as from Cervantes and his Don Quixote, who use, in her view, forms of direct, simple and yet mag-ical communication that seem to let go of the need and demand for understanding. She consequently suggests that perhaps what makes something magical, and what enables a true dialogue unobstructed by fear, memory, desire and the need for understanding, is when "the intellect dwells in the heart."

In the **second dialogue**, Michal opens by examining the desire to go on being and the fear of ceasing: their nature, their origins and the unconsciously driven behaviours meant to cope with them. She draws from Klein, Winnicott, Bion, Bick, Symington and others, as well as from ancient Buddhist Pāli texts and concepts, forming an integrative perspective on the phenomena of fear of annihilation and the self's attempts to cope with it and to go on being. She offers a vignette that demonstrates how consistent mental movement may function as a self-holding, second-skin mechanism; and suggests how the connec-tive and projective properties of our mind create an illusion of a solid, continuous self. She points out some paradoxes, such as that the self needs to feel held in order to let go; to acknowledge its impermanence and dependency in order to become integrated, and to be integrative and collected in order to face its disintegrating, essenceless nature.

In response to Michal's paper and to the Covid pandemic, Yorai shows how alienating circumstances annihilate the welcome "mess" of human embodied connectedness: in violating the fundamental con-nection between self and environment, developmentally engrained states of anxiety are evoked by a sense of being lost in (cyber)space. In response to this threat, one of two unconscious psyche-somatic strategies is applied: expulsion of mental contents, leading to a sense of disintegration, or a defensive constriction, leading to psyche-somatic agony.

Contending that "the space of the mind affects its content and vice versa" (Grotstein, 1978, p. 55), Yorai suggests that the cultivation of internal spaciousness – as promoted in contemporary psychoanalytical approaches – is a determining factor in the psychotherapeutic process. More specifically, when properly cultivated, the emergent sense of spaciousness helps therapists and patients transcend the seemingly insurmountable dichotomies of individual vs. eco-environmental, life vs. death, and emergence vs. diffusion. This approach, strongly supported by cardinal Buddhist tenets, promotes psyche-somatic at-one-ment between therapist and patient. Thus, co-jointly making space for the mess of humanhood, it nurtures and enhances both the experience of and the capacity for going-on-being. A clinical vignette, Haiku poetry and quotes from Kohut further demonstrate the afore-mentioned ways of being and attending.

In response to Yorai, Michal offers some thoughts on the development of mental space, as it may be supported by one's stance towards physical and psychic realities, capabilities and constrains. Inspired by the Buddha's teaching, by Becker's (2022) concept of True Other and by Lazar's (2022) discussion on meaning-making of the body's otherness, she suggests relating to the body as a true other: not as "self" but as an intimately felt other, which, given the right point of view, manifests the deepest truths regarding the world and ourselves. Following Sella's (2022) call for embodiment of the natural elements, which elaborates on Balint's (1979) ideas concerning the therapist's mental space, Michal discusses the Buddha's instructions for developing a state of mind as receptive and unshakable, as non-rejecting and non-desiring as the earth, water, fire and wind; and as un-fixed and un-fixated as space. Openness to engage with the full range that stretches between the far edges of human condition enables us to become providers of space, time and nourishment.

Michal then reflects on how the Corona pandemic air travel constrictions prevent some of the psyche's spontaneous gestures from being "joined up with the world's events" (Winnicott, 1960, p. 146), and thus may affect mental space and its capacity to expand. Finally, she demonstrates how the four limitless states, according to Buddhist thought – selfless love, compassion, sympathetic joy and equanimity – bring together boundless vastness and nourishment, thus exemplifying how the mental space or place of being intersects with the mental contents or substances that saturate it.

The **second "associative trialogue"** revolves around the essential role of the other's quality of attention, verbal and non-verbal communication, and presence, for the healing of trauma and the restoration of distorted truths.

Clara begins with Laub's (1992) claim that severely traumatized individuals had lost the internal witness that makes possible an internal dialogue and testimony of the actual trauma. And therefore, only a sympathetic other, fully present, empathically and ethically connected other – what Ferenczi called "benevolent and fully present observer" can re-present this displaced and divided truth. She distinguishes trauma caused by human agency from trauma caused by natural disasters, accidents etc., and following Liotti (1995) and Steele & Steele (2008) states that dissociation occurs only in the former. It is there that the human bond of trust has been destroyed, and only there can it be recollected and reexperienced in the context of a new therapeutic, healing attachment.

Clara describes how in order to psychically and emotionally survive, having suffered evil one distorts the kind of truth which one finds impossible to accept. A dissociation between the self and the body occurs, forming the basis for somatizations and psychosomatic reactions. Furthermore, complicated dynamics of introjection and of the victim-persecutor dyad, as well as re-externalization and redirecting of aggressiveness, create much misery for the traumatized person – including self-harm and depressive feelings – as well as for others, producing potentially endless intergenerational transmission.

Truth must therefore be redeemed, and this depends on the right presence of an other. She describes the neurobiological aspect of this process, which involves complex mirroring, right brain communication and empathic intervention through mind-body-brain as "embodied witnessing." She quotes Shore, Cozolino and others, and offers a clinical vignette to demonstrate the importance of being properly engaged with mind, body, voice and gaze.

Mitchel responds with a deeply moving vignette and suggests quite provocatively that "truth is in the I-You relation, and the relation is in truth. They are one until the moment of trauma, where the psyche can not fill in the missing parts to complete the picture of union. The crack is too deep to be mended." Mitchel proceeds to discuss the presence of uncontainable dread in the heart of therapist and in the basic fabric of our society.

From this evocative formulation, Michal then draws a possible new angle on the definition of trauma caused by human agency: "interpersonal trauma entails a schism between truth and relation, too deep to negotiate or bridge or reconcile. Healing, therefore, involves their reunion." This reunion entails "a dynamic relation of non-exclusion, of co-existence and co-creation that is reinstituted or reclaimed". Supported by Buber (1923), Ghent (1990), Benjamin (2004) and Buddhist thought, she ends by suggesting the essential link between truth and trust, and the links that they themselves form.

Following this trialogue, we had two conversations with Paul R. Fleischman, where we discussed Clara's ideas and our own understandings. The ending text of this chapter is the result of these conversations – a trialogue within a trialogue. We start by discussing the prevalent sense of social isolation felt in post-modern society and the profound meaning of true dialogue for those sensing alienation. This moves us to reconsider the meaning of trauma as a function of the values of society. Societies contain and interpret their emotional scars in specific ways, which are transmitted verbally and non-verbally as messages. These messages, in turn, effect the nature of trauma and healing, a process which is culturally, contextually and personally dependent, and hence relational. Similarly, according to Paul, every phenomenon – be it matter, energy or communication – is interactional and therefore a relational event.

Mitchel offers a clinical vignette, in which the therapeutic dyad truly co-created thoughts, emotions, poems and wordless meaningful sounds. We wonder what in our world allows for a mutual effort of witnessing and containing, and what prevents these processes, leaving the individual unseen, unheard and alone.

The third dialogue of this book offers further angles and elaborations on the dialectic between the word and the wordless. It addresses some of the verbal and non-verbal aspects of interpretation and their effects on the patient-analyst relation and on contact with and digestion of truths. The chapter begins with Hilit's discussion of what she terms "the minimalist interpretation," whereby the analyst proposes a brief, concise interpretation. As the psychic truth is elusive and is a retrospective formulation of past experience, she suggests that the required interpretation frequently occurs in the blink of an eye, akin to a Haiku poem. Hilit examines the possibility of experiencing the psychic truth from a Bionian perspective, with an affinity to Haiku poetry and with references to Freud's and Bion's respective concepts of the caesura.

This directly relates to the immanent "cleft tongue" (Amir, 2013), which opens up in therapy at the moment when truth is formulated into words and interpretation. It is the analyst's ability to process psychic experiences into alpha elements that enable the patient to experience a truthful encounter with himself together with the return of the psychic movement. This encounter, much like a Haiku poem, encapsulates the existing and the absent, summoning a humbling and momentary contact with the psychic truth and its ever-changing essence.

In her response to Hilit, Hagit suggests that although the psychic truth is elusive, transformative and in constant motion, and although we do not have direct contact with it but merely with its evolving stages – still, every a priori attempt to attain a particular modality of interpretation, every pre-planned construction and search for a formula narrows and shuts down the psychic openness, receptiveness, movement and intuition. An informed search for a brief and concise interpretation might, as with any other construction, become a diminished and saturated intention, memory and desire.

Hagit maintains that an encounter with the psychic truth and the ability to formulate a meaningful, resonating interpretation should by no means be pre-constructed, whether it be shape, form, length, rhythm or temperature. She illustrates her line of thought by means of a clinical description and a poem. They both present a minimalist response, in a breath-long moment, though one is affecting, connecting and imbuing an emotional meaning; while the other is remote and distancing, isolating and tormenting.

Our final **"associative trialogue"** is a contemplative, often poetic text. It begins with Mitchel's fresh look at Martin Buber's I-You link, proposing that our most natural instinct to hold onto experience is the way we leave the other as an "it," an object to be possessed. If this is so, does true encounter with a true other – a meeting with no memory, no understanding and no desire – take place beyond experience? Is it therefore too unformulated? Dissociative? Rare, and ultimately exhausting?

Responding to these reflections, Michal elucidates three modes of meeting experience and the other, through which we may alternately pass: a "conventional-confined" mode, a "streaming" mode and a "temporarily selfless" mode. Truly meeting and meeting truth, she claims, involve non-conventional self-states and perception; but this does not imply neither regression nor dissociation. Instead, the second and third modes entail being with experience while being with an other. And the more one manages to let go of the first mode – to let go of grasping and possessing – the truer the encounter becomes, growth supporting and vitalizing.

A poem by Paul follows, and offers reflections on "the love of all things" and on "the laud static" of hatred and impassivity that disrupts love and life. The poem invokes further discussion between all three writers, touching subjects such as "savage receptivity," "natural fusion" and the ability to "ride the waves of experience" in the therapy room. It becomes clearer and clearer to the writers that maintaining "the love of all things" is inherently a continuous, laborious yet highly precious task. When confronted with otherness and our love for all things, we are simultaneously overwhelmed with the fear of loss and change. Our need for sameness and the basic instinctive competition over life giving elements calls us to grasp and dearly hold on to an I-It relation. And yet, even in those moments of existential angst, the deep call for knowing a True Other may still be heard and answered.

Note

1 Makom in Hebrew. One of God's denotations in the Mishna – referring to the divinity in its absence, in its namelessness.

References

Barnea-Astrog, M. (2017). *Carved by Experience: Vipassana, Psychoanalysis, and the Mind Investigating Itself.* London: Karnac Books.

Becker, M. (In Press). You Are Requested to Raise Your Eyes and See": The Reconstruction of Religious and Psychoanalytic Belief during the Analytic

Encounter. In: L. Aron & L. Henik (Eds.). *Answering A Question With More Questions: Contemporary Psychoanalysis and Jewish Thought*, vol. III. New York: Routledge Press.

Becker, M. & Shalgi, B. (2005). Sameness, Difference, Play and Fear in the I-You Encounter. *The Psychoanalytic Review* 92(5): 747–757.

Becker, M. & Shalgi, B. (2006). The Dialectic between Self-Determination and Intersubjectivity in Creating the Experience of Self. *Psychoanalytic Study of the Child* (Vol. 61). New Haven: Yale University Press.

Buber, M. (1923). *I and Thou*. Translated by W. Kauffman. New York: Charles Scribner's Sons, 1970.

Freud, S. (1901b). The Psychopathology of Everyday Life. *S.E 6*(vii): 296.

First Dialogue

Creation and the True Other

Mitchel Becker and Rina Lazar

Chapter 1

The Birth of a True Other

Mitchel Becker

To Hadas
Who awakened a dormant wish for a true other

When does dialogue begin? When is truth born? Is truth born when the intrapsychic digests a truth? Does truth need a twoness? I do not know. I have struggled with this question for many years. Doesn't truth need a dialogue? Or does dialogue need truth? Bion would say truth needs no speaker. Only a lie needs a speaker for it to exist. And yet my soul insists on believing that truth is connected to the heart of an other.

I have been reading my friend Rina Lazar's articles for some 25 years. We have spoken together about our lives and thoughts for some 10 years. We have taught together. And dreamed together.

Several years ago, Rina wrote an article called, "In the beginning was love?". The question mark for Rina is crucial (as a question to Julia Kristeva's book by the same title without the question mark). Rina writes of love, beginnings, primary scenes, envy and potentials. But most importantly, when reading Rina's work, the reader gets a sense of an unsettling and a grappling with the naked truth of our human existence. In the beginning there is love? Or perhaps an urgent need to create?

Lazar (2006) wrote:

> The woman therefore represents primordial and cosmic chaos as well as the ability to switch from such a state to a clearly delimited and organized state. The woman is a transformation marker as its opposite – a chaos marker. She is the one capable of moving along

DOI: 10.4324/9781003325499-2

the chaos-structure axis. What is frightening about her is that she can move in both directions - from No-name ('nameless dread') to naming and back. This reversibility is awe-inspiring.

(pp. 397–398)

Our quest to create is indeed awe-inspiring. Rina speaks of the woman's inherent capacity to create the other, both in birthing and in "naming." The catastrophic potential as well as the growth-enhancing capacity. And the simultaneous need for a dialectic between chaos and structure. From these thoughts on creation, I begin a journey in the quest of a true otherness. I feel that our existential search for truth is fundamentally co-existent with a true other, and that to create, was, is and will be forever present in poetic harmony with Martin Buber's I-You. And it is my contention that Buber saw the birth of the dialogue in the words of the creation of Adam and Eve in the book of Genesis.

In the beginning, there was a pure truth.

In the beginning, there was a G-d of truth still uncomplicated by an other or by any human. A pre-human world created with perfection. G-d was at his best without us to make the pure ever so murky. And then on the sixth day came the creation of the human.

It is strange to say, but after 62 years of living and 57 years of reading the book of Genesis, I am proud to admit "I Still Don't Get it."

Trust me when I tell you that there are two completely different stories told in the sequence of Adam and Eve's creations, and most people completely unaware will say, "huh?, No way!"

How can we read something even several times and not get it?

I "get" the stated facts but still don't get the meaning.

The facts of the narrative are that in the initial creation, Adam and Eve are created together after a previous breathtaking six days of world creation. All of the world in its natural glory, including all plants and animals, are in place, patiently waiting for the coronating entrance of the human. Adam and Eve are created seemingly equal, and they come to a full world and are given the world to rule.

And then, the world is given the Sabbath on the seventh day.

And after this complete rendition of creation, a new creation is described. And this time, before there is a plant or tree, Adam is created completely and totally alone. Alone without plant, without animal and without Eve. G-d plants the garden and says that "it is not good for man to be alone." G-d brings animals, but man finds no solace. Then G-d puts man to sleep, takes from him a rib and from the rib creates Eve.

Two basic origins, two basic ways to experience the world.

Until this very moment of writing, I have never emotionally understood what my analytic self has tried to conceptualize about these two phenomena. In previous writing and thought, I have spoken of the plentiness and royal majesty of Adam I versus the emptiness and poverty of Adam II. I have spoken of a sameness in birth and in perception, Adam (I) and Eve born together into a known world, versus a deep understanding of difference (Adam II).

But what do I emotionally internalize?

I suddenly really feel the awesome birth of dialogue. I sense the story of creation as seeking to discover dialogue. In the first creation, Adam and Eve are given the world and each other "on a silver platter." They could not possibly know of dialogue because allness is there to be had. Recognition implies a capacity for absence and thus the need for Adam II and his rich and painful existential journey. Adam and Eve go through a whole new way of becoming, a whole new phenomenology. Suddenly, there is an aloneness that creates a new potential. Out of the no-ness, I recognize an other.

This is Buber's movement from an I-It world of objects (Adam I) to an I-You world of seeking otherness via the dialogues of Adams. Suddenly, it is clear to me that this is our lives. We move back and forth between attempting to possess and master objects and seeking a partner to dialogue. This is a movement from a place of objects that we either rule or desire, to an existential aloneness in which we seek otherness.

And so the two typologies meet.

Where and how do our parts meet? And when must they part? What does "dominator of objects" have to say to the "seeker of dialogue?" Why is dialogue sought? What does the aloneness of man mean and why did G-d, and thus man, deem the aloneness as not good? Is dialogue sought to solve loneliness or does dialogue seek truth? Does the "dominator of objects" occupy himself with issues of truth?

It strikes as wondersome how many times we may read this story and not take in its simple truth. Two creations! We can easily somehow miss the text. But how can that be? Actually very simply, we see what we are ready to see. And truth???

Truth. Hmmm. I once imagined the psychoanalyst's encounter with truth. It went something like this:

ANALYST: Dear Truth, you hide yourself so well in bright colorful emotion-full costumes.
TRUTH: Spoken as a true coward.
ANALYST: I have my fears.
TRUTH: To drink from my fountain?
ANALYST: You know how many wells of water have been poisoned! How shall I know from where to drink? Truth: I am who I am.
ANALYST: And your look alike?
TRUTH: Huh?
ANALYST: Lies!
TRUTH: Oh him-he dresses like a psychoanalyst, pay no attention.
ANALYST: Thanks, reassuring!
TRUTH: Beware of the preacher.
    Beware of the ego.
ANALYST: So where!!
TRUTH: Be still!!

How do we know if we are on a path to awareness or a path of false mirrors? In this imagined dialogue, I reveal to you, the reader, my genuine fear. I fear to be in falseness and not even to be aware that it is false. I seek via Adam I and Adam II to understand the basic building blocks of relation.

The two Adams are a dialectic of two typologies of being as described by Rabbi J. Soloveitchik (1965) in his reading of the two creations of man from the book of Genesis. Each typology experiences a particular challenge that is unique to that inherent aspect of being. Adam I is in search of mastery over a world that is seemingly beyond control. For him, chaos, as in the paranoid-schizoid, is something to be reckoned with until the end of his time. It is as if his inborn drive to rule, conquer and control stems from the basic truth that the world is chaotic and frightening, where helplessness is the feared unknown truth. He conquers what seems different and unknown and melts it down into knowable sameness. The depressive state is the moment of concern when a soulful tear has managed to pierce the armour of his embattled life.

Adam II seeks to know what is different from him and thus unknown. The world is an endless "library of Babel" which entices and excites the epistemological pursuit. For Adam II, control is a sort of death in which the knowing becomes temporarily finite. The infinite is engaging and vitalizing. Here, the paranoid is not chaos but a stifling order of mirrors reflecting the sameness that deadens.

How do these two typologies co-exist? Their essences seem to be mutually unapproachable. Adam I seems to be born a prince. The infinite possibilities of life energize him to conquer his next adventure. Along the way, he meets new partners and challenges, which he gradually brings under his control. His birth rite is always moving him to hold onto a true identity of majesty – each action a new mode of being the ruling royalty. Those less fortunate in their birth rite will forever attempt to upgrade their place in society.

Adam II was born of dust in the desert of being, like a reptile in its egg buried safely in the sand. As he peaked out of his shell, he felt overwhelmed by the endlessness of the world. He gradually senses the cosmic presence of an awesome entity whose spark he marvels. But who hid him in the sand? And for what purpose? Every move he makes is to discover and define, not to secure and not to empower, but rather to know intimately.

These are two personas. They are equally basic and essential, both born with a purpose. One seeks conquest–dominion over mother's love and father's identity. The other thrown alone to the desert in an adventure of knowing, he seeks to know his mother's and father's heart and soul. One seeks to master his surroundings, and one seeks to know them.

The mastery of Adam I paradoxically assumes sameness – we are of one goal (my goal), and I love you for that. The notion of submission arises when there isn't a win-win situation. Then mastery demands victory and conquest. The "other" is the prince's "subject" (i.e. object) either by will or against will. Difference for Adam I is always a challenge and a source of conflict. Difference immediately challenges mastery and invites the struggle for territory. Difference is not a welcome visitor for Adam I.

For Adam II, the seeking of knowledge lives naturally with and is nurtured by difference. Seeking of meaning is surrendering to the other's difference. Adam II is in conflict with sameness. Sameness is at best a comma or a pause in the pursuit. At worst, there is a sense of painful withoutness or emptiness, a loss of one's purpose and meaning. The dialogue is dead.

Suddenly I am frozen.

From where shall I find the soul to speak of a true other? Dare I? "Remove your shoes from your feet for the place you seek is vitality of life." Breathing in the other without an agenda and within this struggle, hospitality is born. It is suddenly clear to me that in order for Adam I to meet Adam II, we must expand our perspective to Adam and Eve I meeting Adam and Eve II. No true meeting of selves is done without otherness. My study of Rabbi Soloveitchik's work was lacking the relational turn that I had made and yet had not successfully incorporated into Rav Soloveitchik's "Lonely man of Faith." He discussed Adam I & II, and now I see that it is not just terminology. Adam I & II are seriously lacking.[1] Adam and Eve are the essence. Adam and Eve I born together are totally alike in a mutual experience. Adam and Eve II are born totally apart and in search of the other. And then I begin to reprocess by quoting Rina's conceptualization of the woman as a marker of transformation and chaos.

When can the encounter with an other become true? And what can our two stories of the human's creation uncover in our quest? Is it possible that there is a moment in which the desired sameness of the couple that is Adam and Eve I and the desired difference of Adam and Eve II meet? And in this meeting place a true encounter becomes? The biblical Sabbath of the text is a metaphor for this encounter. But what happens here? Majesty and dust swirl into a moment. And for that moment, time, person and place are no longer relevant. The masters and seekers are one – an encounter of souls spiriting.

Buber (1923) asks us to become beyond experience. No experience. No I as I and something. I-You has nothing. I-You becomes truth. (I am using the concept truth as Bion uses the symbol "O." Bion (1970) states, "I shall use the sign O to denote that which is the ultimate reality, absolute truth ... O does not fall in the domain of knowledge or learning save incidentally: it can become. p. 26.") But this meeting place I am for now calling the place of spiritual rest (the Sabbath) is not "out of nothing," ex nihilo, nor is it nothingness. It is the capacity to contain the meeting place of the two Adam and Eves. Winnicott's (1971) transitional space and transitional experiencing come to mind:

> It is an area that is not challenged, because no claim is made on its behalf except that it shall exist as a resting place for the individual engaged in the perpetual human task of keeping inner and outer reality separate yet interrelated.
>
> (p. 2)

In the context of Adam and Eve I & II, the Sabbath bridges together the two primordial experiences of the other. You are just like me, and you are completely different from me. But as in Winnicott's transitional space, the bridge between the two experiences is to contain the paradox and not solve it. Thus, the dyad can approach uncertainty and the unknown of the encounter without needing to reify their encounter. And in that Sabbath, sitting at the Sabbath meal, along with the Sabbath guests in the moment of rest, a dialogue is born.

It is the place to share a meal of uncertainty. Suddenly, Adam and Eve I and Adam and Eve II are capable, as a linked whole, to contain uncertainty. The poetess Eeva Kilpi (1972) writes, "When do you know it is love? When being together gives you more freedom than being alone." The dialogue of Adams and Eves or of all humans begins when each becomes aware that the other is the key to discovering.

I am now ready to define "true otherness":

True otherness is the place or state of a relation in which the couple are able to contain, process and digest truths that each individual on their own could not achieve. These truths are born of pain and hurt, fear and hope, and joy and ecstasy, and they concern the basic and infinite conflicts of existence as seen through the prisms of subjectivity, intersubjectivity and objectivity. The couple's immersion in trust forms a mutual surrendering to the encounter, which in a seeming paradox brings forth freedom. True otherness in its ultimate fruition creates a relational freedom to become.

> True otherness is when the presence of an other brings an other inside of us who is not available otherwise. So being with someone in a relationship leads not only to mutuality and connection and giving and taking, but at a certain point also to a state where

something is revealed out of both participants that otherwise could not exist.[2]

I want to discuss why this place and state of relation is so difficult to achieve, and why we are so frightened of emotional freedom; but I realize that no further meaningful progress can be made unless my own personal struggle with truth speaks his piece. The walls of my dissociations began to crumble some ten years ago. My soul sought to put the unconnected parts together. And in the search for this "connecting," our (my ex-wife and I) marriage began to grasp what was ungraspable: that my wife and I suffered from parts missing (Thomas Ogden wrote a novel, "The Parts Left Out," and a psychoanalytic article, "What I would not part with." He describes a place of being barely alive and a place of being wholly human). We knew we were dead and I sensed that true otherness never had a chance. We divorced four years ago after 33 years of marriage. And new transformations were born.

I very much ponder how I got into an unauthentic relationship. A false otherness. Not horrific trauma but a place of falsehood. I wonder if I could have known much earlier, and sadly I feel that indeed I could have known. And I guess I really did not want to know. The incapacity to know? The fear of knowing? The fear of being without? The fear of shame and of rage? Or emotionally not knowing something better? Or feeling unworthy of something better? Unworthy of love? Afraid to discover joy? Afraid to know what it means to be free? Or all of the above.

When I am at my most innocent, I can naively ask, why are we afraid to open our hearts? And then, I find myself writing:

> wherever recognition was sought
> there you shall sense tears of alienation.
> wherever the drums of freedom roared
> there you shall find the blood of revenge
> wherever hope was sung
> there you shall learn to bear the pain of the mourner

Adam and Eve I meet Adam and Eve II, and the dialectics of recognition and alienation, freedom and fear, and hope and pain bring our soul to tears. The cycle of discovering, resistance to the discovery and the need for dialogue is interminable. We are endlessly seeking true otherness and just as persistently hiding from or even attacking the other. We fear the pain of alienation, aggression and loss. We seek recognition, freedom and hope. The Sabbath and the transitional space afford a hope to contain these strains of growth. This journey is beautifully described in a poem by Eeva Kilpi (2014, p. 15) called, "He stepped inside my door":

> Let me know right away
> if I'm disturbing you
> he said
> as he stepped inside my door
> and I'll leave the way I came
> Not only do you disturb me,
> I answered
> You turn my whole world
> upside down.
> Welcome.

I sit with a group, and I invite the naivete. Letting go of the need to possess, the need to hold on. A searching for a place where the two Adams and Eves join to accept uncertainty, chaos and loneliness. Hearts are open. Vulnerability is at its height. And I hear a group member[3] say, "When the individual cannot bear his truth, they may need to borrow the truth of an other." This relational freedom is always vulnerable, we are always seeking to "Escape from Freedom" (Fromm, 1941). We are always trying to put freedom, truth and the other into a concept or a reification. To make it "containable." To put it into a category, a bottle or a box. This is natural. But I think often-times the weight is thrown to certainty, routine and security. Can we face the face of an other? Can we call to an other and simultaneously answer "hineni" – Here I am to be found.

A poem by Rabi'a (an 8th-century woman Sufi mystic) describes a worshipper who prays that his devotion to his Lord will not be for fear of punishment or desire of reward, but rather for a pure love of his heart and the passion to sense the face of his G-d (In: Hirshfield, 1994). The struggle is in our dialogue and relation to true otherness.

It is my contention that we are born with a basic true otherness. A truth that is, that needs no memory, because it is clear and present. This truth is in constant danger to become an empty concrete entity, because we are frightened of staying in an innocent curiosity to the unknown uncertainty of the infinite truth of the other and its interminable metamorphoses. We desperately attempt to take hold of the other and make it our object. One manner of objectifying is by making the quest for a true dialogue into a rigidity, a preaching a polarization into the good or desired and the bad or untouchable. I find myself struggling with this defining of "this is authentic, and this is unauthentic." The language of the persecutory superego seems to have infiltrated. In essence, there is no freedom in the land of a moralistic proselytizer. No freedom, no creativity and no dialogue. The protest for absolute and ideal freedom inhibits liberation.

And a true dialogue between Adam and Eve I and Adam and Eve II: how does it transpire? Adam and Eve I & II were born to absolute uncoverings of realities. Absolute enriched sameness and absolute isolated aloneness. As I mentioned, this absoluteness is inherently problematic. Their experience is a metaphor to the experience of a baby's innocent discovering of all the world's truth in a non-verbalized absolute truth. The baby too experiences the bliss of at-one-ment and the dread of total isolation. The baby somehow apprehends all, and in their knowing eyes, the caretaker who gazes in their eyes sees the infinite. Truth discovered but undigested. However, naturally, Adam and Eve I & II were unable to "take in" their truths, and eating the tree of knowledge could not magically implant the knowledge. Knowledge was in their stomach but not metabolized. For modern persons, this is hearing words and seeing images of inspiration provided in endless media (love, freedom, modesty, basic human rights…) spoken or visually shown, but no message is heard. Words are spoken, images are presented and they remain a collection of concrete signs representing the thing itself, the object without subject without connection or relation. "The thing in itself."

In our story of Genesis, Adam and Eve I &II are helpless to truly recognize the meaning of their discoveries. The fullness of their discovery makes recognition impossible. There is no dialogue because there is no space and no time. Fullness is undigestible. It is like musical notes without any silence or absolute silence without a note. In order for a dialogue to begin, a bridge between worlds must be constructed. Thus, the Sabbath. The Sabbath allows for contradictory absolutes to co-exist and allows for the encounter of otherness. The Sabbath is the playground, a transitional space, where uncertainty and the infinite have their moment of mutual containment. Where mastery and modesty, knowing and curiosity, join in a mutual need to recreate each other. Abraham Joshua Heschel (1951) in his beautiful masterpiece on the Sabbath writes that the Sabbath holds for us the concept of time. And, "Time is otherness" and "it is only within time that there is fellowship and togetherness of all beings" (p. 99). An I meeting a You.

> We sit at the meal of uncertainty
> a true other arrives
> freedom to breathe, think, feel and dream
> freedom to surrender to knowing each other with all your heart soul and strength.
> freedom to move away knowing your movements' waves will encounter her again and again and again

And then I hear Leonard Cohen singing, "Dance me to the end of love." Dance me with love until the very end. If love is in my heart when the violin is burning, and the loss and the void come to visit, then I will die while still alive. In the beginning, there was love. Shall we dance to the end of love?

Notes

1   Thank you to Hadas Arbel for her comment on Eve's absence.
2   Personal communication from Gabriela Gusita in response to my above-stated definition.
3   Mishael Chirug.

References

Bion, W. (1970). *Attention and Interpretation*. London: Heinemann.
Buber, M. (1923). *I and Thou*. Translated by W. Kaufman. New York: Charles Scribner's Sons, 1970.
Fromm, E. (1941). *Escape from Freedom*. New York: Discuss Books, 1971.
Heschel, A.H. (1951). *The Sabbath*. New York: Farrar, Straus, and Giroux.

Hirshfield, J. (1994). *Women in Praise of the Sacred: 43 Centuries of Spiritual Poetry by Women*. New York: HarperCollins.

Kilpi, E. (1972). *Perhonen Ylittaa Tien*. Translated from Finnish by R. Saari. Jerusalem: Carmel, 2007.

Kilpi, E. (2014). *A Landscape Blossoms Within Me*. Translated from Finnish by D. Adamson. Todmorden, UK: Arc Publications.

Lazar, R. (2006). In the Beginning Was Love? *The Psychoanalytic Review* 93(3): 393–410.

Soloveitchik, J.B. (1965). *The Lonely Man of Faith*. Northvale, NJ: Aronson, 1997.

Winnicott, D.W. (1971). *Playing and Reality*. Middlesex: Penguin.

Chapter 2

Meeting the Ultimate Other

Allowing the Creation

Rina Lazar

What are we talking about when we phantasize about meeting the ultimate other in a creative way? Is it synonyms to playing as a way of being alive as Winnicott (1971) so eloquently said: "Playing is an experience, always a creative experience. And it is an experience in the space-time continuum, a basic form of living?" (ibid., p. 59)

In my dialogue with Mitchel Becker's paper, I wish to examine our supposedly most intimate relation – the one between our bodies, our language and ourselves. I see this complex partnership as a relation between "Intimate Strangers," examining it through the experience of illness and the transgender patient's experience.

I do this through reading Mitchel's thesis regarding creation – the creation of the Earth – the Place[1] – and the creation of Man. Moreover, I add Eve to the cycle of creation. I write about our "bodymind" and "creationism" not only as a response to a coincidental meeting with Mitchel's paper (although nothing is coincidental in our meeting); I do this because these themes seem to me as the central ones to Motherhood in large and to our "mothering" (caring, minding) our bodies in particular. Hence, Eve's trespassing God's place (what I call creationism), which she actually does twice – in the Garden of Eden and in giving name to Cain – is, from my point of view, a central pole in our dealing with our bodies as a strange intimate other in times of disease and in the process of transforming our gender. Themes of confrontation, creation and protest are inevitable ingredients of these life's events: in which our bodies are sensed as either a "primeval matter," as "the clay in the potter's hand" (Jeremiah, 18:6), or as "finished product" a datum, a kind of "dead end." Adding to it the theme of God as the [absent]

DOI: 10.4324/9781003325499-3

Place² while looking for our psychic home on earth. The one that would fit our body, soul and heart.

Dear Mitchel,

I try to follow your scheme of thought while using my associations in order to meet your otherness with my words. To create out of your affluence a point of departure for my thoughts, to find my way and to articulate my idiom of being as a person and as a therapist.

You begin "The Birth of a True Other" with a question: "Where does dialogue begin... When is truth born?" You base your answer on two narratives of creation (the Creation of a Myth). The first one is from Genesis 1: the creation of Man ("Adam" in Hebrew) "in His own image... **male and female** he created them" (Genesis 1: 27). This was on the sixth day of Creation, out of plenty. There is no interdiction, no transgression and no curse. It is a blessed world without Gan Eden (the Garden of Eden) or any reference to human language or a dialogue. We are at the providence of God and its founding sayings – its truth, "the voice of the living God" (Deuteronomy, 5: 22). The second narrative relates to Chapter 2. **Man** comes to the empty void of the universe – a creation out of emptiness. Then, God planted the Garden of Eden, put Man there in order, "to dress it and keep it," allowing him to eat from every tree of the garden freely except from the tree of the knowledge of good and evil. This is the first Godly decree. The big No. Its trespassing would bring death on earth.

Thereafter Man's loneliness was presented as a problem (in contrast to the first narrative). God looked for a "help meet for him": first, the animals whose names were given to them by Man. Man has a language though only at the level of signs. Then the Woman. The animals were not enough. Man was alone (maybe inherently alone in the world of a transcendent God, and not only technically). The Woman was created out of Man's rib – a bone of his bones a flesh of his flesh (a part object). That is why Man named her Woman and cleaved to her, "and they shall be one flesh" – naked and not ashamed.

We can see here four modes of creation – in God's image (in Chapter 1), out of dust (Man), out of Man's rib (Woman) and by enacting law or giving name – Midrash Shem (all in Chapter 2).

I start from this point and go directly to the story of Eve, moving between her being a speck – a part of Adam's rib – on the one hand, and the one who takes part in the creation and in the human dialogue on the other hand. I present human (Woman) language both as a means of creation and of destruction: "Death and life are in the power of the tongue" (Proverbs 18:21). With the story of Eve comes the first death – Abel's murder (Lazar, 2006; Pardes, 1996).

In Chapter 2, Man is the name-giver subject to all living creatures on earth including Woman, according to God's will. Woman's name becomes Eve in Genesis 3 after their transgression, the expulsion from the Garden of Eden and God's curse: "I will greatly increase your pains in childbearing, with pain you will give birth to children. Your desire will be for your husband, and he will rule over you" (Genesis 3: 16). Only then was she named (by Adam) as the "mother of all living" – Eve[3] – and not just a Woman.

In Chapter 4, Eve gives birth to a child and names him Cain, saying, "With the help of the LORD I have *brought forth* a man"[4] (Genesis 4, v.1). From a name-given object, she turns into a name-giving subject. She is becoming part of creation, and this is precisely where the trespassing occurs. The Hebrew root, which is translated here as "brought forth," has two meanings: "acquire" and "create." God is therefore presented here as a partner to the act of creation, not as the central and pivotal axis of creation. Eve's position among the creators allows her to feel the "personal closeness of divinity to her soul" (Cassuto, 1965). By using a Hebrew verb, which in all of its other occurrences signifies divine creation, Eve ascribes the same position to the birth of her son as to the creation of Man by the Lord. She defines herself as the creator and by so doing in fact shatters one of the premises of the scriptures: the Lord's exclusiveness in the process of creation. The other recipient of her statement is Man. "With the help of the Lord I have brought forth a *man*" (and not a child) is, among other things, a reaction to Man's words when he named Woman[5]. Cursed and expelled, she became a subject – The Other.

Naming is a sort of life giving, the perpetuation of life. However, once the Woman becomes the name giver she also becomes capable of potentially not only giving life but also taking it away. The lack of explanation of the name of Eve's second son "Abel"[6] is presented by Pardes (1996) as a prediction of its bearer's short-lividness (since the

Hebrew root of Abel, H.B.L., means "short-lived"). This is a dark parallel to the creativity, that is inherent in Cain's name, but it also insinuates Eve's passive complicity in the sacrifice of Abel. The lack of a name explanation for Abel is even more conspicuous, when we consider the name explanation[7] provided for the name of her last son Seth, who was born after the death of Abel and the curse of Cain. We are told that "Adam lay with his wife again, and she gave birth to a son and named him Seth[8], saying, God has granted me another seed in place of Abel, since Cain killed him" (Genesis, 4, v.25). Moreover, the Lord is the subject in this name explanation; he is the one who gives the seed; the Lord's usual status as the Creator is therefore recovered here. Unlike in Eve's first name explanation, which dramatically inaugurated the act of name giving by the mother by relating the feminine power of creation to cosmic creation, her second name explanation seems more moderate. Eve no longer sees the Lord as a partner. He remains the Creator. The boundary between human and divine has been restored; the sacrifice has already been made – Abel – hence, it was necessary for all that follows.

Could we read also the preceding story of the Garden of Eden as a necessary phase in founding the human being as a subject of his or her life and not only as subject to God?

Fromm (1966) views the expulsion from Eden as the necessary emergence from embeddedness. Only when Adam and Eve broke the law of God, transgressed God's scheme, they became separate subjects – Others (in Aron, 2005). Soloveitchik (2000), by contrast, views submission to law as the basis for intersubjectivity and mutuality in human relations and in relations between humanity and God. He speaks of Adam I and Adam II as two ideal types: the one is a part of nature and lives a non-reflective, instinctive existence, an object among objects rather than a full individual person. The second is a human person, a subject relating to a personal God. He is the lonely man of faith, capable of being an intersubjective partner. The critical change occurs when God addressed and commanded Man confronting him by law and by limits.

Mitchel adds the distinction between the master and the seeker accordingly: Adam I desires to master his surroundings, and Adam II seeks to know them.

Basing myself on Fromm's "reading" of the expulsion from Eden, I take the paradigm of the "seeker" one-step forward. I assume that being subject **to** the Other (God) and accepting its laws are not enough in order to become a subject (the owner **of** one's self). The transgression itself is the changing point, transgression and shame – the eating of the forbidden fruit, opening their eyes and knowing that they are naked. All of these transformed Adam and Eve into being subjects: the ones who have chosen, rebelled and purchased knowledge, even though through being tempted and punished for that; the ones who search for their place in God's scheme, seeking equilibrium and truth, and ready to pay the price, knowing that there is a price. The pains of travails and desire, of separation and dependence, of toil and sweat, and the pains of living **corporal life** and knowing **death**. Death of thyself and death of your offspring.

Being autonomous human subjects, our autonomy is based on rebellion, expulsion and interdependence. Knowing competence, vulnerability, destructiveness, helplessness, fright and death (human destiny), we need partners to this voyage on earth; we long for intimacy while facing the "predicted" unknown.

Are these the components of human intimacy, of this so yearned for disturbing relation[9]? Is this what makes intimacy into what it is – inherently transgressive, arising from fantasized access to the "primal scene" (the "tree of the knowledge of good and evil"), a way of being together in the "other [psychic] room" (Britton, 1998)?

In this room, we imagine a wild world of passion and creation; it is the room of imagination, the imagination as a room without boundaries or limits, from which we are excluded – the parental room of the primal scene (Freud, 1918). This is not the Winnicottian "potential space" between the mother and her infant, the *space* of illusion, the space of creation beyond questioning and the space of separateness in unity (Winnicott, 1971). It is a *place* that includes the desiring subject, its object (or another subject) and the observing gaze (Lazar, 2013). It is the place where the one who is not there yet is always present. Though we yearn for it, we are taken aback by this place. We will weave our fantasy around it; we will fashion it as the never-reached land, an assumed wholeness somewhere out **there.**

However, such an intimacy will inevitably crack: not owing to an infraction from the outside, but from inside, from the knowledge of otherness, which it conceals, the forbidden knowledge, which is so hard to bear (Lazar, 2010). This otherness is not just on the level of a required partner who will affirm our creation and will bestow meaning on our life in this place, but also the otherness of the language we know best – our Mother Tongue. As Derrida (1966) so eloquently says: "I have but one language – yet that language is not mine" (ibid., p. 33). Law and transgression, shame and expulsion are at the very root of our human existence as individuals (as "bodyminds") and as parts of thirds, groups and dyads.

The Intimate [Ultimate] Other

Talking about intimacy, the "other room," transgression and shame, I want to look at our supposedly most intimate relation – the one between our bodies, our language and ourselves. I want to relate to them as "Intimate Strangers," examining this relation through the experience of illness and that of the transgender patient.

It can seem as a strange pair. Why them? I choose them "by chance" – going through cancer and treating Male to Female and Female to Man transgender patients; however, both these experiences are not so far apart. In both of them, the body is an intimate stranger to the subject – the body and its apparent health and gender. Both could be seen as generic experiences – as metaphors – and not as personal ones. I do not imply in any way that transforming our gender is a kind of disease, although it is not an easy project neither to its subject nor to the surrounding others. Rather, we could think of it as one characteristic of our "liquid modern world" (Bauman, 2011).

Cancer and transgender become so frequent nowadays, that we need to reconsider our conceptualizations regarding health and illness on the one side and normality and perversion, on the other. As Muriel Dimen (2001) asked so eloquently some years before she passed away (due to cancer): "Perversion is us?" Moving on with Dimen's (2000) so picturesque phrase – "**the Body that stinks and the Body that thinks**" – I want to relate to the body as we think it and the body as we experience it.

Our bodies are both given to us *and* made by us, and embodiment is always mediated through discursive practices (Durban et al., 1993). Although they may not be fully our possessions, we experience them as ours and as incontrovertibly "real."

The body is, on the one hand, the product of cultural inscription (Butler, 1993) and of historical contingency (Foucault, 1976). On the other hand, it is the brute and immutable materiality that straightforwardly derives from its constitutive biology, organs, chromosomes, hormones, etc. (Saketopoulou, 2014).

Going through cancer, we find ourselves encountering our psyche's limits and our brute existential ones. There is a body there and potentially imminent death. It is its play. We have to cooperate. We are our body self, but the body sometimes is almost an alien to us. It has its rules of play and its anomalies. We have to learn to live with them. Our psyche has to cooperate if we want to live through this phase of our life. Paraphrasing Winnicott's well-known prayer: "Oh God! May I be alive when I die" (1989, p.4), I would exchange "die" with "being ill." This exchange is not an accidental one. Being ill with cancer, you are going to meet the dread of death face to face. Death is our true other. The Real one. The Ultimate one. It does not lie to us. It is our lot – not incidental but inevitable. The story of the Tree of Knowledge enforces the human being to know corporality deep inside – its nakedness, seductions, hunger, dependency, pains and finality. All in all, to know shame, guilt and dread.

However, our "capacity to come to terms with internal and external reality in a playful way, which makes reality bearable to the individual, so that denial can be avoided and the experience of living can be as fully realized as possible" (Winnicott, 1989, p. 4) is not always at its best. "Playing can be said to reach its own saturation point, which refers to the capacity to contain experience" (Winnicott, 1971,, p. 61). Using words like surrender and playing, we refer to our psychic work – what Freud coined "working through" – with our physicality, its ramifications and associations. Our body is always constructed by our "dreaming" mind, even when we do meet it as a natural phenomenon with its inner circadian rhythms. As Becker (2020) said it so beautifully: *There is no spiritual psyche. There is a spiriting of the psyche.* We can even experience it sometimes, especially at times of threatening disease, as "bare life" (Agamben, 1995). A life that had been stripped of the protection of the law and lies wide open and exposed to any intervention, a potential platform indifferent to the countless possible forms of human existence, present with the full burden of its impermanence, with its full vulnerability and with its death that already murmurs within it.

Being so exposed to dread many times while being ill or moving on with lots of tests and threatening states, I often felt simply lonely and ashamed though there were many good and friendly eyes around me. I know the theory about accumulative trauma. I met it as a child and as a grown-up living in Israel, and I meet it also as a therapist. Illness had a special colour of loss and pain for me since at the age of eleven I lost my father, who died of heart disease. I used to talk to God, asking him to bring my father back to life even only for a moment or two, promising to give him back after that, to give up. There was no response. Since then, illness and the "True Absent Other" or "The Ultimate Indifferent Other" became an agglomerate in my mind. However, it feels different to experience it in single first person. Here, body and language coalesce, though in these so traumatic states we cannot talk with dread. We are speechless in a way. It is a deaf partner, but it is our sole partner in these states. We have to wait until it comes to its term. We are meeting "bare life."

I wrote this paper before the coronavirus pandemic relating to my personal experience with cancer. Today every word reverberates like an orchestra of trumpets and drums. Cancer seems like an old-timer acquaintance, a family friend. The one we long to be with in troubled times, times of misfortune. The epidemic puts us all on the edge: both the virus and the corona-impacted body are now a real foreign territory to the ill persons as well as to the scientists and doctors that deal with it. It's a bare and unconquered piece of land, and a very dangerous one to individuals and to society. It would take us time to speak about it and to see the whole picture. Right now, we are almost verbosely mute. In Hebrew, we talk about Nagif[10], which has the same root as Magefa (epidemic/plague) and relates to "impingement," which was translated into Hebrew as Negifa (Kolker & Gilan, 2014). "Going-on-being" in these times is an uncanny experience.

How do we feel when we are required to contain otherness that does not threaten our life but shakes our stable matrix regarding gender, putting us at the territory of "gender as soft assembly" (Harris, 2005), and enforces us to use our Mother Tongue differently? Our ground is slipping. We do need to adapt to this situation or to use denials as our default strategy as long as it works. We are expelled from our home base although in very different ways: when we are diagnosed with cancer, we have to learn that we are not the masters of our body.

Our psyche has an important role, but it is not the queen there. Not at all. We come to know our limits and the gap between our psychic functions and capabilities and our body in a harsh way: "… for dust thou art, and unto dust shalt thou return" (Genesis, 3: 19). Choosing to transform our gender, we are on another track: we try to create ourselves in the form we do feel would fit us more.

We could say that being ill and being born with a specific gender are things that happen to us. We are not responsible and it is not our blame, although there is a widespread literature that almost preaches about our psyche's share in being ill and its power to fight it against all odds and about our gender as a cultural construct. Having said that, we still have to assume that our psyche and spirit have their share in our life for better and for worse, although in different directions: on the one hand, acknowledging illness' otherness and our psychic limits, surrendering to our bodily selves while being ill. On the other hand, creating ourselves while transforming our gender according to our core feelings and belief. Anyway, we need to accept the harsh fact that after all we are only human beings – flesh and blood. Yet, surrender, according to Ghent (1990), "implies not defeat but a quality of liberation and 'letting-go'" (p. 134). We do not submit. We do try to relate in a more benign way to our bodies and ourselves. To move differently in our life. We try to be "seekers" rather than "masters" (Becker, in this volume). We do not have other choice if we want to live and not just to survive.

Are trans phenomena an example of this so human yearning for letting go, the longing for rebirth, seeking our place on earth? Transgression as an option for re-finding and/or re-founding ourselves, for being in harmony with our body-mother-self? According to Durban (2017), the body as a mother to our self – "MoBody" – is a phantasy of the foetus, which afterwards is projected onto its mother – the phantasy of being mother and body together. The primary object body (the "MoBody"), which the uterus triggers its creation (the placenta), is initially equated with the mother's body, when the baby is born and has to move on from primal experience of omnipotence to dependency. A reasonably secure bodily home paves the way for lodging in the other.

Alternatively, we could ask, is "transing" a way to put on ourselves a "second skin" (Bick, 1968)? Is it a way of dealing with "anxieties of being" and knowing that we have to rely only on our own resources, replacing dependence on the important other by a pseudo-independence, by the inappropriate use of certain mental functions or innate talents for creating a substitute for the primal skin (internal mother), the container function?

These anxieties are typical to developmentally damaged early mental states and include experiences, such as falling forever, going to pieces, having no membrane or skin, being full of holes, losing orientation, having no relationship to the body, burning, freezing, liquefying and dissolving (Durban, 2017). We do have the taste of these "anxieties of being" even when we are not developmentally damaged. After all, impingement is our human lot.

Originally and starkly biological and sexual, the psychoanalytic body has all along carried other, often-discordant meanings (Saketopoulou, 2014). Both mind and body inhabit culture. Culture is shot through with power. Bodies are inscribed with ideas and values that announce to self and other what a person is and is to be. Shame determines the conditions of the subject's existence, since it marks what is out of its scope: unrecognized and culturally negated. However, shame is not only a measure of subjugating the subject to the social order. It could also be means of resistance to this subjugation (Ziv, 2008), to resist the threat to his or her identity (Agamben, 1999).

The trans–queer alternative allegedly enables its subject to feel a kind of victory over her shame since she could be the owner of her identity – acknowledging her active participation in this choice and in her pleasure, hereby unravelling (undoing) the chains of shame and playing with the classification system itself. However, undoing shame does not mean that it stops being part of the inner dialogue of the subject. Moreover, trans experience is not a victorious one. It is hard and painful. You gain something, but alongside the loss of your conformed belonging to the social order you also lose your so called "natural" or habitual gender, its appearance, gestures and language, even if they were hurtful and conflictual. They were part of you.

Treating M to F and F to M patients, I found myself many times in the beginning of our acquaintance stumbling over language issues. It felt like a struggle over language. It reflected feelings of confusion, doubt and objection, as a reaction to an implicit subversion and the threat of "eternal" disruption, together with a search for new ways of being together and a hope for better ones. These phases were not easy; not to her, to him and not to me; I really did my best and failed time and again. However, this enabled another way of knowing each other, maybe a truer and deeper one.

Saketopoulou (2019) argues for the conceptual and clinical utility of a psychic territory she calls *overwhelm*. Overwhelm is brought about when escalating excitations are pushed to the limit. Unlike malignant dysregulation, overwhelm is a driven state that mostly issues from within an attuned dyad. Contrary to malignant too-muchness, overwhelm is more likely to arise through limit consent's[11] reliance on the interpersonal conditions of attentiveness, passibility[12] and surrender. It is an extreme state that can bring about ego shattering, a radical unbinding of the ego that unravels previous translations that may be at an impasse, in order to make room for new ones. Sexuality, she suggests, especially sexuality in its transgressive and perverse renditions, may be ideally equipped to incite overwhelm. Saketopoulou uses the term perverse not as a marker of pathological sexuality but in its original analytic meaning, to denote sexuality that is polymorphous, has exchangeable objects, is fragmenting and is not organized reproductively or hetero-genitally. She bases this argument on Stein's (2008) plea for the rehabilitation of the place of excess in sexual experience, emphasizing its transformative potential.

We came to the point where the body is "as the clay in the potter's hand" (Jeremiah, 18:6), and painful experience is no more Eve's curse by God but her own choice. It is a way to find new modes of being in human dyads. Again, transgression is a way out of the Garden of Eden to human life, to idiosyncratic ways of life, those that Eve creates for herself and gives them a name, her own. Talking about "limit consent" and "overwhelm," this is a form of transgression and radical receptivity at the same time. We could call the open acceptance of changing gender, which is internally demanded, "transability" (as a paraphrase on "passibility" and "possibility").[13]

Relating to trans experience, we can use Saketopoulou's terms. Especially where we do find attuned dyads. That is to say, intimate relations, a place to feel at home and to come to terms with excitations and shame – a limit consent.

Talking about disease, we really talk about "malignant dysregulation" (both literally and metaphorically). It pushes us to our limits and over them (physically and psychically), exposing us to feelings of dread, helplessness and shame. We are literally naked, publicly exposed with our weak spots. Yet, it is also a phase that enforces us to look at things differently: to adjust to our vulnerability, dependency and mortality – to surrender to human life necessities.

Disease and trans play with limits, borders and excess. In both of them, the limits are on the front stage: the limits of our bodily and psychic capacities, the materiality of our body and its being a process, a place for fantasmatic creation, as transgressive. We need to move between accepting our limits, protesting against them and creating our alternative ways of being.

However, they are not just alternative ways: they are particular, personal and intimate ways of being, which can be found only in the presence of another – maybe of a True Human Other (when we are dealing with the Ultimate Indifferent one). In addition, it requires the creation and adaptation of language by both partners, which will allow the transformation to be creative instead of negative, giving name and not only losing one, recognizing and being recognized.

Are we then in the Garden of Eden or in hell? Maybe we are treading on a new terrain, still a human one. "All too Human" (Nietzsche, 1878).

Notes

1 Makom in Hebrew. One of God's denotations in the Mishna – referring to the divinity in its absence, in its namelessness.
2 Makom in Hebrew. One of God's denotations in the Mishna – referring to the divinity in its absence, in its namelessness.
3 Hava, חווה
4 Kaniti ish et yehova, קניתי איש את-יהוה
5 We can read it also as a reaction to the inverted "primal scene" (or even Primal Sin) of God and Man while creating Woman. Now Eve and God are the creative couple.
6 Hevel, הבל
7 Midrash Shem.
8 שת : Seth. In Hebrew, it means to give, to put and to grant.
9 "Let me know right away/ if I'm disturbing you/ he said/ as he stepped inside my door/ and I'll leave the way I came/. Not only do you disturb me,/ I answered/ You turn my whole world/ upside down./ Welcome." Eeva Kilpi (2014, p. 15).

10 נגיף.
11 Limit consent does not centre on (re)producing an experience of satisfaction but, instead, works to facilitate novelty and surprise. In contrast to its affirmative counterpart, it does not hinge on respecting limits but on transgressing them.
12 Lyotard (1988) has coined the term *passibility*. Passibility is not opposed to activity. It is akin to the radical receptivity that Ghent (1990) described as surrender, which he carefully distinguished from masochism and submission.
13 Merav Roth – personal communication.

References

Agamben, G. (1995). *Homo Sacer: Sovereign Power and Bare Life*. Stanford: Stanford University, 1998.

Agamben, G. (1999). *Remnants of Auschwitz: The Witness and the Archives*. Translated by Daniel Heller-Roazen. New York: Zone.

Aron, L. (2005). The Tree of Knowledge: Good and Evil Conflicting Interpretations. *Psychoanalytic Dialogues* 15(5): 681–807.

Bauman, Z. (2011). *Culture in a Liquid Modern World*. Tel Aviv: Hakibbutz Hameuchad, 2014.

Becker, M. (2020). Allowing the Creation. In: W. Pearson & H. Marlo (Eds.), *The Spiritual Psyche, Mysticism, Intersubjectivity and Psychoanalysis in Clinical Practice* (pp. 202–216). London: Routledge.

Becker, M. (in this volume). The Birth of a True Other. In: M. Barnea-Astrog & M. Becker (Eds.), *The Birth of a True Other: Relational Conversations on Meeting and Becoming*.

Bick, E. (1968). The Experience of the Skin in Early Object-Relations. *International Journal of Psychoanalysis*, 49: 484–486.

Britton, R. (1998). *Belief and Imagination: Explorations in Psychoanalysis*. New York: Routledge.

Butler, J. (1993). *Bodies That Matter: On the Discursive Limits of "Sex"*. New York: Routledge.

Cassuto, U. (1965). *The Book of Genesis – From Noah to Abraham*. Jerusalem: Magnes.

Derrida, J. (1966). *Motolinguisme de l'autre*. Translated by Moshe Ron. Tel Aviv: Resling, 2019.

Dimen, M. (2000). The Body as Rorschach. *Studies in Gender & Sexuality* 1(1): 9–39.

Dimen, M. (2001). Perversion Is Us: Eight Notes. *Psychoanalytic Dialogues* 11: 825–860.

Dimen, M. (2014). Both Given and Made: Commentary on Saketopoulou. *Journal of American Psychoanalytic Association* 62(5): 807–813.

Durban, J. (2017). "Home, Homelessness and Nowhere-Ness" in Early Infancy. *Journal of Child Psychotherapy* 43: 175–191.

Durban, J., Lazar, R. & Ofer, G. (1993). The Cracked Container, the Containing Crack: Chronic Illness – Its Effect on the Therapist and the Therapeutic Process. *International Journal of Psychoanalysis*, 74: 705–713.

Foucault, M. (1976). *The History of Sexuality Vol. I*. New York: Vintage Books, 1980.

Freud, S. (1918). *From the History of an Infantile Neurosis. Standard Edition* (Vol. 17, pp. 1–124). London: Hogarth Press, 1917–1919.

Fromm, E. (1966). *You Shall Be as Gods*. New York: Holt, Rinehart & Winston.

Ghent, E. (1990). Masochism, Submission, Surrender: Masochism as a Perversion of Surrender. *Contemporary Psychoanalysis* 26(1): 108–136.

Harris, A. (2005). *Gender as Soft Assembly*. New York: Routledge, 2009.

Kilpi, E. (2014). *A Landscape Blossoms Within Me*. Translated by D. Adamson. Todmorden, UK: Arc Publications.

Kolker, S. & Gilan, O. (2014). Linguistic Introduction. In: D.W. Winnicott (Ed.), *Deprivation and Delinquency*, 1965. Tel Aviv: Bookworm.

Lazar, R. (2006). In the Beginning Was Love? *The Psychoanalytic Review* 93(3): 393–410.

Lazar, R. (2010). Infinite Conversation: The Work of the Unconscious. *Ma'arag: The Israel Journal of Psychoanalysis* 1: 199–218.

Lazar, R. (2013). Intimate Strangers in "The Other Room". *Sihot – Dialogue. Israel Journal of Psychotherapy* 2: 140–147.

Lyotard, J.F. (1988). *The Inhuman*. Stanford: Polity.

Nietzsche, F. (1878). *Human, All Too Human*. Translated by Jacob Gottschalk and Adam Tenenbaum. Jerualem: The Hebrew University Magnes Press, 2008.

Pardes, I. (1996). *Countertraditions in the Bible: A Feminist Approach*. Tel Aviv: Hakibbutz Hameuchad.

Saketopoulou, A. (2014). Mourning the Body as Bedrock: Developmental Considerations in Treating Transsexual Patients Analytically. *Journal of the American Psychoanalytic Association* 62(5): 773–806.

Saketopoulou, A. (2019). The Draw to Overwhelm: Consent, Risk and There-Translation of Enigma. *Journal of the American Psychoanalytic Association* 67(1): 133–167.

Soloveitchik, J.B. (2000). *Family Redeemed*. New York: Ktav.

Stein, R.A. (2008). The Otherness of Sexuality: Excess. *Journal of the American Psychoanalytic Association* 56: 43–71.

Winnicott, D.W. (1971). *Playing and Reality*. Middlesex: Penguin.

Winnicott, D.W. (1989). *Psychoanalytic Explorations*, C. Winnicott, R. Shepherd & M. Davis (Eds.). Cambridge, MA: Harvard University.

Ziv, E. (2008). The Dialectics of Shame: Between Subordination and Resistance: The Dialectics of Shame Apparatus. *Theory and Criticism* 32: 99–128.

Chapter 3

In the Beginning There Was an Other

Mitchel Becker

All creation seems to have stopped, there is no place to go and we have landed in Sartre's "No Exit." Sartre meant for this to be hell, i.e. our lives. This place has no movement, no process and no surprises. This is the ominous and pernicious Garden of Eden where the naked is not bearable and the cloth is a betrayal. But "No Exit" is when the other is a thing with no emotionally true link. Hell is all dressed up to go on forever to nowhere for no thing.

It seems to me that for Rina (Lazar, 2023), meeting the ultimate other always implies a confronting of strangeness. We ache for a homeward bound and yet trespass boundaries way beyond home, and then we are homeless. But why? Is this a repetition compulsion to return to the primary scene which can never be totally contained? Or is it a genuine need to escape an incestuous existence and discover new worlds? Could our relationship with our bodies, as Rina discusses, actually encompass this dialectic of intimate and foreign?

I imagine Rina's discussion of illness and gender transformation as a discussion of hospitality. Inviting to our psychic awareness, a prospect of death and of birth of a new gender to our self's playground. "Welcome please, won't you please stay with me? I feel all alone and ashamed. Can you stand it with me? Because I can't stand it alone."

Each time I read or hear Rina's voice, I am immediately enwrapped in the core conflicts of relation. Sure, there is the simple and the petty of all relations, but each time Rina's voice is heard by my soul, I know there is a bitter and sweet truth of recognition and alienation; of the incapacity to know and the endearing and magical wish to truly know.

We are enigmatic, but not to conceal; we are enigmatic because we believe that we are uncontainable. A hybrid of Bad Me and Not Me,

DOI: 10.4324/9781003325499-4

in which the Bad is somewhat containable and the Not is most certainly not what we can stand. The I that is mortal and the I that lives in false identity are in need of an I-You. And thus Rina concludes that there are "particular, personal, and intimate ways of being which can be found only in the presence of another, maybe of a True Human Other." How is an other to join my journey?

We are forever unfettering the tie to the other, not letting the intimacy in. My patient wonders: "Why bother if he will one day just take his leave? And with him a part of my heart." I too wonder in my thought, "Yes, why bother? One could stay untouched, be in a relationship untouched, so that when he leaves, he takes nothing with him." My patient smiles, as if reading my reverie. She left a "safe" relationship which never dared to enter a sincere dialogue. I think of her parents – of the primal scene. She feels there never was much to see in their shared bed. No one overwhelmed or whelmed at all. Her parents were never in fear of the uncontainable; their lives were always suffocatingly under control. In juxtaposition, there are so many ways in which life and relationships can lead us to a sense of the uncontainable: death, dread, shame, abandonment and complete overwhelment. The psyche in terror immediately responds: "This cannot be a part of my narrative." And so it invites denial, rage and desperation to avoid the uncontainable.

Another patient, whom I have known for many years, enters a place that is uncontainable. There is a pain of love in which both of the lovers were unable to accept the simple fact of their mutual love. My patient was closer to this awareness than his friend, a wished-for partner. His friend rejected him without even acknowledging that he was rejecting. My patient enters a world of psychosis in which he sees himself as the messiah. He sees no connection to the romantic hurt he experienced. He is discharged from the hospital and comes to see me. He talks about the different patients he met on the psychiatric ward, and I ask him how he understands the phenomena of psychosis. He says, "Psychosis is the desire for the other and the other betrays and does not appear." His words cut through all the words and touch the most basic inner turmoil. A soul alone.

And now I reflect again on Rina's thoughts and feelings. The self senses a pain as a result of being told directly or indirectly that something in the Me is not right. A "Not Right" that is in the eyes and perception of the other. My cancer or my gender causes anxiety in the other. When that anxiety is apparent but bearable, the self is experienced as a "Bad Me," and when that anxiety seen in the eyes of the other is unbearable, or totally dreadful, then the self is experienced as "Not Me." The other is then seen as unable to accept the "Me" and its body's struggles. But this other also lives inside me, an internal other.

In the middle of a seminar that I was giving, I found myself saying, "The vital self is twoness." It fell upon me like an ocean wave rushing over my head. What is the essence of the Good, Bad and Not Me? That the Me is an entity as long as the Other's relation is present. A non-relation means the deadness of my Me.

We give names to things when they become or have the capacity to become absent. What is present does not need to be named. As long as ourselves are present in the eye of the other, we need not name the phenomenon of selfhood. We are forced to call ourselves "a self" because in some way the Other has emotionally gone, has become absent. And in his or her absence, we name ourselves as in relation to them.

The psychoanalytic model of Me-ness in which I determine who I am by the face of the other is an expression of us trying to decipher the meaning of the many ways we sense an absence or a mismatch or a misattunement. Since the vital self can only be alive in a twoness, in a passionate link, s/he will desperately seek that aliveness of relation. Thus, being named as Good or Bad are ways to be. I am alive in a relationship in which the other sees me as Good or as Bad. The look in the face of the other is of harmony or disharmony, of pleasure and confirmation or of discord and disapproval.

But what happens when it is clear that the other ceases to process? When I become undigestible and incomprehensible? Then, I desperately try to become digestible. This may lead to attempts to trigger up Good Me or Bad Me – whatever works, whatever can bring things into comprehensibility for the two of us. But the Not Me is not, by virtue of this attempted distraction, undone. The place of Not Me, dissociated from the vitality of twoness, stays lurking in the memory. A memory of the face of the Other as a blank stare or a face that simply crumbles or a face whose light has been extinguished. And the wish for a True Other becomes ever more fierce. Yet the fear and dread of more Not Me interactions leaves the self resolved to not grow for fear that any hint of movement and creativity will result in the repetition of Not Me. Thus, we come to the paradoxical conclusion that a bearable deadness is adopted to prevent an unbearable deadness.

So, whence I go when I know the Not Me is within me? The catastrophe persists in my very essence. I sense that something in me is bereft of the right to exist, and thus a part of me must and will desist. Does every significant change entail a capacity to contain catastrophe? This is a simple difficult truth. Transformations in self and in relation always entail a sense of birth and death. Destruction and creation are always hand in hand, and for those who seek, there is no escape from destruction. There is no way out, other than to hug destruction as one of the inevitable guests of ourselves and of our journey.

And just when I think that I have begun to understand why Rina chose to speak of cancer and transgender issues in response to my chapter on "The Birth of a True Other," I sense a deep sadness and hear Rina's childhood recollection, "I used to talk to G-d, asking him to bring my father back to life even only for a moment or two, promising to give him back … There was no response. Since then, illness and the True Absent Other… became an agglomerate in my mind." Can the Absent True Other declare of truths unknown to the present psyche? Does the acute pain of what is desperately missing inform the soul of what is missing? Yes and no. Yes, we are aware of the present when it is absent. But the absence can only be felt when there was a previous presence, if only for a brief Garden of Eden glimmer of a True Other.

I am two years old. I have gone through an eye operation to straighten my crossed eyes. It is 1959, and parents were not seen as essential to a child's recovery. They said I would cry if my parents would come visit. A hospital with no hospitality. So for several days, eyes bandaged, I see no face and hear no known voice. And in my psyche, I am that hybrid of a Bad and Not Me. Bad and therefore punished for having eyes that need to be fixed. Not and therefore abandoned. Shame seems to synthesize the Bad and the Not of my Me. My body is sick and in need of transformation. And the other? No Other was able to contain or see my uncontainable. The nurses say I was the perfect child. Fifty years later, my aunt, who came with my mom to take me home, says she had never seen a child so quietly overwhelmed.

In the lone night, when the bearable and unbearable become indistinguishable, we desperately need a mate to bear the truths of our lives. And in those very spaces of deep despair, if we are somehow still left with hope and have fortunately, if but for a moment, sensed True Otherness, we seek an other. A true other who can fathom our unfathomable. "That is why a man leaves his father and mother and cleaves to his wife, and they became one flesh. And they were both naked and felt no shame" (Genesis 2:24–25).

How rare and dear to feel no shame when the eyes of a True Other see almost all of our soul and we sense that our multiple "Me's," the Good, the Bad and even the Not, are truly containable in their eyes. How incredibly magical when an encounter with a True Other safely transgresses the boundaries of the known and seeks new overwhelms of being.

References

Genesis The Holy Scriptures (1984) Jerusalem: Koren Publishers. 2:24–25.
Lazar, R. (2023). *Meeting the Ultimate Other: Allowing the Creation*. In: M. Barnea-Astrog & M. Becker (Ed.), Relational Conversations on Meeting and Becoming: The Birth of a True Other. London: Routledge.

First Associative Trialogue

I Call Out to You

*Irene Bleier Lewenhoff, Michal Barnea-Astrog
and Mitchel Becker*

Irene

The first book of poems I published was titled *You*. I was calling out
to you. Desperately. This was the purpose of my writing: at first,
when I was very young, and now, close to the end of the road – to get
a reaction, to feel alive, to meaningfully exist.

I have published six books so far. Three in Uruguay, my homeland,
in my language. Three here, in the local tongue. All six were thin. All
six were not promoted. And they all hid, as I now see it, two big lies.
The first involved denying the reality of my life: I was already living
in Israel, but still published my book in Uruguay. The second was the
refusal to seek recognition. I denied my need for a response. Because
I was calling out to all of *you*, but I was afraid of not getting an appropriate answer. Of not being properly understood.

Why do we write? What is worth writing for? These are two very
different questions, and the answers reflect the circumstances of
the writer's life. As for me, I am always suspicious of my intentions.
Mostly, I suspect myself of covering the truth. I don't really know
where this suspicion stems from, and I admit I have taken this habit
way beyond my own good. I came to learn that sometimes truth covers can protect and make things easier, softer. And mainly, that they
should be forgiven.

So why do I write? And why do I read? Right now, to gain temporary clarity, only to immediately resume searching. This much is clear
to me, and it fills me with curiosity and joy: coherence is beyond me.
And the act of searching is the only bearable one, when haunted by
the fear of lying that accompanies my need for articulation – the fear
of denying truth.

DOI: 10.4324/9781003325499-6

An act of articulation is an act of clarification. But it is also an ending. Every word I write is the last word I will ever have. By this word, an enormous sorrow is erased, gone, buried; it is named and is no more. Everything that was, everything I saw and everything that sizzled through me – all of that dies when I choose a word. Because when I write "tree" – what is left? What is erased? What became unliving? And at the same time, what is nevertheless formed?

Far away from keyboard, screen and paper, words appear in sequences that I want to keep. They disappear or change when I am facing the paper or the screen, in the very same way that I'm changed by the presence of others, sometimes having my very being erased. And there is also the effect of translation. Complete sentences appear in my home language, in Spanish, and I translate them into Hebrew; but then, in a way, they die. They are lost to me, and something inside me dies along; and I try to live, which means writing. But the dead words are not good material for life to spring from.

Skyscrapers consistently grow around me. Glass and steel. They hide the sky and the clouds. Cement covers the soil and the earth. Where does the power of the earth go when it is covered? There is a wall in the south of Tel Aviv, smooth and grey and tall, maybe four stories high. And in the middle, far from the ground and far from the top, there is a tree that I've watched grow over the years. And sometimes, through the cracks, a living plant may emerge. One can never know how the life force may find its way through the covers, when and where and in what form it will spring. And I would like to be able to live and write in the light of this fact. I would like to be less compelled, or at least to attribute some hidden good intentions to my being compelled.

Being pushed to put everything – sensations, sounds, colours, thoughts – into words, burning with the desire and urge to share every discovery, every conclusion, every realization and insight and revelation – to what extent is it a manifestation of the eternal desire to be, to vanquish the approaching end? I ask myself this question, and the wonderful and terrible expression "to escape forward" crosses my mind. Perhaps this is what we sentient beings are always trying to do: to escape forward. To escape forward from ourselves, from terror and fear into other people's arms. Into their soul and body and voice and warmth. To escape from death, into their embrace.

And perhaps the need to turn every phenomenon into words expresses a life force, like the one that pushes the blood through our veins, or the one that pushes the tree to grow tall against all-powerful gravity. Perhaps the word, the language, the primal scream or the simple sound that we pour into conventions is the core of our being. Or perhaps, for some of us, they became this core by necessity. The necessity that emerged from chronically living in unclear, unreassuring circumstances, which we had to endure without any choice or satisfying explanation. When this is the case, one seeks refuge in language expecting some kind of an answer or a response – from eternity, from one's surroundings and from everything one is a part of: the cold, the heat, the stars, the dust, the light and the storms, the everlasting, incomprehensible movements that encompass us all.

Reading and writing turn the world into a liminal space. Not reality, not a dream. Both reality and dream. The same rules and laws apply to life and to the acts of reading and writing, including the law of constant change. I change them or they change on their own. I control them or they control me. But this is not a game. Not if a game is an action without actual results. And anyway, for me, every action, even a game, has consequences. These find their way in through the dialectic movement between distance and closeness of the writer and the reader, the speaker and the listener; between receiving and projecting and transmitting and knowing that information and experience arise codependently from here and from there, from this side of the text and from the other.

So I write in order to move between the two sides, between myself and others. To constantly break the eternal divide. I don't want to write in order to justify my existence, nor to use others for that purpose. I don't want to always remain there – my self, my needs and my yearnings – as a divide. But can it be avoided? If we do write for others, can we be clear enough? Can we move out of the way once in a while and, in a sense, leave ourselves behind?

Then we can write words that are at once empty and full. Full of meaning and intentions. Understandable and empty enough to contain whoever meets them. Open and wide and precise enough to be easily written and read – enough to enable a fruitful encounter, enough to simply bring joy. But the roads of our lives are ever twisting. Sometimes we walk steadily, to a clear destination that calls us.

And then the road disappears, and the destination no longer gleams in the distance, or else it seems ridiculous and unworthy or even forbidden. And we fall into an abyss, which is always there; we fall down and crash or we hang from a branch, perhaps a blossoming branch, which cares not that we fall. And sometimes, while our hand still clutches the branch, we rest. And then we can begin to carve out a new road, which simultaneously continues the old path and diverges from it. And such is the road of writing that a writer is placed upon, in a way that might be mysterious to her while very clear to others; perhaps clear to the life force that enables her to walk, fall, rise, rest and carve out again and again until she reaches the final abyss or resting place. Perhaps.

Meanwhile, I chase the possibility of triumph when I know there is only surrender. I hunger for the truth, and I run away from it with all the tricks I've learned and inherited. And it is this circle, which one can never exit – or else exits with no sense of triumph – that brings me back, time and again, from the last word to the next, like in this very moment. From the last to the next, to the word that right now gives me a new hope. The hope that someone may be immersed in the words – the same words that were supposedly mine before I wrote them, but are no longer my own. The hope that the words will close the distance between us and make our connecting strings tremble, and there will be no need to shout, perhaps no need to hear. Then the words will cross all the dividing between us. Then we can truly meet.

Michal

Sometimes words are used in ways that create a mental space and cross it at the same time. Internal space and intermental space, through which the unspoken and the unthought can travel: in the world, in the mind and between minds. This space encompasses plenty of intervals, but it is not void. It is ethereal as it is watery, and there are solid and fiery elements to pass by or to stumble upon. All kinds of messages – felt and unseen, seen but unheard, heard but not sensed, sensed but not grasped by the intellect – move there in all directions. They travel like light and colour, like scent or sound, like heavy ships drenched in black oil, barely managing the turbulent sea. They travel and reach some kind of shore, and dock there, absorbed by someone's body–mind. At least momentarily. Or they don't dock and are not quite absorbed, but merely touch its fringes. Or they don't touch them directly but through foam. And as they do, it changes, producing new territories and atmospheres to reach and to absorb and to move across.

Turning O into K – or rather, being with O until it is poured into a K stream on its own – whose job is it? The analyst's? The mystic's? The thinking person's? The poet's? It is about making room for something that has no concrete body. It is about bringing a back stage, underground matter to the front. It is about treating darkness as glorious, and letting it shine through the known and the blunt.

The habitual and automatic are always there. They can go unnoticed, be dismissed, taken for granted. After all, they are not perceived as life itself, but only as the veil through which life shows. Only as the bounded route through which life flows; only as the enzymes and intestinal tissue that take life's substances apart so that they can be properly used. Only. But our habitual, repetitive reactions and ways of perceiving, of ingesting and of formulating meaning – are in many ways what create life and keep us going on.

What is already known is of no further consequence (Bion, 1967). It has lost its relevance to the present moment and therefore is not a fertile soil to dwell on. The thing is, that very often what feels so familiar to us – so habitual, so automatic, so known – is actually mostly outside of our awareness. We may know some of its overt aspects, but its deeper truths are hidden, all the while operating us from within. It is an unknown disguised as known. This is one reason for us to be self-suspicious. Mitchel expresses such suspicion too: "How do we know if we are on a path to awareness or a path of false mirrors? ... I fear to be in falseness and not even to be aware that it is false."

The seeker of truth is often suspicious of his own hidden agendas, not only of others'. I flip this suspicion on its side and turn it into curiosity. Sympathetic curiosity. Something is repeatedly happening (in me, in you and in the person sitting with me for a while every Monday afternoon), and we don't even see it. Or we only see a few of its ends sticking out on the surface, and we are so tired of it and of what it consistently leads to, that we just wish for it to be gone. But it has its good reasons to go on. It has its truth. So I blur the focus of my mental vision, and don't invest too much in the overt surface, and try to remain open to the evolutions of the obscure present. Until something becomes something. Until something that gradually or suddenly takes on a form or a meaning, filters through. Like in the following instance.

She sits in front of me, experiencing and describing sadness and shame regarding her relations with her mother, which echo in her relations with her daughter. Her mother never sees her; she's incapable of seeing. She feels invisible wherever she goes. Now her daughter accuses her of not seeing her too.

After a few minutes of being in touch with this deep pain, everything fades away. Tiredness comes; disengagement and fog replace the acuteness of life. She tries to bring it back by remembering certain situations and people and by telling me some more, but the strong emotions and the clear links have dispersed. It all slips through her fingers.

She's disappointed with herself. It's the same old routine over and over again. All too familiar, all too known. And it shouldn't be this way. But I'm most curious about this foggy, tired, disengaging stream. I tap into it, and I say that I do. I say how interesting and significant this familiar dynamic that we both meet so often in her seems to me, and suggest that we stay with it and follow it wherever it takes us. She hears the words and sees my facial expression, which confirms my intentions and state of attention. We are in the fog of the unknown disguised as known, but there's a shift. She feels she doesn't have to push away what's really happening, nor try, without success, to do or to be something else. She feels seen.

What appears before us is universal as it is personal, private and idiosyncratic. It is brought about to the front through our reflective capacities – the capacity to allow spaces of nothingness and vague lumps of rawness, which may eventually meet our verbal, meaning-making capacities. It does not have to be discursive or otherwise comprehended by the intellect as it emerges. Quite the contrary. At first, it often bypasses reason and control. There are unseen passages that can be regularly cleared, so as to allow the underground unknown matter to filter through. This doesn't mean that the entire mind is cleared, nor that these passages are cleared forever; just that there are the ability and skilfulness and commitment and good fortune to have some metaphorical tunnels or airways, created and maintained momentarily, available to facilitate the movement of substances across mental space.

Then we can meet truth while truly meeting. Then we can deeply communicate. We can communicate realities with ourselves and with others – with ourselves who are others and with "true others" (Becker, 2023, see Chapter 1) who make us more ourselves. These realities may be delivered in words, enveloped as words; but they travel through the unseen passages as waves, as oscillations, as coordinates marking vast fields of meaning. The fields of meaning come to life inside us – inside private individuals – but they cross boundaries of personality, space and time.

I'd like to place here some words of others as such coordinates.

Arendt (1958) writes:

> Because the actor always moves among and in relation to other acting beings, he is never merely a "doer" but always and at the same time a sufferer. To do and to suffer are like opposite sides of the same coin, and the story that an act starts is composed of its consequent deeds and sufferings. These consequences are boundless, because action, though it may proceed from nowhere, so to speak, acts into a medium where every reaction becomes a chain reaction and where every process is the cause of new processes. Since action acts upon beings who are capable of their own actions, reaction, apart from being a response, is always a new action that strikes out on its own and affects others. Thus action and reaction among men never move in a closed circle and can never be reliably confined to two partners.
>
> (p. 190)

The effect moves beyond the apparent doer and done to. The doer herself is a "done to." And the waves and particle of action or reaction travel in many seen and unseen directions and touch multiple layers of experience and of the world.

At this moment, between us, the action is conversing or reading and writing; but it is also internal speech, conversing with imagined others, with internal objects and with self-parts; and it is also any volitional mental action that underlines or accompanies the act of conversing, as the Pāli term "kamma" (which means "action") indicates. Mental action in this sense is not synonymous with contemplation or to thought, which classic western perspectives traditionally distinguish from action – since in Buddhist view, mental action is the foremost action that carries actual results in the world (Barnea-Astrog, 2017).

Regardless of its specific content, an action always creates a relationship. This is why it has an inherent tendency to break through all boundaries (Arendt, 1958). The external physical actions depend on the internal mental ones, and what happens in a relation affects all parties and spreads beyond them. Complex dependency characterizes all conditioned phenomena, all that lives and dies in the context of relations.

Another coordinate (bear the leap, if you will), this time by Bion (1970):

> Since thought liberates the intuition there is conflict between the impulse to leave the intuition unexpressed and the impulse to express it. The restrictive element of representation therefore obtrudes in transformation $T\alpha{\rightarrow}T\beta$ of preverbal material. One man achieves the transformation; the other, who cannot tolerate restriction, does not. He therefore forfeits the relief from frustration that thought, were he able to tolerate it, would give.
>
> (p. 11)

> The impossibility of communication without frustration is so familiar that the nature of the frustration is forgotten. [...] difficulties become more marked still when the material to be communicated is pre- or non-verbal. [...] The pre-verbal matter the psycho-analyst must discuss is certain to be an illustration of the difficulty in communication that he himself is experiencing. Ability to use points, lines, and space becomes important for understanding 'emotional space', for the continuance of the work and avoidance of a situation in which two inarticulate personalities are unable to release themselves from the bondage of inarticulation.
>
> (Bion, 1970, p. 15)

Articulation matters. But there's a whole field between the vitalizing force of articulation and its deadening potential, between its capacity to link or to detach and between its ability to cross over, to break through boundaries (of self and other, of conscious and unconscious and of self-parts) or to keep apart. How far does this territory stretch and what does it include? It must include our reactions, our mental actions and our relations. It must include our needs and intentions, what we consciously and unconsciously try to **do** with words.

Here is the voice of Bernard, from Virginia Woolf's *The Waves* (2000 [1931]), towards the end of his life, who lived on articulation and relation, on story weaving and storytelling as the medium for living and relating:

> Thin as a ghost, leaving no trace where I trod, perceiving merely, I walked alone in a new world, never trodden; brushing new flowers, unable to speak save in a child's words of one syllable; without shelter from phrases – I who have made so many; unattended, I who have always gone with my kind; solitary, I who have always had someone to share the empty grate, or the cupboard with its hanging loop of gold.
>
> But how describe the world seen without a self? There are no words. Blue, red – even they distract, even they hide with thickness instead of letting the light through. How describe or say anything in articulate words again? – save that it fades, save that it undergoes a gradual transformation, becomes, even in the course of one short walk, habitual – this scene also. Blindness returns as one moves and one leaf repeats another. Loveliness returns as one looks, with all its train of phantom phrases. One breathes in and out substantial breath; down in the valley the train draws across the fields lop-eared with smoke.
>
> But for a moment I had sat on the turf somewhere high above the flow of the sea and the sound of the woods, had seen the house, the garden, and the waves breaking. The old nurse who turns the pages of the picture-book had stopped and had said, "Look. This is the truth."
>
> (pp. 161–162)

Now all these words, all these points, lines and intervals, all these coordinates of fields of meaning, hover inside me, above and around me, and perhaps you too. Now they create a multi-dimensional space where particles and waves can travel, where we can move amongst various, partial, tentative truths – briefly landing on one and then on another, like butterflies. Or we can blur the focus of our vision and sense them all at once, our minds expanding with the vastness that extends between and beyond them, with no need for inclination or preference towards none.

For a while, we can live in space and time without fixating on any of the coordinates that mark and form them. We can live in real time. With those who wrote these words, although they are long gone. Because the effect of an action is boundless. Because something that was created depending on their lives and actions (in body, in speech and in mind) is still pulsating in the universe. And it can reach shores of consciousness and touch and transform them. It can create space and traverse it at the same time.

Mitchel

Here I begin to write, and clearly the other is present. Can one write without the other? Can one think? These are not questions for the philosopher on the couch; these are the essences of our existential being.

I read again and again what Irene wrote. Each time the "process" becomes more and more a whole. Can you sense this? Irene began by seeing her writing as an expression of her natural need to actualize her very own existence. A form of, "I write therefore I am." But this formula quickly unfolds to a search. A search for what? A solution to death? To meaninglessness? To loneliness? All of these are proposed. And all of these are indeed our lives. But then I sense a metamorphosis in midst of her thought. She begins to ask: where do these words go? What do these words want? How does one understand the dance between oneself – the writer – and one's readers?

I then read Michal's thoughts and perhaps sense her sensations. She challenges the reader to ponder the concept of space. There is a private one. And there is a couple's dialogic space, and finally, a hard to imagine universal space extended to an endless time. Michal then writes:

> For a while, we can live in space and time without fixating on any of the coordinates that mark and form them. We can live in real time. With those who wrote these words, although they are long gone. Because the effect of an action is boundless.

These words move me. They represent for me a faith that is so crucial to our existence and yet so difficult to bring to fruition. But I am more and more convinced that this faith is born of dialogue.

Thus, the process proceeds to its destination: a wish for a true dialogue. In this case, a dialogue in which Irene speaks and the reader in their inner contemplation continues to ponder and evolve. But this dialogue is not a "one says and then another answers." Irene expresses something, in my opinion, far more profound. The moment that souls truly meet. Barriers fall away, and a truth touches two at the same moment in a way that no ego can ever understand.

Michal responds to Irene by allowing herself to unravel her mind from words. As Virginia Wolf's character that Michal cites, single baby syllables bear the truth while actions seek the other. But how does this really happen? X does Y to Z. What does this mean?

A couple comes to therapy. Their language is uni-directional. X does to Y or Y does to X. The sense of give and take isn't necessarily "bad;" it just lacks a spirit of true mutuality. Even a more complex circular dynamic doesn't capture what I seek. I see you, so you see me. This makes for decent business partners. Nothing to belittle. And yet I seek more. So what do I seek? A couple being an intersubjective entity, an entity that co-digests and co-dreams. A place in which the unconscious of one speaks with the other's unconscious in a way that both can grow. When the relation is with an adversary, this can be a true nightmare. When romantic partners are adversary, there is a sense of misrepresentation, coercion and a sense of one's self being taken hostage. The rageful tones come from a deep hurt from these three overlapping experiences.

Misrepresentation

The partner feels that the revealed intimacy has been cast in a negative maligning manner. "You will not say that about me!" or "you will not see me that way!" My dreams have been misrepresented.

Coercion

The unconscious dance implies that the couple are mutually registering cherished unconscious material. Because the relation is adversarial, each one senses that, against their wish, they are induced into an undesired dance which ruthlessly touches raw emotion without any hope for safety. The most intelligent response to this experience is helplessness.

Being Taken Hostage

After being misrepresented in one's sense of self and then coerced into acting in a manner that feels foreign to one's self, the final step is a kidnapping in the middle of the night. Not only does the individual feel they are living a narrative that is not them, but ultimately there is a sense that the real self is tied up in the cellar, mouth taped shut and barely able to breathe and no one is there to save the imprisoned self.

How did I get here? From a wish to be free to write and create, I tell a story of enslavement. The wish becomes the jail in which the soul is taken hostage. The wish for love, recognition and understanding, the wish to connect, attach and link, becomes the place of empty nurturance and decimation.

Emptiness, a sense that what should be is not, evolves into a hatred of the other who refuses to be the source of all that is desired. And a deep resentment of the other is born. Misrepresented, coerced and being taken hostage – the master and slave begin to drown in hatred.

Toni Morrison (1970) wrote of hate and prejudice, and of the trampled flower called love. In her first book, she opens with a harrowing passage involving two young sisters desperately attempting to care for the young Pecola, who is pregnant with her father's baby. The young innocent sisters planted marigold seeds, and when the seeds failed to grow, they thought it was because of Pecola and then because of their own tormented souls. They could not know that the deep hatred of prejudice planted in their adult world prohibited any seeds to grow anywhere. They dreamed up magical words to repair their broken world but to no avail. Due to the annihilating relations of racism, all growth failed, and with that failure, hope and love died as well and so did Pecola's baby.

With her first virgin words, Toni Morrison began her illustrious career of digesting hate and prejudice.[1] It is hard for me to grasp all of the endless pain that Morrison puts into these words, and the heart wrenching wish for a magic that will repair a torn world. As if the words could magically repair. She asks of us to ponder how the sins of a collective reverberate throughout the natural world.

I read her words again and again. Each time, you and I sense a new pain and a nuance of guilt, rage and deep sadness. How does hate enter our heart and destroy? In her book *Love*, Morrison (2003) writes that hate destroys everything in its path, and that the faces of the haters become one (p. 34). The tragedy is obviously not just how hate looks on the face of the other, but rather how hate regenerates its self. Hate handed down from generation to generation with a sole aim of creating more hate. That fact we all know. Perhaps the real tragedy is that what we see is what we get and what we become. We are a product of relations. What actually happens in deep prejudice racism and bigotry? We become a hopeless mutual destructive relation.

I suddenly realize that I have described the negative of the true other. Hate, emptiness and mutual impoverishment of the other are the ways we diminish all growth. The ways in which one plus one equals less than one. The ways in which hate produces the raping of Pecola.

Is there a similar parallel with the writer? Can hate attack the link between writer and reader? This is the very same writer who wishes, as Irene writes, to touch the reader in a way that allows for a dialogue, between the souls of writer and reader, to be born. How is the dialogue derailed? I want to contend that via misrepresentation, coercion and a taking hostage the writer and reader confront the same challenges of romance. The challenges that confront love.

You will not see me in that way!! You will not contort my feelings into distorted foreign matter. You will not subjugate my soul to the devil or to decimation! The writer declares freedom via a narrative of subjugation. Thus the writer writes, and thus the reader reads. At times the result is utter hate, and at times we sense a found soul mate. At times the author's dreams or nightmares are in direct conflict with the reader's psyche's space. The reader is attacked by every word and every emotion that the writer offers. And at times a true dialogue is born.

How astonishing is this place of dialogue! All the barriers shouting "halt," "yield" and "stop" suddenly evaporate, and the reader is free to dream up the words of the author. Erich Fromm writes that the opposite of love is fear. We are afraid to love. Toni Morrison writes a nightmare of love's distortions and of how fear dressed as hate does the distorting. She uses the eyes and mouth of a child to tell her story. The child expresses her fears, and we are invited to hear and somehow contain the child's unbearable pain. The reader who cannot do this will begin to misrepresent, coerce or take hostage either themselves or Morrison's pain. A true other somehow unexplainably finds the courage to love Pecola. To love a difference containing unimagined pains. The moment of engagement not as hostage but as hosts to the unknown that is I and you. Writer and reader meet, and for that moment, fear is somehow digested and love nourishes all.

Irene

After writing my first text, I waited for Michal's response, and when it arrived, I was afraid I might find she didn't understand me and I feared I might not understand what she wanted to say. Then I waited for Mitchel. Again I was afraid.

And of course I also feared my own thoughts as they occurred when considering this present text, the one I am writing now.

Mitchel quotes Erich Fromm who said that fear is the opposite of love. Mitchel's entire text is about this, and it filled me with amazement. Because as said, most of the thoughts I had in anticipation of writing what I am writing now had to do with fear. Clarifying the different paths that take each of us to her or his text, this time about fear, is the very essence of dialogue. For me, this is the nub of the turbulence that a dialogue can stir in the mind.

Michal, too, examines fear, but this time the fear (whether or not implicit) of truth, and she refers, among others, to Bion. It is this search for truth and for love (after all, can we separate truth from love?) that leads us to suspect the other, but maybe more than anything: ourselves.

But the search for truth is scary and exhausting, and we avoid, scrape by and don't dare. We give up.

Mitchel's and Michal's texts reverberate the therapeutic dialogue, a psychoanalytic (and in Michal's case, at the same time, Buddhist) poetics of constant becoming, where new worlds may be revealed as a space emerges that allows for deep undercurrents, a confluence between time and space. Between therapist and patient. And at times, this flow, this sometimes decidedly non-verbal dialogue, resembles an ongoing masquerade. The masks may occlude love and truth, but sometimes they reveal what we would so much like to suppress. This is what a well-known make-up artist and costume designer said to me; she worked with carnival groups (*murga*)[2] in my country of origin, Uruguay: "Even though the heavy make-up ostensibly comes to camouflage the individual members of the group, it may just be exactly what allows each of them to be fully himself."

It is this same steady undercurrent, which sometimes emerges in dialogue, that takes me to the language of poetry, to sentences which may at times sound hardly coherent, in which literary defamiliarization acts to crush the obvious, the self-evident. Here is a call – open and explicit, at times, at other times not – to stop and re-examine the written words and even to allow oneself to be cast into the unknown. It may also come as a form of contact with the fear (fear of love, fear of no love and fear of truth) this interaction arouses, which threatens to confront us with hitherto unknown inner continents or worlds. The very paths each of us treads, and on which each of us may stumble and fall. And which, every so often, come together to form a shared road.

This is why we are afraid to love. We fear to surrender ourselves, to speak, to remain silent. We fear to overwhelm the other, to be overwhelmed or erased by them.

All this time, I tried to disentangle this thread of fear which went with me. I tried to understand, take apart and also to disperse it the one way I know in the face of fear: with hope and love. And trust. The kind of trust we had as children, leaping into loving arms, knowing the arms would be there. Hope full of love. It is a love that is within us, always, though sometimes hidden from ourselves and others. And love, too, itself, fills us with terror; and sometimes we try to remove it from ourselves, when we confuse it with weakness, with neediness and with erasure. That's how afraid we are. That's how afraid I am.

Can I listen to you, hear you? Can I listen without immediately becoming preoccupied with the words arising in me, with constructing the sentences I will soon use to respond to what I think you said? Am I actually letting you in? Am I really open and willing to receive everything you choose to tell me? Can I listen without letting my memories and desires clog the space between myself and your words, as they turn into a screen – or a wall, or even a background noise – that distorts anything reaching me from you? Because this I know: fear (and memory and desire) gets in the way of the space we need in order to really listen and hear. To let the other in.

I realized I was preparing the words for this text, preparing thoughts, even before seeing Michal's and Mitchel's responses. I asked myself: is this dialogue? Are we always immersed in monologues, exchanging words which are in fact scars; scars of whatever lies underneath them and is now threatened with extinction each time we try to hand over and receive, to pronounce and hear, to interact with an other? Monologues. And we call them "dialogues."

Now I read what I've been writing and am overwhelmed with sadness. Here, just like in my first text, I see that I focus on what I want, what I need and what drives me towards people. I desperately want to connect, to hear and be heard, touch and be touched – but do I have enough space, enough strength, enough freedom and especially enough ability to move away from this instrumentality to what Buber called I-You? Can I move in that direction in spite of the very strong forces that constantly drive me the opposite way?

As I reflect on these questions, which are so central to my life, about how we, humans, fight for our lives (because that's what we do when we are engaged in relationships, more or less successfully – as there is no life without relationships), Lewis Carroll and Alice, as well as Cervantes and his Don Quixote, come to mind: "Eat me" says the cake to Alice, "Drink me" beckons the bottle, "Off with her head!" says the Queen. Is this a mere amusement, nonsense, as Lewis's young readers might feel, or is it a call aimed at adults to soar in the imagination, a return to the infantile psyche? Or is this in fact a manifestation of primary, survival-oriented terror, where it seems we swallow or are being swallowed, kill or are killed? And not just metaphorically.

Don Quixote transforms into a knight, his beloved Dulcinea into a lady, and windmills become base enemies that must be defeated – taking me to the territory between imagination and reality from which we may find ourselves propelled into total love and a truth that is no less clear cut.

I'm listening to what they say, Carroll and Cervantes, to their respective dialogues: they are direct and simple, magical, yet they let go of the demand for understanding, as though understanding is intrinsic to the very wish to hear and to make oneself heard. Because at times, a need and wish – perhaps even a necessity – to be understood issue forth from us in unknown, unclear, mysterious ways.

And then I see what makes something magical: tender and simple lines of music. Lines of music emerging from the intellect that dwells in the heart. I ask myself whether this, perhaps, is one of the paths that lead from me to you and from you to me. When I see you and you see me, unblinded by our neediness. Me and you, you and me. And maybe it is this intellect, when it dwells in the heart, that turns monologue into dialogue. For it is then that a space opens up between our words, a place. And in that place, there are two. Or more. At last.

Notes

1 *The Bluest Eye* (1970) is her first book.
2 *Murga* originates in the annual carnival held in the Spanish city of Cadiz and occurs in similar forms in Tenerife and the Canary Islands. The troupe brings together elements of comedy and protest through song and highly stylized body movement, costume and heavy make-up.

References

Arendt, H. (1958). *The Human Condition*. (2nd Edition). Chicago: The University of Chicago Press, 1998.
Barnea-Astrog, M. (2017). *Carved by Experience: Vipassana, Psychoanalysis, and the Mind Investigating Itself*. London: Karnac.
Bion, W.R. (1967). Notes on Memory and Desire. In: E.B. Spillius (Ed.), *Melanie Klein Today (Vol. 2): Mainly Practice* (pp. 15–18). London: Routledge, 1988.
Bion, W.R. (1970). *Attention and Interpretation*. London: Tavistock.
Morrison, T. (1970). *The Bluest Eye*. London: Vintage.
Morrison, T. (2003). *Love*. London: Vintage.
Woolf, V. (1931). *The Waves*. Ware, Hertfordshire: Wordsworth, 2000.

Second Dialogue

Becoming, Spaciousness and Vitality

Michal Barnea-Astrog and Yorai Sella

Chapter 4

Going on Being
On the Fear of Ceasing and the Need to Go On

Michal Barnea-Astrog

In the beginning, there's separation. In the beginning, there's unintegration and no internal force to hold things together. In the beginning, there's catastrophe. The end bites beginning from behind. Creation sprouts between a seemingly complete and full density and a seemingly endless void.

To go on being, physically and mentally, is one of our most basic desires, and the fear of death or annihilation is its unavoidable companion. In this paper, I offer a few thoughts on some of our human ways to face them. These thoughts are informed by psychoanalytic notions and by Buddhist thought, as it appears in the early texts, the Pāli canon. I'm particularly interested in the following: the place of annihilation and the fear of it in creating our ways of being; mental activity as a second-skin or self-holding function; and the process whereby internal and interpersonal conditions enable trust to emerge, leading to temporary relinquishment of these functions, replacing – even briefly – the strain and restlessness they involve with deep steadiness and peace of mind.

A Sense of Catastrophe

Psychic reality and thinking originate, according to Bion, in a type of "catastrophic emotional explosion" (1970, p. 14) or "Big Bang" (Eigen, 1985, p. 323). As long as the scattered particles resulting from this explosion stay in their raw state – separate in one sense, yet welded together, in another – catastrophe maintains its total, original form: pervasive, meaningless and unprocessed, spreading "through the infantile cosmos with infinite horror, a kind of electrocution from no tangible source" (Eigen, 1985, p. 324). Even when they

DOI: 10.4324/9781003325499-8

are processed, these particles preserve traces of their catastrophic sources (Eigen, 1985).

Disintegration is therefore a product of explosion, and in this sense – evidence of catastrophe; but in the absence of disintegration and primary distance, nothing can emerge (Barnea-Astrog, 2019). This is why, in Bion's view, there is no self without a sense of catastrophe: "the sense of catastrophe *links* aspects of personality[1]. It is the cement that holds personality together, a primordial forming principle, the sea or atmosphere we live in" (Eigen, 1985, p. 325).

The connecting tissue is the result of fragmentation. The catastrophic element is a thread that runs through experience, calling us from the unseen darkness to remember a truth: that coming into being involves a dispersing of particles away from each other and from any imagined complete core. That creation and destruction roam together in the world (Barnea-Astrog, 2019).

Something as strong and as fundamental as this, something as horrifying and unthinkable as this – having been experienced (or not experienced, as Winnicott (1974) put it) – must leave a mark. Unknown as they may originally and presently be, the primordial sense of annihilation and the fear of it accompany us all. More rigidly and intensely (pathologically, one may say) or less, they build our being at the same time as they undermine it. And we find different ways to live along: to avoid them and to meet them; to harden against them or to dissolve. At first, depending on our caregivers and later mostly on our own.

Klein (1946) saw the fear of annihilation as resulting from the inner destructiveness of the death instinct, which is projected and experienced as a fear of persecution. Winnicott (1960) dismissed the applications of the word "death" and the term "death instinct" as irrelevant and unacceptable in describing the roots of destructiveness at these early stages of development. In the beginning of life, so he thought, the two possibilities are "being" or "reacting," and reacting annihilates. The main function of the holding environment is therefore to reduce to a minimum the impingements to which the infant must react with resultant annihilation of her being. Under favourable conditions, she can establish a continuity of existence, realize her "inherited potential" and "become an infant" (ibid., pp. 589, 591). Otherwise, a "fear of breakdown" might take hold (Winnicott, 1974). In Bion's view, it is the mother's containment that serves to moderate the fear component in the fear of dying, which is split off and projected into her: hopefully to be re-introjected as a now tolerable, and therefore growth-stimulating part of the infant's personality; or regrettably as a "nameless dread," a "worthless residue," having been robbed of its valuable aspect (1962, p. 96).

So when the container is sufficiently flexible and receptive, and the infant's mental space, too, enables openness to learning – the fear of death, like any other mental substance, can be used for mental growth. Otherwise, the fear of death and other forms of the sense of catastrophe lose their value as meaningful signals (Eigen, 1985). They cannot serve the psyche's links to truth, but only cause deep anxieties or agonies, as when the holding is bad and reactions to impingements are too strong. Such agonies are associated with a lack of proper sense of boundary, wrapping, skin or existential floor. The person is thrown into an existence where there isn't a reliable psychic skin to hold her personality parts together (Bick, 1968), where there's nothing to stop her inside from leaking out, where there's nothing to stop her from endlessly falling or dispersing into the dark, infinite void.

Something has to be done to survive this unbearable state. The fundamental need for an external object experienced as containing puts the infant in a constant search for sensual objects of any kind that might hold her attention and, thus, her unintegrated personality, even if only momentarily (Bick, 1968). But if the containing-holding-physical-psychic-skin function is not sufficiently available and fails to be internalized, the psyche must hold herself by herself. It must somehow produce a substitutive "second-skin" (ibid.), a sensory "wrapping" (Anzieu, 2016) or a "sensory floor" (Ogden, 2004).

Bick (1968) names three ways by which infants create second-skin: they may focus on some sensory stimulus – a ceiling lamp, for instance – and feel held as if their attention is "held" by the stimulus; they may tense and clench certain muscles to form a tight layer through which, in fantasy, no leakage will occur, or they may use incessant body movement to produce a sense of ongoingness that must not be interrupted or stopped (Symington, 1985).[2] We adults, too, resort to such behaviours in order to feel the ongoingness of being and avoid frightening gaps (Ogden, 2004; Symington, 1985): we stare at the TV by way of a holding sensory object; we tense certain muscles continuously and involuntarily to hold ourselves tight; we make sure there's always music in the background, take the car and drive for hours; engage in repetitive body movements; or speak incessantly or superficially and relentlessly jump from one topic to the next.

Mental Movement as a Holding Function

All three strategies – clinging to a sensory object, muscular tightening and constant movement – have mental parallels and may characterize mental activity itself. The mind can hold itself by immersing in or fixating on a certain mental object (an emotion, memory, image, idea or thought). It may tighten and clench, clustering materials into one solid mass, leaving no gaps in the inner space (Barnea-Astrog, 2019), or shut up defensively, hide information and stick to old ways of thinking or tired clichés (Symington, 1985). The mind too may engage in constant movement, by means of an incessant parade of images and thoughts.

These are all forms of inner holding, of sophisticated second-skin that envelopes the self by means of immersion, fixating, tightening and movement, avoiding intervals – in space and time – in the presence of an unconscious fear of annihilation. They all reflect the system's resourcefulness, and each comes with its own particular toll (Barnea-Astrog, 2019).

Peter: Tightening the Membrane Walls

Peter, a psychologist in his forties, was seeing me regularly for three and a half years in a small therapy group. On one occasion, we touched upon his inner restlessness, something he was very familiar with and at that time particularly preoccupied with. He looked at the incessant motion of his thought, a main ingredient of his habitual disquiet. Curious about its nature, he noted that it typically consisted of his jumping from one thing to another (within the metaphoric space of the mind), as if in search of something. This mental movement, we both noticed, was accompanied by muscular tension around his forehead, his eyebrows and especially in his eyes which moved continuously, along with his thoughts. He felt as though this muscular clamp down served to hold something, that there was something it prevented from being dropped.

He wanted to see what would happen if he managed to stop the hectic mental movement for a while. Since this turned out to be quite impossible, he tried, instead, to relax his eyes and eyelids, hoping this would reduce some of the tension and help his attention not to swerve. Whenever he managed to stop and relax for a fraction of a moment, he would be flooded by adrenalin, his heartbeat would go up and the muscular contraction around his eyes as well as his ceaseless mental motion would instantaneously reappear.

He wanted to know more, and we played with these things for a while. Not trying to change it in any way, but rather, in order to study it, we followed his habitual behaviour: either as it naturally presented itself, or as he intentionally increased it slightly to sense it more clearly, or alternatively, as he tried to do the opposite or withhold it. Increasing the inner movement or further tightening the muscles around his eyes was exhausting, and he left it after a few short trials. Any attempt he made to stop the movement and relax the muscles led to the same chain of reactions: adrenalin flow, fast heartbeats and instantaneous re-tightening. He was unsure whether this was tied to fear or to excitement, and whether relaxing into a focused and quiet state was so hard for him because he was too afraid of it, or because he was too eagerly attracted to it.

Some months later, he came back to his scattered, restless mental movements. It occurred to him that each such movement stretched out towards its inner object like an open hand ready to push. Keeping track of these movements, as one push followed another, he felt as though the metaphorical hands of his mind were pressing against something like an inner membrane, and that in doing so, they were both constituting it and sensing its existence. With a more accurate understanding, this time, he was again curious to see what would happen if he refrained from doing so. When he managed it briefly, he felt as though he disappeared, scattered into space, turning into nothing.

A young baby experiences the loss of mother's attention as being dropped. Suddenly he is not held, suddenly he is falling through space, unprotected, terrified of never being caught again and rescued.

(Symington, 1985, p. 482)

He didn't feel like a baby, nor did he feel the presence of any external object. He felt no contoured self at all. He was just falling through space in an indeterminate state of being, dispersing, ceasing to exist. His instantaneously increased pulse, he later thought, rendered both fear and excitement – the thrill of recognizing the very cusp of a slippery state he simultaneously dreaded and longed for. Like Winnicott (1974) pointed out: those who experienced an early breakdown dread it and try to avoid it, but at the same time they are also attracted to it and seek it, since only through experiencing it will they find relief and improvement, and only in it will they briefly feel themselves as themselves (Kolker, 2009).

Some weeks later, he followed his hectic inner movement once again. All concentrated within, his eyes were either shut or downcast. Then he switched some of his attention outwards and slowly lifted his eyes to meet the five faces that surrounded him: those of the four other group members and mine. His gaze had a fresh, amazed, curious quality, as if he was seeing something for the first time. Then, all of a sudden, his inner state transformed. The hectic movement of his thoughts, his nearly constant burden and companion, had stopped. His eyes and mind dropped their pursuit of an object and rested. His facial muscular strain was entirely gone. He was completely immersed in a deep, wakeful calm with no agitation at all.

We were all very much present. A circle of warm, available, undemanding attention. A circle of quiet, appreciating love. This circle created and held his membrane for him, it occurred to me later, and so the metaphorical hands of his mind could finally stop reaching to form and to touch it. Now that he had an external psychic skin, he no longer needed to strain himself to produce an inner second-skin. In those moments, the huge effort of holding himself by himself became dispensable.

Sustenance

The continuous process of becoming and dying is at the heart of Buddhist thought, and the early texts provide several models describing the substances and forces that support it. In this view, just as the body consumes material food to sustain itself, so does the mind feed on mental food. Mental food is threefold: the contact with our surroundings, that is, the impressions left on us by our incessant encounter with objects from all sense spheres; mental volitions, which are directional actions of the mind, reactions and their accumulations in the form of habits, attitudes and tendencies; and the stream of consciousness[3](SN 12.11). Together with the first, physical nutriment, they make up four "substances" that sustain our continuous becoming.

There's an inherent pain in all four nutriments[4], as one very vivid Sutta (Pāli canon text) portrays. Physical hunger is physical hunger – in extreme conditions, it can make us devour even our dearest ones. Being incessantly subjected to the touch of the world, external and internal stimuli constantly impinge on us – we're like a flayed cow whose exposed flesh is being nibbled wherever she goes. Our habitual reactions are compulsive and counter our own good; they drag us into pain and ruin like two strong men who forcefully drag one into a human-size pit filled with hot-glowing coals. Our constant stream of consciousness tortures us as if we were repeatedly punished by the striking of one hundred piercing spears, morning, midday and evening (SN 12.63). The most basic activities and functions we cling to, identify with, hold so dear and can't imagine living without are compulsive sources of misery. They create and destroy us at the same time. Wherever there's identification and clinging – there's production, reproduction or becoming. And wherever something comes into being – suffering is born with it too (SN 12.15).

All four nutriments are connected to each other, and all have craving as their source (SN 12.11). The contact between our consciousness, our senses and their respective objects evokes sensations, pleasant, unpleasant or neutral; and to these sensations, we react. We react with attraction or rejection depending on the kind of sensation, that is, according to the pleasure principle. These are our volitional mental actions. Reactions of attraction quickly develop into craving (or greed or desire), and reactions of rejection quickly develop into aversion (or repulsion or hate). Both sides of this pendulum motion come under the force generally referred to as craving, desire or, literally, "thirst."[5] Thirst soon develops into clinging, which, in Buddhist view, automatically instigates the process of generation and coming into being (MN 38).

The desire to go on being or to exist or to exist in certain states is one of the three kinds of thirst. The other two are the desire for sensual pleasures and the desire to cease existing or to be rid of certain states of existence.[6] Similarly, the tendency to go on being is one of the four kinds of mental "secretions," "influxes" or "intoxicants,"[7] together with the intoxicant of sensuality, the intoxicant of ignorance and the intoxicant of wrong views[8]. All of these are tendencies, latent or manifest, that run through or below our existence. They stream into our mental blood system (like mental neurotransmitters? Like mental hormones?) and paint it in their hues. They blur our vision, unsettle our internal space and induce us to sense, think and behave in certain ways. It is these desires and intoxicating secretions that pour us into existence and keep us going on.

No phenomenon arises by itself, but only as a result of certain conditions. The conditions for our individual formation, for our specific ways of arising and passing at the onset of life, at the moment of death and in each moment between the two, are our nutriments. Pleasant or unpleasant, beautiful or ugly, beneficial or hurtful – they all converge in the specific material and mental realities that touch us and in the ways of perceiving them, relating and reacting to them that we develop. It's a cycle of creation: we are created, again and again, into a world that our own mental activity took part in creating (DN 27). And destruction is a creation too.

Becoming is fuelled by directional forces that appear as choice and will. Yet it is far from being voluntary. It is automatic, repetitive, compulsive, conducive of suffering and rooted in "non-knowing"[9] – in the misperception of reality (MN 38). We unconsciously perceive the pleasant as permanent, essential and satisfying – so we are pulled towards it, we crave it and cling to it. We unconsciously perceive the unpleasant as permanent, essential and satisfying to get rid of – so we push it away, we resent it and cling to our hatred and to the wish to expel it. We unconsciously perceive our self as permanent, essential and satisfying and so we cling to it, we want it to continue and we want it to possess as much of the pleasurable and as little of the unpleasurable as possible (Barnea-Astrog, 2017).

But if things depend on certain conditions to arise, then in the absence of these conditions – they cannot ensue. And if arising entails suffering, then the cessation of arising is the cessation of suffering (SN 12.15). So the more we are able to see reality clearly and to lessen our blind reactions – the more we can subvert our repetition compulsion and begin to dissolve the habits, the tendencies and the substances that keep us rotating in the same old, limited, painful worlds. And at the same time, of course, develop beneficial mental actions that will feed our becoming with good, nourishing, growth-supporting food.

Spatial and Temporal Aspects of the Sense of Self and the Constant Self as Projection

Like any mental-material phenomenon, we are in space and time. Our sense of self and our identity therefore draw on both spatial and temporal perceptions, images and intuitions: we may feel ourselves, to varying degrees, solid, bounded and essential; we may feel more or less collected, more or less wrapped and more or less whole. Similarly, we have a sense of continuity, of going on being through events in history, up to this moment and onwards into the imagined future: such and such I used to be, then this and that happened, such and such I then became; I wonder or wish or worry about what happens to me next. These two fields of meaning are linked, two aspects of the same phenomenon: if I'm collected and held in space, I will go on being – as myself – through the passage of time.

We unconsciously lean on such basic assumptions, and we have our preferences: we want to feel solid or on solid ground, we want to believe that inside us there is an independent core which is "us," and we feel safer when we perceive ourselves to be collected and held, when our line of history seems apparent, when our identity is clear to us. When these feelings and perceptions are severely unsettled, we are usually in trouble. It may shake us entirely, or it may overwhelm us for a while before being pushed back into the depths by other forces. It may create an undercurrent of unease and anxiety, more or less intense, which will accompany us steadily or appear every now and then.

In the beginning of life, feeling sufficiently collected and continuous is crucial. Good-enough holding – where limbs and head are properly held together, not dangling or flopping – supports a primitive, raw sense of self as uniform, smooth and round, a kind of a circle. Bad holding ruptures this circle, breaking it into body and head, two circles that have become detached (Winnicott, 1987). If this is repeated too often, the infant's "line of life" and sense of "going-on-being"

(Winnicott, 1975b) are disturbed by her reactions to impingements, and the trigger of primitive agonies is switched on. Properly holding the baby in space, that is, taking care of her spatial outlines, gradually makes her feel that she **is**, and that she continues to be in time.

Containment too creates a skin that wraps the personality (Bick, 1968), and therefore it "holds." Internalizing the mother-container creates the three-dimensional experience: perceiving an internal space – the mother's containing mind – which is capable of holding her own and her baby's feelings, leads the baby to sense that she has an inner space of her own (Shaw, 2014). Accumulating such experiences makes us feel that we can somehow trust our continuous existence in space and time. And we need this feeling in order to be well and to be able to connect (reasonably freely, reasonably closely) with ourselves and with others. But growing on fertile-enough ground, there are other truths regarding this so-called "self" to touch upon.

The self is a stream of conditioned elements and functions, incessantly arising and passing away, related in specific ways through complex causality. A sense of a solid, independent and continuous self is therefore an illusion. Our consciousness presents itself as having a connective property (Nyanaponika Thera, 1998), and our perception[10] recognizes and evaluates reality according to past experiences with objects and situations it identifies as being similar or identical (Barnea-Astrog, 2017; Hart, 1987). We therefore perceive a flow of events as a continuous line, as if it possessed a cohesive identity that remains constant through time. We fill in the gaps. We connect the dots. We relate to a stream as if it were somehow complete or as if it contained an unchanging core.

Freud referred to this connective, gap-filling, bridge-building property as an aspect of projection, which is characteristic of our everyday mode of thinking and feeling (Ornston, 1978). This function of the mind draws lines between sense impressions registered in the present and past experiences stored in memory, thus tying together conscious and unconscious, perception and memory, present and past (Freud, 1913). We may also say that, basing itself on what it has already experienced and knows, this function extends the line forward into a future it supposedly foresees. Projection as a defence and as a form of object relation and communication is usually thought of as emerging later than second-skin mechanisms and their likes; but this connective function is most elementary, I believe. It characterizes consciousness and perception as such – regardless of their level of maturity.

Since physical reality is discontinuous, the sense of psychic continuity, too, requires projection (Rapaport, 1944). And this, we might say, is what produces our illusion of a solid and constant self (Barnea-Astrog, 2017; Mitchell, 1993): a self that is "one" or "essential" or is in some other way collected in space; a self that is constant or permanent or in some other way goes on being through time, from moment to moment, maintaining some kind of a core identity; a self that believes it is somehow independent and therefore in control; that relies on pleasurable internal and external objects for its happiness and gratification, under the illusion that they too are somehow solid and may therefore be preserved and owned.

Seeing permanence in the impermanent, satisfaction and happiness in what is bound up with misery, selfhood and essentiality in the conditioned-dependent[11]– these, according to Buddhist thought, are basic misperceptions or distortion of reality (AN 4.49); and this is the stuff that the I-sense is made of.

Reaction and Desire as Generative Forces

Winnicott said: reactions to impingements annihilate. Buddhist texts say: reactions to impingements generate. And paradoxically, according to Buddhist thought, the desire to cease is yet another factor that keeps us going on. Desire is desire, and whether it is directed at sensual objects, at existence and certain states of existence or at annihilation of existence or of certain states of existence – it is a generating force.

Peter's constant mental movement was meant to create a holding membrane. It was meant to avoid holes in attention, which would perforate existential holes he might spill through, scattering into the wall-less, floor-less, ceiling-less space. It was meant to prevent the catastrophic cessation and to keep him going on. And it did: even if he wanted to get some rest and ease, he could never stop.

This was a survival behaviour meant to maintain Peter's sense of continuity, to preserve his self, and it actively produced the way he **came to be**: early impingements in an untrustworthy environment, I suppose, produced mental and physical reactions, which turn into automatic habits as a result of their necessity and countless repetitions; and these reactions and automatic habits created for him a restless, agitated, untrusting world.

This is a specific individual instance that is derived from and points at a broader rule: the psyche depends on its own actions, reactions, desires and clinging for its continued existence. It depends on them for its very survival (Barnea-Astrog, 2019). "From reaction as a condition, consciousness arises" (MN 38): from our mental reactions, habits and deep-rooted tendencies, the residues of past actions that have become engraved as patterns of mental behaviour – from all this flows consciousness, which is experienced as the internal space that differentiates us from what we perceive as external, the space that produces us as subjects. "From clinging as a condition, becoming arises" (MN 38): it is through our attachments that we are repeatedly born.

Keeping Together and Falling Apart: Some Paradoxes

Psychologically speaking, the self's emergence and integration are developmental achievements. At the same time, if we follow Klein's account of the depressive position, this integration involves the realization that actions have consequences and that history cannot be magically re-written, the recognition that loss is inevitable and the ability to reflect death (Klein, 1975a, 1975b; Ogden, 1986). It therefore involves a certain measure of disabuse from the illusion of omnipotence, and a certain measure of realization of the self's (and other selves') impermanence.

From a Buddhist perspective, the self's contoured identity is an illusion, and the ability to see through its apparent essentiality and solidity and to realize its impermanence, its unsatisfactory nature and its lack of independent core, is the achievement that frees. For this to happen, the self should be analyzed, taken apart into its components, processes and contents, all of which are to be experientially observed as they arise and pass away, come together and fall apart, momentarily decay, cease, die.

But the ability to penetrate illusive solidity and to see through it depends, among other things, on sufficient collectedness of attention and on other integrative qualities of the psyche. As Epstein (1988) puts it, the disintegration of the "representative" aspects of the self – those that maintain the narcissistic illusion of a solid self – depends on the development and enhancement of what he calls the "functional" aspects of the self – those that are responsible for processing experience, assimilating and integrating it. So the meditator who tries to follow the Buddha's path trains herself in collecting her mental energy and attention in order to disintegrate her sense of solidity and continuity. She focuses her attention, concentrates it, harnesses and controls it, and fastens it to the selected object of meditation – in order to dissolve her adherences and attachments, in order to be able to let go.

According to Buddhist thought, one of the factors that collectedness of mind relies on is faith or trust[12] (Ledi Sayadaw, 2009). Until this factor is sufficiently established, the mind is, to some extent, scattered, agitated or fixated on unbeneficial objects. The ability to soberly (as opposed to blindly) trust and surrender evolves through repeated experiential realizations of the true nature of things. It emerges from a growing clarity and in turn supports it. This clarity and the attitude that accompanies it have to do with coming to terms with the fact that there are so many things over which we have no control. In the present context, this brings about calmness and peace rather than desperation or fear; and these calmness and peace increase concentration and the ability to direct our mental activity to consciously chosen beneficial routes. Trusting and feeling held – even if the holding object is rightly recognized as impermanent and lacking in essential, ever-satisfying core – is necessary in order to be able to let go. Letting go paradoxically leads to collectedness of mind and to deeper self-control.

When Peter felt held by the right kind of external attention, when he felt he was surrounded by a soft, loving, potent membrane – a deep sense of trust emerged in him. This trust naturally and effortlessly turned into surrender. He didn't need to tighten, to constantly generate elements that would hold him, to be watchful and to control. Temporarily leaving these led him to immerse in a peaceful, concentrated state he felt so rarely and so immensely longed for.

We could say that he was able to stop investing in the envelope and to afford to lodge in his kernel (1975a, p. 99). We could say that he was able to drop into deep absorption and calmness (Pāli: samādhi) since some disturbing factors, such as fear, doubt, restlessness as well as overly active thinking, subsided in him temporarily;[13] or that his trust grew stronger and therefore contributed to the subsiding of his mind's wavering, resulting in tranquillity and steadiness of mind. Either way, something vital and nourishing was received; something effortful and restless was consequently dropped; and a valuable, longed-for state suddenly became available.

One last paradox, for now: anxiety and fear are the result of clinging to an ever-changing, perishable phenomenon misperceived as enduring, as satisfying and as possessing essential, independent selfhood; and one is free from fear only to the extent that one is free from clinging and misperception (DN 1; Dhp 210–216; MN 138; SN 11.3;). But there wouldn't be fear if it wasn't for some back-of-the-mind knowing that our objects of desire are bound to be lost – a knowledge based on past experiences of loss. The sense of catastrophe is imbedded in us since we immerged from catastrophe, since explosion is our source. The dread of annihilation, of leakage and dissemination, of disintegration and unintegration is part of us simply because we are, by nature, ephemeral phenomena in an ephemeral universe: non-solid phenomena that disperse into space, falling apart from moment to moment, created and decomposed, born to be gone (Barnea-Astrog, 2019).

We are therefore always in search, unconsciously, of an anchor, of something to hold on to, of some line to follow: like a baby who fixes her attention on a monotonous sound or on the light of the lamp in order to fend off the catastrophe of being dropped when she losses her mother's attention, we pursue sense objects to cling to. Like a baby who keeps moving so as to have a sense of going-on-being, we try to always be in motion, to keep doing things, avoiding a frightening full stop. Like a baby who contracts her muscles to feel tight rather than diffuse – we contract ourselves around ideas, dogmas and beliefs that our experience had again and again proved harmful and wrong (Barnea-Astrog, 2019).

And how do we relate to all of this?

Symington (1985) mentions that when a patient uses very early self-holding mechanisms, they are usually experienced and interpreted as resistance to the therapeutic relationship. When the therapist fails to understand the survival function of these behaviours, she suggests, the patient experiences it as a lack of holding and his need for self-holding and the associated behaviours consequently grows.

We can take this understanding further and relate to such primitive fears and behaviours softly and empathically – not only for the sake of this therapeutic purpose, but also because they are so universal and shared by us all. Because clinging to the delusion of solidity and continuity is our default condition, and this very clinging is what keeps us going on being. Because even those of us who are not so strongly driven by the primitive sense of catastrophe and fear of annihilation are propelled by the thirst for existence and by the fear of annihilation. Because even those of us who have less rigid self-holding and second-skin mechanisms are constantly engaged in self-holding, self-wrapping, self-determining and self-constituting. Fearing dissolution and cessation, projecting essentiality onto the essenceless, independency onto the conditioned, and solidity onto the constantly changing and fluid – we are all in the same boat.

Notes

1 Even for those whose self and sense of catastrophe failed to properly appear or appeared but then seemed to have disappeared (Bion, 1970; Eigen, 1985).
2 Tustin (1980) also describes how the psychotic child clutches a hard autistic object when the total fear of annihilation arises in her. She also finds and states that in certain circumstances, when seeking to address those very deep layers of the psyche, terms such as "ego" and "projection" become inappropriate and are "misused to plug the holes in our understanding. As such, they are pathological autistic objects!" (ibid., p. 36).
3 Pāli: viññāṇa.
4 Pāli: āhāra.
5 Pāli: taṇhā.
6 Pāli: kāma taṇhā, bhava taṇhā, vibhava taṇhā.
7 Pāli: āsava.
8 Often non-literally translated at "taints." Pāli: kāmāsava, bhavāsava, diṭṭhāsava, avijjāsava.
9 Pāli: avijjā.
10 Pāli: saññā.
11 Also: seeing beauty in the not beautiful (AN 4.49).
12 Pāli: saddhā.
13 Buddhist texts account in detail the factors that prevent or lead to concentration and insight. "The five hindrances," for example, prevent the meditator from entering the initial state of concentration, which is also necessary for initial clarity and insight. These hindrances are

sensual desire, hatred and malice, laziness, drowsiness and dullness, restlessness and worry, and sceptic doubt. When these are temporarily suspended as a result of proper meditation (and gradually get weaker and weaker), they allow for calm and concentration that enable insight. Entering yet deeper concentration involves a temporary pause in discursive thinking. Like this it goes on.

References

AN 4.49.

Anzieu, D. (2016). *The Skin-Ego*. London: Karnac.

Barnea-Astrog, M. (2017). *Carved by Experience: Vipassana, Psychoanalysis, and the Mind Investigating Itself*. London: Karnac.

Barnea-Astrog, M. (2019). *Psychoanalytic and Buddhist Reflections on Gentleness: Sensitivity, Fear, and the Drive towards Truth*. London: Routledge.

Bick, E. (1968). The Experience of the Skin in Early Object-Relations. *International Journal of Psychoanalysis* 49: 484–486.

Bion, W.R. (1962). *Learning from Experience*. London: Tavistock.

Bion, W.R. (1970). *Attention and Interpretation*. London: Tavistock.

Dhp 210–216.

DN 1.

DN 27.

Eigen, M. (1985). Toward Bion's Starting Point: Between Catastrophe and Faith. *International Journal of Psychoanalysis* 66: 321–330.

Epstein, M. (1988). Deconstruction of the Self: Ego and "egolessness" in Buddhist Insight Meditation. *Journal of Transpersonal Psychology* 20: 61–69.

Freud, S. (1913). *Totem and taboo. S. E., 13*: vii-162. London: Hogarth.

Hart, W. (1987). *The Art of Living*. Washington, DC: Vipassana Research Institute & Pariyatti Publishing.

Klein, M. (1946). Notes on Some Schizoid Mechanisms. *International Journal of Psychoanalysis* 27: 99–110.

Klein, M. (1975a). Some Theoretical Conclusions Regarding the Emotional Life of the Infant. In: R. Khan (Ed.), *Envy and Gratitude and Other Works 1946–1963* (pp. 61–93). London: Hogarth & the Institute of Psycho-Analysis.

Klein, M. (1975b). Envy and Gratitude. In: R. Khan (Ed.), *Envy and Gratitude and Other Works 1946–1963* (pp. 176–235). London: Hogarth & the Institute of Psycho-Analysis.

Kolker, S. (2009). Introduction to "Fear of Breakdown". In: E. Berman (Ed.), *True Self, False Self: Winnicott DW, Essays, 1935–1963* (pp. 287–291). Tel Aviv: Am Oved.

Ledi Sayadaw. (2009). *The Manuals of Dhamma*. U Nyana Sayadaw, Baruna Beni, U Sein Nyo Tun & U Saw Tun Teik (Trans.). Igatpuri: Vipassana Research Institute.

Mitchell, S.A. (1993). *Hope and Dread in Psychoanalysis*. New York: Basic Books.

MN 38.

Nyanaponika Thera (1998). *Abidhamma Studies: Buddhist Explorations of Consciousness and Time*. Boston, MA: Wisdom Publications.

Ogden, T.H. (1986). *The Matrix of the Mind: Object Relations and the Psychoanalytic Dialogue*. Oxford: Rowman & Littlefield.

Ogden, T.H. (2004). *The Primitive Edge of Experience*. Lanham, MD: Rowman & Littlefield.

Ornston, D. (1978). On Projection: A Study of Freud's Usage. *The Psychoanalytic Study of the Child* 33, 117–166.

Rapaport, D. (1944). The Scientific Methodology of Psychoanalysis. In: M.M. Gill (Ed.), *The Collected Papers of David Rapaport* (pp. 165–220). New York: Basic Books, 1967.

Shaw, J. (2014). Psychotic and Non-Psychotic Perceptions of Reality. *Journal of Child Psychotherapy* 40(1): 73–89.

SN 11.3.

SN 12.11.

SN 12.15.

SN 12.63.

Symington, J. (1985). The Survival Function of Primitive Omnipotence. *International Journal of Psychoanalysis* 66, 481–487.

Tustin, F. (1980). Autistic Objects. *International Review of Psychoanalysis* 7, 27–39.

Winnicott, D.W. (1960). The Theory of the Parent-Infant Relationship. *International Journal of Psychoanalysis* 41, 585–595.

Winnicott, D.W. (1974). Fear of Breakdown. *International Review of Psychoanalysis* 1, 103–107.

Winnicott, D.W. (1975a). Anxiety Associated with Insecurity. In *Through Paediatrics to Psycho-Analysis* (pp. 97–100). London: Hogarth & the Institute of Psycho-Analysis.

Winnicott, D.W. (1975b). Primary Maternal Preoccupation. In *Through Paediatrics to Psycho-Analysis* (pp. 300–305). London: Hogarth & the Institute of Psycho-Analysis.

Winnicott, D.W. (1987). *Babies and Their Mothers*. Cambridge: Perseus Press.

Chapter 5

Making Space for the Mess
The At-One-Ment of Going-On-Being

Yorai Sella

When Michal asked me to dialogue with her chapter, I knew – being somewhat familiar with her work – that it would be a stimulating and challenging experience. Since Michal kindly gave me free rein to free-associate, what follows is a flow of elaborations on my psychotherapeutic, psychoanalytic and meditative practice, with a sprinkling of Taoist and Zen Buddhist thinking. The latter have helped me cross the boundaries between the somewhat solipsistic reality of mindful meditation and the paradoxical nature of applying one's mind to the process of at-one-ment with another, so as to conduce a sense of going-on-being within a therapeutic setting.

So, here goes.

Anxiety, Binaries and the Welcome Mess

The anxiety that pertains to *not* going on being is all encompassing; it is "the anxiety" *par excellance*, the total angst. It is different in this respect from an anxiety concerning *something*, which is foreclosed or encapsulated and thus definable. It relates to the totality of our biological–mental body–mind functioning: being the organismic testimony to life itself, the psyche-somatic aliveness of going-on-being is an irreducible concept. Going back to Freud (1920), it has to do with both "[...] the libidinal character of the self-preservative instincts" and "[...] Eros, the preserver of all things [...] by means of which the cells of the soma are attached to one another" (ibid, p.55).

What a succinct image for "going-on-being"! The individual libido, in preserving itself, erotically connects with the environment, which, in turn, serves to hold the personal soma together.

DOI: 10.4324/9781003325499-9

What a trial. What a life challenge to sustain. What a challenge for us therapists.

Literally speaking, going-on-being is not inevitable nor is it a trivial affair. In the history of the human race, there have been two instances in which it was close to being wiped of the face of the earth. On one of them, apparently, only a few hundred human beings survived. What is true of the human race is all the more so as pertains to the unique somato-psychic phenomena of "going-on-being," born of sets of causes and conditions, of coincidental circumstances and contingencies. Michal's chapter would have us understand these conditions as pertains – particularly, but not solely – to fragile, vulnerable individuals; it urges us to understand – and then embrace – these causes, effects and contingencies. Having embraced them – I would suggest – we may be in a position to nurture the conditions which enable us to embody their vicissitudes; having embodied their vicissitudes, we might be able to implement them in the tandem of our therapeutic work.

I am reading Michal's text on "the fear of ceasing and the need to go on" in the midst of the corona pandemic. I am keeping in mind Michal's reminders that going-on-being requires maintenance of life via "a sensory wrapping": As Anzieu (1989) tells us, this external sensory wrapping is derived from the ectodermic connection of both skin and central nervous system (brain) with the outside world. In the empty alienation of our neighbourhoods, in anxious eyes peeping over protective masks and in the plastic texture of gloved un-touching hands, I find testimony to the fact that modern humanity's second skin, technology, is striving to fulfil the task of maintaining a vital, inspiring–expiring, steady, liveable equilibrium.

A sensory wrapping is the function that technology and personalized mass communication now usurp, enveloping us in a second skin that brings us together when setting us apart; a second skin whose aspirations to contain are delimited within its two-dimensional container. As Marshall McLuhan writes, while "all technologies are extensions of our physical... systems to increase power and speed" (1994, p.90), telecommunications are specific extensions of our nervous systems and, as such, affect the whole psychic and social complex.

In adopting an artificial, surrogate, isolating skin, we dismiss the messiness and comfort provided by depth, by bodily humours, by porous liquidity and by flesh. Consequently, contemporary French philosopher Francois Jullien (2016) maintains that "technology, in multiplying presence, atrophies it" (ibid, p. 15). Those of us who are familiar with attachment issues are sadly reminded of the heart-wrenching dilemma in Harlowe's famous experiment: should one choose a wire surrogate (strictly physically) nourishing mother or a furry tactile – albeit (physically) un-nourishing –one: in our current human predicament, communication technologies aspire to be a nourishing wire mesh container, withholding much of the rich contents of human sensuous, container-contained encounters.

In this aerial ethereal mode of communication, the media is a void inhabited by invisible waves, an all-abiding phlogiston infected by an overwhelming miasma of impending contagion; in this emptiness, the yearning I experience is to be enveloped anew in the mess, in the gushing voluminous, sensuous world of yesterday, in touch, in the rich exchange of tinder and tender body fluids, in espressos, health smoothies and cocktails, in holding and containment. As our current situation persists over the weeks and months, it has become a sad, ongoing reminder that some of us "have always wanted to run away from our bodies," from "being together in a messy way, and now we are given a chance" (Turkle, 2018, p. 15).

"In a way, a real mess would be welcome," tells us Michael Eigen (1997, p. 32) in a piece so aptly named "A Bug-Free Universe;" and yet – wonder upon wonder – many of us have qualms regarding a return to the "mess;" many of us, and many of our clients, cling to going on being just as we are now: alone, in seclusion and locked down. Moreover, in the recurring Zoom sessions, many seem to be more open, more relaxed. This would suggest that the mess I yearn for, this aliveness, this hallmark of psychic life and health, is no trivial matter.

Put differently: when the environment is in a mess and the mess threatens to invade us, when interaction with the environment *per se* is perilous, what are the options? Following Bion, Michal posits two punishing and tragic strategies that serve to prevent or mitigate the environment's impingements on the body–mind: one is an expulsion, an expelling of unwanted, invasive mental contents. Within this strategy, space is equivalent to unholding, to nothingness and to a loss of psyche-somatic integrity. The other is a defensive constriction, a psyche-somatic constraint and restriction leading to a life of constant strain.[1]

I shall elaborate on these two positions:

1 One is open-ended, with no sensory holding, no containing boundary, invoking a fear of *the* undefined, of chaos and of a Sisyphic, repetitive, relentless eternity. Winnicott points to this state – depicted as an eternal fall, a "falling forever" – as invoking unbearable anxiety; Bion proposes that psychotic patients psychically project into a space so vast that all sense of self-other experience is lost. Therein lie the terrors of space and time, "*les silence des ces espaces infinis*," the endless solitude that Bion (1970, p. 46), quoting Pascal, attributes to Coleridge's accursed Ancient Mariner, fated to endless foreverness. Under such circumstances, Bion warns us that we are threatened by a looming inferno-hood, a mortal fear of an infinite dispersal in space and time, within which rational, linear knowledge no longer prevails.

   Whilst some of us find inspiration in the capacity to transcend limitations of space and time, others find themselves incapacitated by this prospect.

   Thus, at the other end of the continuum lie density and constriction.

2 In an anthology inspired by the work of Esther Bick, the editor, Stephen Briggs (2002), poses the following question: "What does it mean to survive space?" Briggs suggests that for some infants, "infinite-space/dispersal" is countered by constriction, by a shutdown and by a close-knit, restraining wrapping. At approximately the same time, Gianna Williams (1997) – also of the Tavistock Clinic – wrote about "the no-entry system of defence," suggesting that trauma engenders a state of being wherein both mental apparatus and bodily apertures shut down due to a painful penetration, or the ingestion of foreign bodies: it is thus often the case that eating disorders and sexual abuse form a co-morbid state of distrust, a closing down and a general constriction in regard to the outside world.

   In this context, the existential reality of residing within the space of a human environment entails a vulnerability often engendered by or leading to neglect and abuse. This coincides with Michal's

Buddhist imagery depicting "the inherent pain of searching for sustenance," subjecting us "to the touch of the world, external [...] stimuli constantly imping[ing] on us."

Briggs emphasizes skin and musculo-skeletal shut-down mechanisms, unrest, fidgety second-skin bodily armour defences, against loss in endless, unbound apace; Williams emphasizes the specifics of closing down, avoiding interaction with the environment. Both recognize that these mental or psychic survival strategies entail painful mental constriction, and often extreme, unexplained, physical pain.

Both poles of this binary delineation – the open-ended one, invoking the anxiety of un-containment and that of a psyche-somatic shutdown invoking the sensation of constriction and restraint – preclude going-on-being. Both may, in fact, approximate psychological death.

Let me give an example through a client of mine who taught me much concerning transitions between these binaries.

Orr, a successfully self-employed woman in her 20s, was referred by her psychiatrist with a diagnosis of OCD. Persistently seeking completion and perfection, she incessantly reconstructed events in her mind in order to reach a "hundred percent certainty" or, failing that, to assume "a hundred percent guilt" for thoughts and actions that she could not, *ipso facto*, prove were non-existent. The torturous would-be panacea was constant self-awareness and constant thinking.

And, at moments in which these conscious processes relaxed, hunger set in, then stomach aches; pains set in – then shrill headaches.

As our work progressed and all of these were – tenuously, momentarily – held at bay, Orr would stretch forward, exercising her calf muscles.

"Why are you doing this?" I would ask, incredulous.

"So as not to waste time," was Orr's response.

It gradually became clear that Orr's persistence in maintaining an intensity of sensation *or* emotion *or* pain *or* intellectual efforts was interchangeable, as long as some tangible experience, on some level, persisted. As this surfaced, her overwhelming guilt feelings and anxiety reframed themselves: her real anxiety – she confided – lays in the fear of **the arrest of time**, of "losing her lifeline," her temporal continuity itself.

Losing a lifeline: what eloquent words for the cessation of *being*, for death, for the "ultimate fear"!

"I need to maintain this lifeline, this is my timeline, If I exit it, **I am left with nothing, nothing...**"

There was more sadness than fear in her tone.

Incessant doing, incessant feeling and undulating discomfort or pain were all unconscious efforts at keeping the passage of "empty time" – of a sense of nothingness – at bay. If time were empty of an intensity of feeling alive, fear of death set in: Orr felt "clueless," "unconsciously search[ing]" – in Michal's words – for "an anchor [...] something to hold on to [...] some line to follow." Being clueless equalled death, being relaxed equalled death and daydreaming equalled death. Being without pain equalled death. Time spent with no thought or action felt tantamount to death itself. Stretching, aching, thinking and doing were efforts, in fact, at allaying death. A far cry from the conventional DSM-based construal of an OCD symptomatology!

Orr's ordeal underscores Michal's speculations concerning a co-joint temporal–spatial state in which the emergence "of inner holding, of [a] sophisticated second-skin that envelopes the self by means of immersion, fixating, tightening and movement" serves the purpose of "avoiding intervals – in space and time – in the presence of an unconscious fear of annihilation." It is a sobering thought: a sense of spaciousness in and of itself does not support a sense of well-being, since the attendant sense of calm often serves as a signifier of "nothing," as a precursor to a sense of threatening emptiness. As in the case of Peter, the antidote is "tightening the membrane walls."

It is the therapist's task to distinguish between "space" and "empty nothingness," between the capacity to embrace infinity and a sense of eternal, undulating agony. It is the therapist's task to engage in allowing enough space for these binaries – spaciousness and restriction – to co-exist, accepting and embracing the tension between them as conducive rather than destructive, de-capacitating or crippling – to life.

At-one-ment: The Role of the Therapist

What need we do, how may we be, in order to avert these contingencies?

Michal, quoting Eigen, stipulates:

When the container is characterized by sufficient flexibility and receptivity, [...] the infant's mental space, too, enables openness to learning [...and...] mental growth. When this is not the case [...]

any [...] sense of catastrophe lose[s] [its] value as [a] meaningful signal caus[ing] deep, primitive psychic pain". Stemming from these stipulations I would suggest that it is the therapist's role as container that requires cultivation.

It is the cultivation of an internal mode of being and the therapist's ability to go on being himself, in attunement with his client, an attunement striving towards what Bion (1965, 1970) terms "at-one-ment," which I shall now examine and describe.

Cultivation of Internal Space

Nagarjuna, the forefather of Buddhism's doctrine of non-duality, postulates: "By a misperception of emptiness, a person [...] is destroyed, like a snake incorrectly seized, or like a spell incorrectly cast" (Garfield, 1995, p. 68). In this instance, as in many others, Buddhist catechism dovetails with psychoanalytic developmental theory: if not internalized and embodied in a safe environment, spaciousness may lead to a sense of empty nothingness, to decay, loss and abuse. How may the benign aspects of spacious emptiness be learnt?

Let's begin here. Eigen – aka "The Psychoanalytic Mystic" – reminds us that, in Winnicottian terms, emptiness often equals nothingness. Winnicott (1989) leans on Eliot's "Wastelands" to establish the fact that a life filled with empty actions, thoughts and gestures is drained of meaning, creating what for Eliot are "hollow men." When this is the case, connections, links and a sense of continuity are all loosened and one "can connect nothing with nothing." The word "nothing" resonates in Eliot's text, connoting an empty, eerie, hollow feeling. Eliot's Hollow Men demonstrates how a chain of mutual connections may be depleted of emotional meaning; only fiery, feisty momentums keep them moving: and as the world burns with mindless momentum, the speaker pleads for someone to free him from this hell of nothingness.

Consequently, in order to start relinking, we must first rethink the concept of the mind's "spaciousness" as opposed to "emptiness;" of the mind's capacities of "infinitude" as opposed to the suffering of "eternity." More specifically, I propose we distinguish between "mental contents" and the mind's containing capacity, between what the Satipaṭṭhāna Sutta calls "contents of the mind" – which are representations of ideas, feelings and affects – and "mental contents," i.e. the state of the mind, its hues and characteristics, and above all – its capacity to contain. In doing this, we are looking at something which psychoanalysis is only starting to name, i.e. the capacity of the mind that relates neither to ego functions nor to psychic contents but, rather, to **the nature of the mind itself** in health and in disease. These are what the Satipaṭṭhāna Sutta in "contemplation of consciousness" refers to as: "The shrunken state of consciousness [...] the distracted state of consciousness [...] the developed state of consciousness [...] the concentrated state of consciousness" and, ultimately, "the freed state of consciousness" (Soma Thera, 1998).

Over the last two decades, psychoanalysts, such as Thomas Ogden (1989) and, more specifically, Ricardo Lombardi (2010), relate to a *"real, bodily space-time,"* conducive to *"an internal body-mind dialogue"*[2] (p. 906). In an article called "Inner space: Its dimensions and its coordinates" – that, to my mind, has not received the attention it deserves – Grotstein (1978) tackles this issue. For him, "psychic space is an important, albeit neglected, aspect of mind, having many far-reaching [... implications...] which are worthy of psychoanalytic study. [...] the space of the mind affects its content and vice versa" (ibid, p. 55). Grotstein (ibid, ibid) continues to stipulate that "the epigenesis and ontogenesis of space dimensions is of great practical, as well as theoretical, importance in psychoanalytic thinking," since, without them, there is no space from within which, and unto which, one may project.

What has this space to do with binary positions and with going-on-being and, more specifically, with the therapist's capacity to cultivate these attributes?

I would suggest that Grotstein's intuition is part of a wider strain within contemporary psychoanalysis, which, implicitly, already espouses non-binary terminology and configurations concerned with the plausibility of non-linear attributes of space and time (I have previously termed this theoretical paradigm "the unitary turn." [Sella, 2018]). This psychoanalytic paradigm incorporates a supraordinate position, one that is implied in Grotstein's and Bion's work, a new link between the personal and transpersonal spheres, a personalized "O," reshuffling and consequently redefining the experience of space and time. It is this position that needs to be cultivated in order to maintain a non-binary, continuous going-on-being existential mode. It is within this position that the therapist's body–mind serves as an extension – in space–time – of the client's.

Beware: this undercuts a predominant psychoanalytic presupposition relating to the temporal trajectory of mental development: dormant within psychoanalysis's punctuation of space–time lies the supposition of benign linearity, a step-by-step development, a forward-moving trajectory that, by its very momentum, creates an illusion of solidity. Under "ordinary" conditions, a cessation of this vector approximates finality and death, the fear of an ultimate boundary. Under conditions of trauma and stress, however, this fear is reversed, replaced by a fear of an eternal, undefined boundary-less time–space, a relentless infinitude and a sense that one "on a lonesome road, doth walk in fear and dread" (Coleridge, in: Bion, 1970, p 46).

But if not temporally progressive and finite and if not spatially self-enclosed, what are our safeguards, what protects us and what is our stimulus barrier, our protective shield? And what are the prerequisites for their emergence within a therapeutic relationship? Or, in reference to Michal's chapter, "In the right internal and interpersonal conditions," how and where does "trust [...] emerge [...] replacing [...] strain and restlessness [...] with [...] steadiness and peace of mind"?

Zen scholar Shigenori Nagatomo (1992) suggests that the answer lies in a dialogical relationship of attuned psyche-somatic mutuality, which is encoded in the Japanese ideographs of kan-no-do-ko, the four characters comprising it being "feeling-response-paths-intersect" (ibid, p.147). The term is pertinent in that it reflects the embodiment of at-one-ment as an interactive mutuality of going-on-being.

Based on the premise that the mind's spatial–temporal attributes provide the mental container for the mind's intolerable contents, while keeping the notion of mutuality in mind, it behoves the analyst, seeking to provide space, to become space; in the less familiar part of Bion's famous injunction (concerning knowledge, memory and desire) is a prompt, urging the therapist "to become infinite," right now, and right now again, over and over again, moment by moment. Beyond the provision of a fruitful metaphor, I understand Bion's infinity to be an embodied position, cultivated moment by moment through the therapist's becoming, through his unceasing. In this rendering of

Bion's terminology, the space of the mind broadens inasmuch as the therapist cultivates his own spaciousness of mind. Quoting Grotstein (1978) again: "All growth and maturation can be seen as expansions of the sense of the *ultimate space*[3] of the self" (ibid, p.60). The therapist's capacity to cultivate and embody these qualities creates a space within which – in at-one-ment – the contents of the patient's mind may transform.

Making Space for the Binaries

Separateness and Mountain Winds

In a conference debate between Tibetan Buddhist monks and imminent psychoanalysts held in the 1980s, the psychoanalytic cohort stressed the instinctual faculties as underlying ego development and the skin's function as an ego barrier. The Tibetan monks were aghast: "If you haven't sorted out the interconnected nature of body and mind and the concomitant mutuality of two psyche-somas interacting with each other, how can we convene here to discuss issues of transcendence, transformation and interconnected relationships?" was their message (Epstein, 2000)[4].

Do our boundaries and foreclosures insure our going-on-being? In a dojo where I used to practice Aikido and Shiatsu, the welcoming haiku was this:

> Mountain wind
> Is blowing
> Even now

This was comforting to me, a stranger in a strange environment. It was a reminder of the fact that the natural world persists in its going-on-beingness even in my moments of strife and suffering. Once practice commenced, I was reminded, through it, that our very relationship to the world inevitably – outrageously – defies the illusion of separateness between self and world, self and otherness. We are dependent on the world for our going-on-being, for our very sustenance: breathing, nourishment and procreation – all defy the solipsistic illusion. Within this framework, our ability to note the wind blowing is a token of our immersion in the universal, thus defying the illusion of a self-contained organism, an enclosed-within-a-skin body–mind.

This is also true in other spheres. We cannot but realize this in a globalized world, with the largest influx of refugees (driven by conditions wrought by global warming and natural calamities) since WWII, with concomitant xenophobia, agoraphobia and claustrophobia generating inner–outer, friend–foe, containable–uncontainable divisions and splits, on all levels. The intertwining of the natural world – in the sub-Sahara, in Syria and in the Bengal Bay – with ecology, politics and human psychology has never seemed more strikingly obvious.

How can we apply this perceived affinity between the web of ecological connectivity in its broadest sense and the pervasive experience of inherent separation? Kohut (1959) takes a hesitant step, teaching us that "some psychological processes [...] lie closer to the movement of the water as it interacts with rocks and gravity" (p. 469). As if personifying "mountain winds," Kohut (1966) mentions that to breathe is to inspire, much as in meditative practice one allows "the circulation of energy activated by the bellows of breathing [to] take over from discursive consciousness" (Seo & Addiss, 2010, p. 9). Winnicott (1954, p. 252) teaches us about such a moment of realization in a clinical vignette that included a "phase in which there was no mind and no mental functioning [...] in which the breathing [...] was all [...] because I was holding her and keeping a continuity by my own breathing, while she let go, gave in, knew nothing [...]."

I imagine Winnicott (1949) holding Margaret Little's head, breathing for her? Breathing with her? Being breath itself?

If and when un-held, Winnicott tells us, people lose their ground, experiencing dissociation and vertigo (1952). It is the function of the elemental mother earth and – by implication – of the therapist, to replace the steady ongoingness of mothering–holding by a repetitive, continuous steady beingness. It is the therapist's role, tells us Balint (1979), at times, to be earth, whose "chief characteristic is indestructibility" (p. 136); within this paradigm, the therapist must be prepared "[...] to carry the patient like water carries the swimmer, like earth carries the walker" (p. 167), embodying the elements, creating the incessantness of continuous flow and emulating the wind and the mountains.

The Binary of Life and Death

It is often our task to acknowledge the unbearable finality of death and trauma on the one hand and the insurmountable infinitude of going on living in suffering, on the other.

Having lost a beloved daughter, Issa wrote:

> This dewdrop world
> Is a dewdrop world
> And yet, and yet...

In this moving haiku, Isaa, poet and Buddhist hermit, poetically and plaintively holds the inevitable tension between the conventional and the absolute, finality and timelessness, and eternal suffering and transition. How can this seeming paradox be resolved?

A stupendous effort towards such a resolution may be found in the writings of 13th century Zen teacher, Ehei Dōgen. Dōgen maintains that, in holding the tension we create space; in creating space for mental events, we transform the tension. Dōgen tells us that both human sorrow over death *and* human acknowledgment of finitude reside within human presence, within being in time and within going-on-being.

Dōgen proclaims: "A fish swims in the ocean, and no matter how far it swims, there is no end to the ocean. A bird flies in the sky and no matter how far it flies, is the sky" (Tanahashi, 1985, pp. 71–72). By inference: everywhere the human mind wanders is the human world, is being present, in life as in death. In fully dwelling within each and every time–space unit, with its own past, present and future, and in fully allowing the flow between these spatial–temporal units, going-on-being is not defined by temporal binaries but by a moment-by-moment continuous presence. (One is reminded in this context of Winnicott's words, "May I be alive when I die.")[5] In this context, the mind's attributes of spaciousness and its contents are not two separate things.

Dōgen thus resolves Western philosophy's riddle set up by Kant: the co-ordinates demarcating the human mind are inseparable from its contents. If its form is perceived as limited by the passage of time or by mortality, its contents are the binaries of life and death. However, if its contents are the actualization, through body and mind, of things as they are at present – there is total exertion, total involvement and total intimacy; in this portrayal, undivided activity is the interwoven continuum of "**time**-being" manifesting as going-on-being, as "**being**-time."

Therapeutic attention thus construed is epitomized in the Chinese term of "I Nian" (意念), literally translated as "attention" yet figuratively portraying **"the sound of the heart right now" or "the nowness of the heart's sounds."** Within this terminology, marking and creating time–space, going-on-being in going-on-beingness, in attention and in mindful holding, are rendered an existential reality, nurturing, via a non-linear presence, the existential moment-by-moment reality of another. One can imagine the implications for the therapeutic encounter: with each moment in time manifesting as a treasured meeting[6] entirety goes on being, "the entire world is not unchangeable: it flows" (Tanahashi, 1985, p. 80).

The Binary between Emergence and Diffusion

Some hundred years ago, Europe emerged, hurt and scathed by the First World War. As the corpses of lives not completed lay in the battlefields, Freud (1916) was concerned with the actualities of the cessation of lives and the implication thereof on the living. Walking through the "smiling countryside" with his companions Rilke and Andre Louis Salome, Freud wondered: is there solace in the thought of inevitable ending and death, of a final diffusion? Does it make life hideous or does it endear it all the more, as Freud, ultimately and somewhat atypically, preached to Rilke?

Years after Freud's WWI meanderings on mortality, Bion (1963) postulated the emergence from Eden – tantamount to the human encounter with mortality – to be one of the formative mythic pillars of western civilization. Within this construal, the emergence of human individuality is anathema to a transcendental unification with the infinite approximated, according to Bion, by the openness of the godfigure, of O.

Within this context, the I-ness of the ego, juxtaposed against the openness of O, literally, metaphorically and figuratively demonstrates what Raanan Kulka (2003) perceives as the oscillation between emergence–separateness and diffusion–allness. Kulka reminds us that a striving towards the ultimate can in itself be restrictive and wounding. To quote Nagarjuna again: "Without a foundation in the conventional truth, the significance of the ultimate cannot be taught" (Garfield, 1995, p. 68).

What one therefore seeks is a supraposition enabling the transition between these two states of being: the painfully human and the blissfully open and infinite. In Kulka's words: a "permanent oscillation between emergence states of the individual self and the state of dissolving into transcendental selfhood" (ibid, p. 267) takes place, where "emergence" denotes a dualistic constitution of reality, and "dissolution" points to a non-dualistic psyche-somatic reality, an idea that a going-on-being "of selfhood contain[s] the free movement between experience as a non-organized essence and experience as a formed and structured organization" (2003, p. 170). Within this paradigm, the ability to return to the supraposition of potentiality, preceding binary determinations, is the hallmark of going-on-being.

The Unbroken Beat

In my clinic, I am seeing a woman whose passion is dance, who is a dancer. Bewilderingly, for her, she finds herself moved by electronic control keyboard panels and similar simulation technologies.

"The instrument that will give a focus to my next project will be a break-beat drum," she informs me.

She responds with a smile to my association with a breakdance movement, and later, we elaborate.

This woman was traumatized by close family members, and her life shattered.

"At times like this a fog appears, a haze through which I am unable to see."

"Unable to see?"

She is silent.

"Unable to speak... but the beat... the break... like that of Afro-Americans," I inquire–suggest; "like them, you are drawn to figuratively and performatively declare the desolation, the devastation, the demise, the 'breaks' of your life."

She does not respond to this, or, more accurately, she does not respond overtly to this. There is no verbal response. Yet *I sense*, within me, a slight clinching of the belly, a sense of impending cold. I image a cold winter approaching, for which I am unprepared, and I breathe as if touched by frostbite, a shrill, sharp, shallow gasp.

"Like now," I pronounce, "... as the fog sets in..."

"Like now," she mumbles, my words hers, and her – mine.

Not only does the mother's containing mind help the baby sense that he has an inner space of his own, as Michal says; within this premise of going-on-being, moments of connection between **two minds**, two echo chambers, ensue. They are non-verbal intuitions of at-one-ment, conducing the existence of a mutual, interconnected continuous process of a – paradoxically – discrete becoming. If and when the therapist's mindful psyche-soma creates a communal continuity in space and time, it continually monitors, regulates, inspires, heats and rhythmically paces; not only does it contain the mess in areas of intense trauma and stress. At times of loss in space, of emptiness, fog and haze, and in moments of unbearable constriction, it creates a notion of inseparate continuity, a continuous embodied realization of life's continuity.

Within this paradigm, the self is undetermined as a separate "life" and the oscillation between emergence and diffusion finds its resolution in the constant pendular swing between one and another. For me, Laozi's Taoist Yin-Yang symbolization most succinctly demonstrates this, declaring that, within this state of shared psyche-somatic temporal spaciousness, "no determination coincides any longer with itself but finds its point of departure in its opposite" (Jullien, 2016, pp. 42–43).

Quoting Laozi, Jullien (2016) says:

In forcing, I call it great
great is called (means) leaving,
leaving is called (means) distanced,
distanced is called (means) returning.
(Jullien, 2016, p. 90)

***

In my response to Michal's chapter, I have allowed myself to free-associate and to transition between acknowledging both the limiting constraints of our present, global, plague-ridden predicament and the vast expanses of spacious infinitude. I have drawn attention to our current alienating circumstances, paradoxically connecting us to each other, and to the manner in which the wide expanses of inter-connectedness seem to annihilate the oh-so-welcome mess of human embodied connectedness.

And I have suggested that, in order to negotiate the polarities of empty spaciousness on the one hand and restrictive holding on the other, it is the therapist's task to cultivate his or her own becoming. To this end, emptiness as an echo chamber or as a potential state of mind needs be wed with the substance of spaciousness, **with spaciousness as the mind's contents.** When the body–mind continuously allows itself to be filled and fulfilled by the contents of mindfulness, then emptied, as in the movement of an inspiring–expiring bellows, as in the mindful breath accompanying a Chi-Kong exercise, a co-joint going-on-being is generated.

In at-one-ment, as Eigen (1992) mentions, we keep our core alive, surviving "our own opening as we O and O and O" (p. 285). This process of expansive at-one-ment incorporates both one's self as an individual emergent entity and O as an endless, diffused interconnected becoming at its heart. I have suggested that, in the embodied oscillation between client and therapist, it is the therapist's capacity in moments of spaciousness, in moments of infinitude and in instances of disavowing discursive, binary thinking that creates space for the client's soma-to-mental contents, rhythms, anxieties, hopes and fears – for the whole mess in short – to transform from potentiality to a nascent reality, and, gradually, to generate an ongoing experience of going-on-being.

Notes

1 Using this dichotomy, we can relate to the immense sense of freedom some people experience lying on the couch, facing a vast expanse delimited only by a ceiling or sitting on the meditation cushion facing the wall, and the all-encompassing panic of others in these very circumstances.
2 Italics in the original text.
3 Italics in the original text.
4 Private communication in a discussion with Mark Epstein during the "Psychology of Awakening" conference held in Dartington Hall, Devon, U.K. in 2000.

5   This poem was handwritten by Winnicott at the end of his paper "Playing and Culture."
6   This is epitomized in the Zen saying "一期一会," connoting the uniqueness and precious qualities of life's encounters.

References

Anzieu, D. (1989). *The Skin Ego*. Yale: Yale University Press.
Balint, M. (1979). *The Basic Fault: Therapeutic Aspects of Regression*. London: Routledge.
Bion, W.R. (1963). *Elements of Psycho-Analysis*. London: Heinemann.
Bion, W.R. (1965). *Transformations*. London: Tavistock.
Bion, W.R. (1970). *Attention and Interpretation*. London: Tavistock.
Briggs, A. (Ed.) (2002). *Surviving Space: Papers on Infant Observation*. London: Karnac.
Eigen, M. (1992). The Fire That Never Goes Out. *Psychoanalytic Review* 79(2): 271–287.
Eigen, M. (1997). A Bug-Free Universe. *Contemporary Psychoanalysis* 33:19–41.
Epstein, M. (2000). *Personal Communication during the Psychology of Awakening: Buddhism, Science, and Our Day-to-Day Lives*. Schumacher College.
Freud, S. (1916). *On Transience. S. E., 14: 303–307*. London: Hogarth.
Freud, S. (1920). *Beyond the Pleasure Principle. S. E., 18: 1–64*. London: Hogarth.
Garfield, J. (Ed.) (1995). *The Fundamental Wisdom of the Middle Way: Nāgārjuna's Mūlamadhyamakakārikā*. Oxford: Oxford University Press.
Grotstein, J.S. (1978). Inner Space: Its Dimensions and Its Coordinates. *International Journal of Psycho-Analysis* 59:55–61
Jullien, F. (2016). *The Philosophy of Living*. London: Seagull.
Kohut, H. (1959). Introspection, Empathy, and Psychoanalysis: An Examination of the Relationship between Mode of Observation and Theory. *Journal of American Psychoanalytic Association* 7:459–483
Kohut, H. (1966). Forms and Transformations of Narcissism. *Journal of the American Psychoanalytic Association*, 14: 243–272.
Kulka, R. (2003). Between Emergence and Diffusion: A Psychoanalytic Kōan of Body-Mind. Paper Presented at *The Body in Psychotherapy – Occidental and Eastern Perspectives Symposium (Collaboration of the Department of Psychology and the Department of East-Asian Studies)*. Tel Aviv, Israel: Tel Aviv University.
Lombardi, R. (2010). The Body Emerging from the "Neverland" of Nothingness. *The Psychoanalytic Quarterly* 79(4): 879–909.
McLuhan, M. (1994). *Understanding Media: The Extensions of Man*. Cambridge: MIT.
Nagatomo, S. (1992). *Attunement through the Body*. New York: New York State University.

Ogden, T. H. (1989). On the Concept of an Autistic-Contiguous Position. *The International Journal of Psychoanalysis*, 70: 127–140.

Sella, Y. (2018). *From Dualism to Oneness in Psychoanalysis: A Zen Perspective on the Mind-Body Question*. London: Routledge.

Seo, A. & Addiss, A. (2010). *The Sound of One Hand: Paintings and Calligraphy by Zen Master Hakuin*. Boston: Shambala.

Tanahashi, K. (Ed.) (1985). *Moon in a Dewdrop: Writings of Zen Master Dōgen*. New York: North Point Press.

Thera Soma. (1998). *The Way of Mindfulness: The Satipatthana Sutta and Its Commentary*. Kandi: Buddhist Publication Society.

Turkle, S. (2018). Changing Attitudes about Sex: A Dual Inheritance Perspective. In: V. Tsolas & C. Anzieu-Premmereur (Eds.), *A Psychoanalytic Exploration of the Body in Today's World: On the Body* (pp. 17–28). London: Routledge.

Williams, G. (1997). Reflections on Some Dynamics of Eating Disorders: 'No Entry' Defense and Foreign Bodies. *International Journal of Psycho-Analysis* 78:927–941.

Winnicott, D.W. (Ed.). (1949). Mind and Its Relation to the Psyche-Soma. In: *Through Paediatrics to Psycho-Analysis* (pp. 243–254). London: The Hogarth Press and the Institute of Psycho-Analysis.

Winnicott, D. (Ed.). (1952). Chapter VIII: Anxiety Associated with Insecurity. In: *Through Paediatrics to Psycho-Analysis* (pp. 97–100). London: The Hogarth Press and the Institute of Psycho-Analysis.

Winnicott, D.W. (1954). Mind and Its Relation to the Psyche-Soma. *British Journal of Medical Psychology*, 27(4):201–209.

Winnicott, D.W. (Ed.). (1989). *Psychoanalytic Explorations*. London: Karnac.

Chapter 6

The Echo Chamber Is Not Empty

On Limitation and Vastness, Spaciousness and Nourishment

Michal Barnea-Astrog

The state and qualities of consciousness affect the mental contents it harbours. The mental contents affect the state of the consciousness in which they appear. The state and qualities of the body affect the sorts and intensity of sensations that arise in and on it. The sorts and intensity of sensations affect the body. We can't really experience consciousness without experiencing its contents, and we can't really experience the body without experiencing its sensations (Goenka, 2010). The intricate net of ties goes further, of course: along with every mental state or content, sensation flows (AN 8.83); and sensation is the direct outcome of contact with the world – the internal world of mental contents, and the external world that touches us via the five bodily sense doors. So, very quickly, a mental event evolves into a bodily event, external event evolves into an internal event, and the other way around. Mind streams into body and body streams into mind; and what a moment ago seemed to be out there, belonging to or originating in the other, is suddenly experienced as me and mine.

This, in my view, is the mess. A world entangled in countless other worlds, its bits and pieces, threads and connecting tissues, blood and oxygen, secretions and nutriments – all of which are incessantly touched and touching, produced while producing, transforming while transformed. A world entangled in countless other worlds, pulsating together in space and time.

But there are different worlds. There are specific bits and pieces. There are all sorts of threads and connecting tissues, inflows and outflows, nutriments and secretions. Distinction and discernment are not the same as splitting or separation. Formulations of chains and nets of conditioned becoming involve discernment and sharp analysis

DOI: 10.4324/9781003325499-10

at the same time as they indicate the complex relations of influence and dependence.

Space-and-time is where-when phenomena exist (albeit briefly, dependently, essencelessly). Where-when nothing arises and nothing passes, where-when nothing becomes – there's no space-and-time. According to Yorai, "In fully dwelling within each and every time-space unit, with its own past present and future, in fully allowing the flow between these spatial-temporal units, going-on-being is not defined by temporal binaries but by a moment by moment continuous presence." Experience and co-experience thus realized are felt as living, breathing streams, connected though not misconstrued as merged, touched and touching though ungrasped; organized, dissolved and reorganized momentarily, unmanipulated and uncontrolled, constantly shifting while navigated by certain paths of truth.

Earth, Water, Fire, Wind and Space

Yorai wrote, quoting Balint (1979), that sometimes it is the therapist's role

> ... to be earth, whose "chief characteristic is indestructibility" (p. 136); within this paradigm the therapist must be prepared "[...] to carry the patient like water carries the swimmer, like earth carries the walker" (p. 167), embodying the elements, creating the incessantness of continuous flow, emulating the wind and the mountains.

I'd like to say more about this attitude or state.

In one beautiful and quite famous Sutta, the Buddha addresses his son Rāhula, who according to the commentaries was an 18-year-old monk by then. He begins by offering him a concise analysis of the nature of the body, and a sober, realistic way of perceiving and relating to it. In this analysis, the body, like the rest of the material world, is considered in terms of the four great or primary elements: earth, water, fire and air or wind; and the fifth factor, space, which in this context is what surrounds, delimits or confines matter, and in the body manifests as the orifices and tube-like passages[1].

Each element is characterized in reference to the individual's body, and the body parts in which it is predominant are specified and named. Like the external earth element, the interior earth element is anything that's hard or solid in the body. Like the external water element, the interior water element is anything that's watery, fluid or generates cohesion. Like the external fire element, the internal fire element is anything that's burning, heating, ageing, consuming and digesting. Like the external air element, the interior air element is anything that's windy or blowing. Like external space, the interior space element is anything that's spacious or void, that allows matter to pass through. Being internal and thus individual, the Buddha points out – all body parts and elements are perceived as personal and are thus clung to. But in fact:

> The interior earth element and the exterior earth element are merely "earth element". This should be seen as it is, with complete wisdom: 'This is not mine, this is not me, this is not my self.' When one sees the earth element as it is, with complete wisdom, one becomes disenchanted with it, and his mind is liberated from passion towards it.
>
> (MN 62).

The same words are used regarding the rest of the discussed elements.

The four great elements are constituents of the material. According to Pāli Canon thought, every material particle is made up of all four, with each manifesting in particular ways and degrees of dominance, to form, when combined, the characteristics of a specific substance at a specific moment. The material particles appear and disappear incessantly, emerging and ceasing at an enormous rate.

But mind and matter flow into one another, create each other; they are interconnected. They spring together or consequently or otherwise dependently, informed by the preset environmental conditions, mental states, contents and actions and fed by impressions and residues left by past ones. Experientially speaking, we may say that the interface of body and mind is sensation: sensations appear in and on the body, yet it is the mind, which is spread all over the body, ready to receive and perceive, cognize and recognize, that feels. Sensations appear in and on the body, but they are mental factors. Therefore, it makes sense that the elements of which the physical world is made of have mental, experiential manifestations as well. In fear, for instance, the predominantly felt element is air or wind, and one may tremble. In anger, the predominant felt element is fire, and one may get all "heated up." The mind can be dense or spacious, heavy or light, indicating various degrees of the dominance of the earth element, and it may be concentrated and cohesive or diffused and scattered, manifesting higher or lesser degrees of the water element.

The traits of reality, whether physical or mental, internal or external, are, as the above text states, simply traits of reality. They can be clearly identified or not. They can be desired or rejected, adhered to or pushed away, appropriated or disavowed due to identifications and disidentifications based on the delusions of permanence and solid selfhood; or they can be purely noticed, with no additional attribution or reaction – fully experienced, yet not confused as self or as counter-self. Then they are truly seen as they are. Then they are not projected and not manipulated.

After identifying the material elements as they are, Rāhula is advised to take inspiration from them. He is asked to cultivate a state of mind as receptive and unshakable, as non-rejecting and non-desiring as the earth, water, fire and wind; and as unfixed and unfixated as space:

> Rāhula, practice meditation as if you were the earth. For when you meditate as if you were the earth, pleasant and unpleasant contacts that will arise will not take hold of your mind and will not fixate there. Just like, Rāhula, when people toss clean and dirty things on the earth, such as feces, urine, saliva, pus and blood, the earth isn't horrified, repelled, and disgusted – in the same way, meditate as if you were the earth. For when you meditate as if you were the earth, pleasant and unpleasant contacts that will arise will not take hold of your mind and fixate there.
>
> Rāhula, practice meditation as if you were water... Just like, Rāhula, when people wash clean and dirty things in the water, like feces, urine, saliva, pus and blood, the water isn't horrified, repelled, and disgusted – in the same way, meditate as if you were water...
>
> Rāhula, practice meditation as if you were fire... practice meditation as if you were the wind... practice meditation as if you

were space. For when you meditate as if you were space, pleasant and unpleasant contacts that will arise will not take hold of your mind and will not fixate there. Just like, Rāhula, space is not established anywhere, in the same way, meditate as if you were space. For when you meditate as if you were space, pleasant and unpleasant contacts that will arise will not take hold of your mind and will not fixate there.

(MN 62)[2]

But the earth doesn't feel. It doesn't think. It is certainly affected and dependent, subject to emergence and cessation, to ruin and creation and to constant change; but it has no consciousness and it doesn't sense. No wonder it is not horrified, disgusted or repelled. So, in a way, the entire thing is a metaphor, a way of explaining, of pointing to a certain state. And yet, it is such a powerful metaphor. Because it is calling for embodiment; and because the elements to be embodied are the world: we are made of them, and we live in them. And to other sensing beings, we ourselves are elements in the world. For certain people in certain situations and relations, such as parent–infant and therapist–patient, we may be the **primary elements** that make up (or heavily contribute to the making up of) the relational world. So at our best, when we are not horrified nor repelled, when pleasant and painful contacts, while being fully felt, do not take over our psyches and do not fixate there, we can "carry [the other] like water carries the swimmer, like earth carries the walker," "embodying the elements, creating the incessantness of continuous flow, emulating the wind and the mountains," as quoted above.

The Body as a True Other

On another occasion, pointing to similar ideas, the Buddha addresses the ascetic Dīghanakha[3] with the following words:

> … this body is material, made up of the four great elements, born from mother and father, built up from rice and porridge, liable to impermanence, to decay and to erosion, to breaking up and to destruction. It should be seen as ephemeral, as suffering, as diseased, as an abscess, as a dart, as painful, as an affliction, **as an**

other[4], as falling apart, as empty, as not-self. Thus seen, any desire for the body, any lust for the body, and any subjugation to the body are abandoned.

(MN 74)

According to this perspective, which is expounded in various ways throughout the Pāli Canon, a person who is "developed in body and mind" (MN 36) is a person who does not lust after pleasure and does not become distraught and upset when pleasure ceases and is replaced by pain (MN 36). This means that both pleasurable and painful sensations are felt, acknowledged and observed, but do not obsess the mind, overpower or shake it. In the opening dialogue of the book, Rina wrote about "acknowledging illness' otherness and our psychic limits, surrendering to our bodily selves while being ill":

> When we are diagnosed with cancer, we have to learn that we are not the masters of our body. Our psyche has an important role but it is not the queen there. Not at all. We come to know our limits and the gap between our psychic functions and capabilities and our body in a harsh way: "... for dust thou art, and unto dust shalt thou return" (Genesis, 3: 19).
>
> [...] we need to accept the harsh fact that after all we are only human beings – flesh and blood. Yet, surrender, according to Ghent (1990), "implies not defeat but a quality of liberation and 'letting-go'" (p. 134). We do not submit. We do try to relate in a more benign way to our bodies and ourselves. To move differently in our life. We try to be "seekers" rather than "masters" (Becker, 2022, see Chapter 1, this volume). We do not have other choice if we want to live and not just to survive.
>
> (Lazar, 2023, see Chapter 2, this volume)

As Yorai suggested, following Turkle, "some of us have always wanted to run away from our bodies" and from "being together in a messy way." A state of a pandemic, like the one humanity is going through as this book is being written, requires us to be physically separated and isolated, to withdraw from touching each other with all of our six sense spheres, and thus, in some way, enables that. But even when we are socially isolated, we are nevertheless confronted with other "messy" aspects of our bodily reality: fragility, infectiousness, morbidity and mortality are constantly hanging in the air. The clouds of disease hover above us, burdening our day-to-day activities. The body is an affliction, a source of vulnerability and pain. The body is an other that does not obey our reign.

Realizing our "painfully human" state, as Yorai puts it, or that "impingement is our human lot," as Rina has, does not have to entail pessimism, depression, passivity or submission. It is a part of mental embodied development that leads to various degrees of freedom. It may lead to a more secure, truthful and joyful lodging in our mind-body. In the world's womb/open-air home body. And, as Rina wrote, "a reasonably secure bodily home paves the way for lodging in the other." Such development may allow us to live fully rather than survive, and whether we are physically together or secluded – to connect. It may allow us to become a richer and more spacious womb/open-air home for the other to lodge in.

According to Buddhist thought, the body is alien, an other[5] (MN 74); and although it is part of our most intimate reality, an immediate manifestation of the intricate web of conditions that created us and that keep creating us from moment to moment and should therefore be fully examined and felt – it is not our "self." The body and its sensations, just like the mind and its contents, keep changing. They cannot endure nor be ultimately controlled and thus cannot be true sources of gratification and happiness. They are, therefore, defined as void of an independent self-core, as **not-self** (DN 15).

We may see the body as not-self, as an (intimately felt) other. We may see the body as the first other (Mucci, 2018), or as the "radical place of *in-betweeness*" (Mucci, 2018, p. 45) – the essential mediator between self and other. Can we also see the body as a True Other? Not in all aspects, of course, since the connection and exchanges are not with another whole being; but can we see it as an other which, given the right point of view, provides us, over and over and over again, with the deepest truths regarding ourselves and the world? An other that when approached as "seekers" rather than "masters" keeps portraying the truths of emergence and dissolution, of interdependency, dissatisfaction and pain? The truths of the human capacities for restriction and vastness, for harm and nourishment, for deterioration and development?

Remembering that

Mountain wind
Is blowing
Even now

is, in Yorai's words, "a token of our immersion in the universal, thus defying the illusion of a self-contained organism, an enclosed-within-a-skin body-mind." It is also a manifestation of the space created by holding "the inevitable tension between the conventional and the absolute, finality and timelessness, eternal suffering and transition," as Yorai wrote. It is a manifestation of not being perplexed by the coexistence of limitation, mortality and ephemerality on the one hand, and of the vastness of the unknown on the other, the ungraspable multidimensional continuity of all things – ourselves included – void of a stable core as we are, interbecoming and interlinked.

Beyond the two possibilities of what he names "empty spaciousness" and "restrictive holding," Yorai offers a swinging movement between full, embodied I-ness and infinite, diffused I-you interconnectedness. This, ideally, should not be an end-to-end movement, leaving the in-between hollow, and thus maintaining a measure of duality and abandonment. Instead, it should rhythmically pass through the entire range of experience, like the breath and the blood stream provide for every cell. It should come and go, rise and fall, hold and let go like the waves of the sea. Like the mountain wind always blowing somewhere. It is this movement that both reflects and creates the going on reliability of earth, the cohesiveness of water, the fluency of air, the digesting quality of fire and the non-fixation of space.

An Offering of an Embrace

We can move between the possibilities, between "empty spaciousness" and "restrictive holding" and vital, interbecoming I-You-ness. Humans have this capacity. Humanity swings between severe confinement and ultimate freedom, between extreme agony and boundless bliss, between the darkest hellish states and the brightest heavenly ones, and between utter ignorance and complete enlightenment. There's a huge range of realities between the furthest points of the pendulum, and it is evident with reference to both different individuals as well as within each individual. How do we relate to such gaps and swings we detect in others and in ourselves?

It seems, for example, as if only a heavily delusional person would assume that

> Winds don't blow
> Rivers don't stream
> Pregnant women don't give birth
> The moon and stars neither rise nor set,
> But like pillars stand still
>
> (SN 24.1).

Yet the fear of fragmentation is so horrible, that we rather cling to such delusions than to feel it. We know better than this, by our own experience and rational parts; but somehow we manage to go on living and behaving as if things can be stable. Stable for us to have, stable for us to master, stable for us to feel as self. On some level, we know the truth, while on others, we remain profoundly deluded. Do we remember to acknowledge and to gently hold this gap in knowing? Can we feel calm, assured and unperplexed in the face of such different levels of our capacity to know and to experience reality, of such seemingly contradictory coexisting aspects of the capacities that form the very heart of our sense of self? Can we create space for this "mess," a vastness of mind where place and time are lovingly dedicated by the remembering parts to instruct and console the parts that forget?

The Sky Is the (Temporarily Closed) Limit

When I was thinking and writing these words, the Corona pandemic was rapidly spreading and the sky was pretty much closed for regular traffic. The way this affected my mental space raised further thoughts on limitation and the possibility to expand.

There's a certain mode I sometimes go into, where thoughts about faraway places, each with its own particular sights and tastes and scents and sounds, pass very vividly through my mind. I see myself walking there, in those different streets with their different shapes and

colours, with the different textures and patterns of the stones com-
posing their sidewalks, with different kinds of trees and buildings
and building blocks; with different languages spoken by a different
assembly of foreign-looking people, eating and drinking and moving
and thinking drenched in an utterly or slightly different climate, in a
somewhat different atmosphere, with a somewhat different undertone.
Or I see myself walking through the hills and the mountains, through
the creeks and the valleys, with their lush green coating, greener than
anything here, as green as they can be; or sitting at the banks of lakes
and ponds, their waters bluer than anything here, as blue as they can
be; I see myself in all these places, and I'm carried on waves of what
is soon to become a fruitful, creative reverie.

I'm not deliberately or actively creating these images nor am I completely overtaken by or lost in them. They are just streaming there. In
a way, it resembles how I may read a book or watch TV or the people
passing by on a busy city street. There's a kind of inspiration that I
find in sensing other ways of being. There's a kind of an opening for
transcendence, as Roth (2020) described with reference to the reader's
experience, in feeling the worlds of others – a temporary departure
from the constrains of the self. It is an intimate transcendence: not
beyond the worlds of mind and body altogether, not detached from
sense, time and space.

When someone says "the sky is the limit," they mean that there's
no limit. Or that there is a limit somewhere out there, but it is so far
that it's impossible or nearly impossible to attain or touch. So one
is free to extend long arms and reach out for the furthest, to do or
be one's greatest with no hindrance or barrier in sight. When I'm in
my "far-away places" reverie, I'm not immersed in fantasizing the
absent impossible so as to dissociate from the here and now. Instead,
I'm inspired by the vastness of possibility: I may actually travel to
such places someday and be changed by them somehow. There's a
vast space between these possibilities and my here and now, and the
unknown dwells there. Yet I have some tender, elusive emotional tie
with them: they seem like unfamiliar, long-lost relatives or like a priori loved and longed-for strangers; and my will and intention may
take me to meet them. My will and intention may participate in turning these dreams into reality, and this makes a part of me feel free to
extend towards them its long possibility arms.

It is this dialectic that induces my creativity: the mysterious interwo-ven unfolding of dream and reality, the evolvement of an ancient–new relation, of a yet-to-be discovered kinsman, an intimate unknown. And it makes me think of Winnicott's (1960) ideas on how spontane-ous gestures, when repeatedly responded to with attuned sensitivity, enable the illusion of omnipotence and evolve into a creative, vital true self, and how this, in turn, matures into a healthy acknowledg-ment of reality, of limitation and of the uncontrolled other, without leaving behind creativity and vitality, which have already gathered enough strength.

But then the sky got pretty much "closed," and I found that this was preventing the spontaneity of some specific self-parts of mine from being "joined up with the world's events" (Winnicott, 1960, p. 146). Air travel was severely restricted, and even if you did decide to catch a flight, there was always the risk that you'd end up being restricted otherwise: isolated in a hotel room while waiting for COVID-19 test results, or stuck in a locked-down or partly locked-down city where everything is closed, or in a foreign country unable to fly back home due to an unpredicted outbreak or changes in policy – and either way not allowed to freely come and go. And so it happened that during that period of time – for about a year and half, until things became unsta-bly better – my psyche's spontaneous gestures towards faraway places could not be answered by a responsive reality. And without this poten-tial communication, it saw no point in stretching out in these direc-tions. Certain possibility arms had to wait folded and unextended, until the barriers were removed, until the relation between gesture and response and between inner reality and outer reality was renewed. Only then did they feel free to become fully active and alive once more.

Since some possibility arms were kept at bay – which may always be the case, for this reason or the other, for all of us – we may also reverse the thought on this simple idiom, "the sky is the limit," and note that the word "limit" is nevertheless there, alongside the sup-posedly limitless open sky. As if the sky were something concrete, a kind of a ceiling that a truly gigantic creature could feel out. And thus we are confronted with the edges of omnipotence, with the sad and/or protective, comforting fact, that even when the sky is "open," and even for a simple earthling, who normally can't touch the infinite or diffused sky, there are inherent constrains. Because after all, we live with our human bodies, flesh and blood, dust to dust; and additional external envelopes are essential for travelling up there, whether inside the atmosphere or in outer space.

We may internally transgress the threshold of bodily limitations and imagine heaven, where no additional envelopes are needed. Or multiple heavens. And the god or gods or heavenly entities that dwell there. We may imagine ourselves protected by them or nourished by them or becoming ethereal and supreme as they are. Because after all, we live with our human minds, desperately searching for nutriments and envelopes and desperately maintaining them.

And yet we also have our creativity and capacity for transcendence. We are able to feel out our own mental and physical limitations and to use them as links, as sources of knowledge. We are able to treat our bodies as True Others: to follow them closely as they show us the markers of existence, to acknowledge their inherent finitude and pain, and to nurture and care for them while liberating ourselves from the delusion of mastery. We are able to develop our limited minds, to expand them, to dissolve some of their constraining layers and lumps; to turn over old trails, where the ground has gotten too harsh and tight, while ploughing new, more fertile ones. We can touch the infinite; be the infinite; stretch consciousness infinitely, in our minds; encompass the unencompassible, reach all sorts of heavens and dwell in bliss like gods. And we may surpass even our longing for physical and psychic envelopes, for becoming and for not becoming, for the infinite, for heaven, for the warm, ever-protective embrace of mother-god.

"All growth and maturation can be seen as expansions of the sense of the *ultimate space* of the self" (Grotstein, 1978, as quoted by Yorai). And, inserting my own words into Yorai's, who followed Dōgen's: "holding the tension [between limitation and vastness, between virtuality and reality, between ignorance and knowing, between dread and the defenses against it] we create space; in creating space [for such co-existing contrasts] we transform the tension." Then, between the far edges of the pendulum, along its vigorous or feeble swinging movements, a personal and universal human connecting tissue can emerge.

Protective Non-Grasping

The spacious and limitless "as an embodied position," to use Yorai's words, have an important role. They inspire the capacity for reverie, the ability to make space, to hold the tension and to transform. Too much temporal and spatial density (of bodies, of noise, of verbal activity, of events) can be overwhelming. Sufficient temporal and spatial room is needed to effectively be and create. More precisely, it is needed to allow being and creation to emerge and evolve on their own, minimizing the limiting interference of one's limited self. And along with this need for sufficient space – a limitation in itself – there are also states where internal space is so vast, that for a while nothing can clog it, and one can just welcome the entire mess.

And there are also states, when a certain kind of very primitive anxiety or agony arises from the depths and grows so severe, that the only source of relief one can imagine is, as someone once told me, "getting inside a wall." In this horribly diffused state, it seems as if the only possible cure would be the density and finitude of a wall. The need for the earth element in its extremest form! Of course, such all-embracing density can never be achieved, and the relief, which is most urgent, has to come from somewhere else.

Superficial, temporary relief may be found in second-skin, self-holding behaviours, which are certainly not to be dismissed and are appreciated as necessary survival methods for coping with harsh realities, as previously discussed. But these require incessant maintenance, and they claim their toll. Truly transformative alleviation, by contrast, is derived from the gradual maturation of sincere non-grasping. Real protection cannot be achieved by avoiding experience or by otherwise manipulating it, but through the capacity to sense without compulsively reacting – externally as well as internally. This capacity relies on deeper mind-body development. It may be supported by therapeutic relations involving the right qualities and states of attention, and by other good relationships; and it is a primary aim of Vipassana or Satipaṭṭhāna, as taught by the Buddha and briefly referred to in the aforementioned Pāli Canon texts.

Ideally, the person going through these developmental processes is assisted and held by the other's (therapist's or teacher's) clarity of thought, and by her loving, caring, calm, non-selfish attention; by safe physical conditions and, very importantly, by continuity: the continuity and stability of the other's and of one's own perseverance in the face of the changing winds and shifting sands of experience; and the continuity of human search for true contact and true growth, across time and space – a search shared by innumerous people from different lands, speaking different tongues, praying to different gods, wearing different garments, treading different city streets and country-side trails, carrying in their psyches and bodies different bruises, different scars, different impressions of parental kisses and loving caresses.

The Echo Chamber Is Not Empty

For one last consideration of the relation between limitlessness and vitality, and between mental space and mental contents, let's return to the Buddha's instructions to Rāhula. After being instructed to meditate on the analysis of physicality, followed by a practice of extreme non-reactivity inspired by the elements that make up physicality, Rāhula is requested to practice and develop the four limitless states: selfless love, compassion, sympathetic joy (that is, rejoicing in someone else's success or happiness) and equanimity[6]. In this practice, one is training oneself to suffuse one's entire mind with each of these four qualities, to increase them to their highest and vastest manifestation – boundless, measureless and all permeating – and to spread them all around: above, below, across, and to all directions, wishing to saturate the entire world with their qualities (AN 3.65).

These blissful, sublime qualities, we may say, are contents of the mind – they can fill it. But they are states of mind as well. Moreover, they are called "Brahma Vihāra," literally meaning the abodes or dwelling places of the supreme god Brahma. So the mind's contents converge with the mind's state and qualities, to form an actual environment or realm of being, a dwelling space.

Yorai wrote: "...emptiness as an echo-chamber or as a potential state of mind needs be wed with the substance of spaciousness, *with spaciousness as the mind's contents.*" Spaciousness as a state or as a content, as Yorai describes it, seems to imply other associated mental states and contents. And these – provided that the ideas and implementations of emptiness and spaciousness are not perverted, abused or misperceived like a wrongly captured poisonous snake

(MN 22) – are suffused with loving, appreciating, caring, nurturing substances. Similarly, selfless love, compassion and sympathetic joy accompany the profoundly spacious, non-judgmental, non-reactive quality of mental equilibrium. But actually, all four states or qualities are inherently boundless. They are limitless both in terms of their measure and in terms of who they are directed to. They are spacious at the same time as they are nourishing: empty of the constraining density and fog of adherences and selfhood, while over flowing with abundance, imbuing the atmosphere and other echo chambers that dwell in it with soothing, vital, growth supporting mental particles. In Yorai's words: "Marking and creating time-space, going on being in going-on-beingness, in attention and in mindful holding, are rendered an existential reality, nurturing, via a non-linear presence, the existential moment by moment reality of an-other." Thus nurtured, the therapist's mind **together with the client's** creates a "communal continuity in space and time."

This is how we may become providers of time and milieu (Balint, 1979) for others and for ourselves. When we acknowledge and gently hold our human gaps in knowing; when we are calm in the face of the swinging movements between seemingly contradictory, coexisting or subsequent states; when we create a vastness of mind for our remembering parts to lovingly instruct and console the parts that forget – we become providers of space, time and nourishment. This is our sincere attempt to engage with the entire range: with the void and the full, the holding and the held, the containing and the contained.

Because the echo chamber isn't empty. Its walls were not built out of nothing. They carry information from so many impressions marked by so many occasions accumulated and transformed over so many years. They are padded with semi-soft layers made of threads of thoughts and feelings, ingrained with tiny memory pebbles and huge memory boulders, harbouring clouds of heat and cold and drought and moisture and clear and foggy atmospheres. And these layered walls absorb some light and sound waves communicated by the other, letting them land on their cushion-like surface and settle in their dents and pleats, allowing them to finally rest in peace, forever or for a while; while other waves travel freely amongst the inner clouds – with tremendous joy or phlegmatically, or fiercely bouncing from the walls, surging from the floor, swooping across; outrageously howling or eerily whispering or shyly mumbling, pronouncing their incomprehensible wordless sounds. The sense of catastrophe reassumes its value as a meaningful signal. The mess of life and death is welcomed and allowed to move around.

The echo chamber is protective, but it isn't closed. It has its own atmosphere, typical yet changing, that makes it into a sort of indoor space, separated from the outside; but its outer surface is neither blank nor blunt nor numb. It's not really a surface. It oozes. It breathes. It keeps shifting as things touch it. As it is impinged or caressed by body, mind, space and time.

Notes

1 The other kind of space (ākāsa) referred to is the unobstructed, boundless, empty space, used as a meditation object in the first immaterial absorption (jhāna). But this is conceived as purely conceptual and not as corresponding with objective reality. In later Buddhist thought, it is regarded as an unconditioned or uncreated state, whereas Pāli Canon rejects it and sees only nibbāna as unconditioned (Nyanatiloka, 1997).
2 The three dots replace the original full repetition, with slight changes regarding each of the elements.
3 Lit. "Long-nail."
4 The emphasis is my own.
5 Pāli: parato.
6 Mettā, karuṇā, Muditā, Upekkhā.

References

AN 3.65.
AN 8.83.
Balint, M. (1979). *The Basic Fault: Therapeutic Aspects of Regression*. London: Routledge.
Goenka, S.N. (2010). *Discourses on Satipaṭṭhāna Sutta*. Igatpuri: Vipassana Research Institute.
Grotstein, J.S. (1978). *Inner Space: Its Dimensions and Its Coordinates*. International Journal of Psycho-Analysis 59:55–61.
MN 22.
MN 36.
MN 62.
MN 74.
Mucci, C. (2018). *Borderline Bodies: Affect Regulation Therapy for Personality Disorders*. New York: Norton.

Nyanatiloka, M. (1997 [1952]). *Buddhist Dictionary: Manual of Buddhist Terms and Doctrines* (4th revised edn). Kandy, Sri Lanka: Buddhist Publication Society.

Roth, M. (2020). *A Psychoanalytic Perspective on Reading Literature: Reading the Reader*. Oxon: Routledge.

Sella, Y. (2023). *Making Space for the Mess: The At-One-Ment of Going-On-Being*. In: M. Barnea-Astrog & M. Becker (Ed.), Relational Conversations on Meeting and Becoming: The Birth of a True Other. London: Routledge. SN 24.1.

Winnicott, D.W. (1960). Ego Distortion in Terms of True and False Self. In: D.W. Winnicott (Ed.), *The Maturational Processes and the Facilitating Environment: Studies in the Theory of Emotional Development* (pp. 140–152). London: Karnac Books.

Second Associative Trialogue

Is Truth a Testimonial Process? The Need for a Testimonial Other for the Reestablishment of Truth and for Healing of Trauma

Clara Mucci, Mitchel Becker and Michal Barnea-Astrog

Clara

What makes truth a testimonial process, especially after trauma? Why do we need another to empathically contact what has been dissociated, the "left out parts" banished outside of our awareness? What is it that the other provides that helps the subject reconnect to what cannot be remembered, and therefore helps to redeem the truth and retain it as an integrated force? How does the therapeutic process work to move materials from the internal, implicit realm to the external, explicit one, so that they can be encoded in episodic memory?

Laub (1992) argues that the severely traumatized person has lost the internal witness that makes possible an internal dialogue and testimony of the actual trauma. In his view, only a sympathetic other, fully present, empathically and ethically connected – a "benevolent and fully present observer", as Ferenczi, who did not get proper recognition for his trauma theory until recently would have it – can re-present this displaced and divided truth to the consciousness of the traumatized person. But why is it so?

In my view, it is important to distinguish between trauma of human agency, where the human hand has created the fracture or has performed evil against another human, and the kind of traumatization caused by natural catastrophes. It is only the first kind of trauma, stemming from a relationship, that creates dissociation, according to Liotti (2014) and to clinical applications of attachment theory (Steele and Steele (2019)).

Therefore, if what has been destroyed is the human bond of trust, it is that trust that needs to be recollected and reexperienced. Ferenczi (1932) wrote cogently that "abreaction is not enough" (p. 108). He

DOI: 10.4324/9781003325499-12

stressed that only a new relationship – in other words, a new capacity for attachment – that reconstructs trust and hope in humanity, can cure and heal the subject and recollect their fractures or "fragmentations". This is the term that Ferenczi used for what we now would call dissociation, a process that Freud did not really acknowledge or name as such. Severe psychopathology, for Freud, stemmed from repression, which we now understand not as a primary defense but a secondary one pertaining to a more developed or mature psyche; while the more severe outcome of trauma of human agency (Mucci, 2018) is constituted by dissociation and hyperarousal – both of which are neurobiological responses to extreme stress and trauma (see Schore, 1994; 2019).

According to Ferenczi, he who outlived trauma has had to negate what happened and to physically and emotionally disconnect from it – and this is usually the case with regards to long term abusive relationships (which we now would call Complex PTSD, unrecognized by DSM-5). Thus, one may distort and negate reality and truth: either by way of turning guilt and shame against oneself – "it is not him who has done this to me, it is my fault, I am guilty of the evil I have received"; Or by way of denial – "this has not happened to me, otherwise somebody would have come to help me". The traumatized subject, according to Ferenczi, asks him or herself this basic question: "is the whole world bad, or is it just me?" and chooses the latter (Ferenczi, 1932, p. 80). The patient prefers to doubt his own goodness and judgement rather than to believe in our coldness, our lack of intelligence, our stupidity and nastiness (1932, p. 25).

So in order to psychically and emotionally survive, having suffered evil one distorts the kind of truth which one finds impossible to accept. Even the body cannot hold the truth entirely, and so one starts to disavow one's perception and experiences (bodily sensations and emotions), disconnecting from what has happened. A dissociation between the self and the body occurs, and in the long run it becomes impossible to feel and to name emotions. Thus an alexythimic pathway is formed, creating the basis for somatizations and psychosomatic response.

Another very important dynamic that is created by trauma of human agency involves the need to identify with the aggressor, in order to remain in the same abusive environment while in another sense outside of it. This is done by introjecting the persecutor, and then redirecting the aggressiveness: either inwards, onto the self, or outwards, against another. This kind of externalization would, for instance, make a parent abusive or emotionally unavailable for one's children, due to the absence of an emotionally attuned and empathic other within oneself. This vicious cycle can go on forever throughout the generations, unless it is stopped by an elaboration of the emotions and a disentanglement of the distortions of reality enacted; that is, unless the truth – psychic as well as historic – is retrieved.

The introjection of the victim-persecutor dyad, as it is derived from the model of the internalization of the aggressor described by Ferenczi, creates a split part of the self that is identified with a victim, with poor self-esteem, guilt and shame, and sometimes with depressive feelings and a sense of defeat and failure; and another part that is identified with the aggressor, which is filled with aggressiveness and hatred. This latter part manifests in all forms of destructiveness and attacks on one's body – including eating disorders and self mutilation – as well as in violence directed against the other (Mucci, 2018).

Only a truly engaged other, empathic and capable of being present as a sensitive observer without intervening with one's own traumatizations or internal unelaborated contents, can help the subject to get in touch with the distorted realities, with the missing pieces that he or she is reenacting, with the absent or untouched emotional parts manifesting in notions such as "this has not happened to me, I can't feel anything, this truth is erased".

The presence of an other, a fully committed, empathic other, enables the internal split parts to be contacted and felt. Here is Ferenczi's voice once again:

> The analyst is able, for the first time, to link emotions with the above primal event and thus endow that event with the feeling of a real experience. Simultaneously the patient succeeds in gaining insight, far more penetrating than before, into the reality of these events that have been repeated so often on an intellectual level
> (19 January 1932, Ferenczi, 1932, pp. 13–14).

Elsewhere (Mucci, 2018), I have described the neurobiological aspect of this process, which involves complex mirroring, right brain communication and empathic intervention through mind-body-brain as "embodied witnessing":

> The presence of a committed other, empathically connected and ethically present, physically engaged with mind, body, voice, gaze, and so on, creates the space for an internal other who can witness the emotionally unbearable contents of the events while at the same time helping to reconstruct a sensitive, internal object that is benign and caring. The presence of that emotionally tuned and committed other renders that reconnection internal and external, physical and psychical, neurobiological and spiritual, a sort of sacred event, a sacred human space of retrieval, memory, going through and a possible road toward acceptance (and finally forgiving, intrapsychically and possibly interpersonally)
>
> (Mucci, 2018, p. 106).

In the appropriate mirroring between mother and child, we find the neurochemical and psychobiological activation of a rhythmic system of modulation of the nervous and endocrine systems. These modulations, generated by the face-to-face relation, serve as physiologic imprinting of the corticolimbic areas of the nervous system of the developing child. They stimulate the production of endogenous opioids, which mediate the process of attachment (Hoffmann, 1978; Schore, 1994); and at the same time, induce the endocrine changes that influence the growth of the brain, especially the orbitofrontal areas – the areas that will become fundamental for control and decision making. It is this activity of the opiod peptides that regulates social affect (Herman & Panksepp, 1978), imprinting (Hoffmann, 1978), attachment (Steklis & Kling, 1985), play (Panksepp, Siviy & Normansell, 1985), and exploration (Katz, 1988).

Similarly, fine tuning between patient and therapist particularly involves the activation of the right brain (Cozolino, 2002; Ziabreva, Poeggel, Schnabel & Braun, 2003), which is where the retrieval of negative experiences stored in implicit memory takes place. Without face-to-face exchanges and the activation of implicit memory, this dynamic, which is fundamental for the retrieval of traumatic experiences, is impossible.

The traces of the traumatic events are inscribed in implicit-procedural memory in the early developing right-brain hemisphere, specializing in the processing of visuo-spatial information (Galin, 1974). But the right cerebral cortex is also dominant for implicit learning (Hugdahl, 1995), which is the basis of much of what happens interrelationally between the two minds and the two bodies communicating in the therapy room. The peculiar interaction between interoceptive perception and exteroceptive information is mediated and processed at the orbitofrontal level (which Schore considers equivalent to the preconscious in Freud's theory), through connection with the right anterior insula; and the latter receives information about the visceral states and is linked to emotions, motor control and interoceptive and exteroceptive perception. In Schore's words:

> At the orbitofrontal level, complex cortically processed exteroceptive information concerning the external environment (e.g., visual and prosodic information emanating from an emotional face) is integrated with subcortically processed interoceptive information regarding the internal visceral environment (e.g., concurrent changes in bodily states). This cortex thus functions to refine emotions in keeping with current sensory input, and allows for the adaptive switching of internal bodily states in response to changes in the external environment that are appraised to be personally meaningful (Schore, 2003b, p. 207).

Therefore, he concludes, "In this perspective, affectively charged transference-countertransference interactions between patient and therapist represent the mechanisms by which the unconscious mind of one communicates with the unconscious mind of another" (Schore, 2003b, p. 215).

All communicative and emotional processes between human beings involve a special kind of interconnection between the right brain of the one and the right brain of the other. Trauma is mostly encoded in the right brain, in the limbic system; so this interconnection allows both the expression of the traumatic contents – almost the download, as Schore would say about the mother "downloading" the emotional, implicit contents of her amygdala into the right brain of her child – and the regulation of the patient's affects through the emotional involvement of the right brain of the other protagonist in the dialogue, the therapist. I also believe that processes of unconscious or implicit exchange such as enactments may be bodily based or right brain expressions/modalities; and in any case may become particularly powerful in face-to-face exchanges, taking advantage of the complex neurophysiologic exchange of the two bodies in relation in therapy. This is why, with traumatized patients, online, video therapy is not very useful, since it deprives the two in connection precisely of the full bodily aspects of the exchange.

In *Borderline Bodies* (Mucci, 2018) I have described a powerful moment of right brain implicit connection between patient and therapist. In this instance, an enactment took place, to which I referred as the "return of the devil" – a psychotic moment where an internalized split image of the incestual father as good was represented and experienced during the therapeutic session. In that moment, the primary caregiver and the persecutor appeared at the same time. I felt goose bumps and a sense of heat or explosion in the room, and I named it so as to acknowledge what was experienced at all three levels – mind, body and brain – by the two of us. She was feeling the presence of the "devil" in the room, the frightening other that represented the persecutory image of an incestuous father; and I said something about the "beast-like heat", validating the extreme, hellish heat we were both feeling (for the full description of the case, see Mucci, 2018). This powerful exchange gave us the opportunity to finally clarify and give words to the split image of the incestual father as simultaneously good (he was the one who had taken care of her when her mother was depressed) and bad (obsessed with her body and crossing fundamental emotional boundaries).

Contrary to Freud's ideal of a neutral (verging on hypocritical, in my opinion) therapeutic attitude, Ferenczi in his *Clinical Diary* expressed the necessity of making the therapeutic exchange a kind of testimony, where the therapist is able to witness the patient's life experiences, restoring life and truth through the therapist's own benevolent, complete, and committed presence:

It appears that patients cannot believe that an event really took place, or cannot fully believe it, if the analyst, as the sole witness of the events, persists in his cool, unemotional, and as patients are fond of stating, purely intellectual attitude, while the events are of a kind that must evoke, in anyone present, emotions of revulsion, anxiety, terror, vengeance, grief, and the urge to render immediate help.... One therefore has a choice: *to take really seriously the role one assumes, of the benevolent and helpful observer, that is, actually to transport oneself with the patient into that period of the past* (a practice Freud reproached me for, as being not permissible), *with the result that we ourselves and the patient believe in its reality,* which has not momentarily transposed into the past

(Ferenczi, 1932, p. 24. My Italics).

Interestingly, for Ferenczi the lack of support from the environment (the empathic testimony and witnessing of another family figure, or of the survivor's community) constitutes an additional trauma:

Actual trauma is experienced by children in situations where no immediate remedy is provided and where adaptation, that is a change in their own behavior, is forced onto them – the first step towards establishing differentiation between inner and outer world, subject and object. From then on, neither subjective nor objective experience alone will be perceived as an integrated emotional unit

(Ferenczi, 1932, p. 69).

The process of bearing witness cannot leave the witness untouched. I am deeply moved by what Laub (1992) writes about the journey of testimony – both in the context of interviewing Holocaust survivors for the Fortunoff Archive for Video Testimonies that he established at Yale University in 1976 and as a basic structure of the psychoanalytic process with the traumatized:

For the listener who enters the contract of the testimony, a journey fraught with dangers lies ahead. ... Trauma ... leaves, indeed, no hiding place intact. As one comes to know the survivor, one really comes to know oneself ... The survival experience, or the Holocaust experience, is a very condensed version of most of what life is all about. ... The question of facing death; of facing time and its passage; of the meaning and purpose of living; of the limits of one's omnipotence; of losing the ones that are close to us; the great question of our ultimate aloneness; our otherness from any other; our responsibility to and for our destiny; the question of loving and its limits; of parents and children; and so on. To maintain a sense of safety in the face of the upheaval of such questions... the listener experiences a range of defensive feelings ...

(Laub, 1992 in: Felman & Laub, 1992, pp. 72–74).

The Empathic Other as a Way to Reconnect and Retrieve What Was Lost

The witness is necessary on order for the missing parts to be retrieved and reconnected. It is a diadic enterprise, or a dual exchange, based on the empathic and committed presence of the witness. In fact, as in any psychoanalysis, the story that the subject is going to reconstruct is not known to begin with. In fact, this is the precise enigma of the psychoanalytic story, and especially that of trauma – the story of an erasure:

To begin with, the survivor does not fully know what he or she knows. It is only as the testimony emerges that the survivor comes to know his or her full story and the impact it has had on his or her life. Even then, parts that are beyond the imaginable will remain left out or retained as frozen, encapsulated, and split-off foreign images. These are the parts of the story that are not to be told. Off-limits, abysmally cold and empty, while at the same time also threateningly violent, tumultuous, and dangerous, they have no form. These parts of the survivor's story, and thus a piece of human history, are lost to silence. I have earlier searched for words for this muting or loss – and have come to call it *an erasure.*

(Laub, 2005, p. 257, My Italic)

I believe that when some pieces of the individual survivor's truth are rescued, with the help and presence of a caring and committed other – then the canvas of collective history recollects some pieces of truth as well. Therefore, the testimonial process mends not only individuality, but human collectivity as such.

The paradox of the psychoanalytic process, like the challenge of the testimonial process, may be summarized in the following questions: "How does one offer testimony about an experience that has no psychic representation? How does one convey a memory that cannot be registered?" (Auerhahn & Laub, 1998, p. 360). The riddle of us subjects is the same, both after trauma and after birth: In order for us to come into being, we need an other – a committed other. Otherwise, as in the story of Oedipus according not to Freud but to Lacan, we are doomed to endless repetition of a story unknow to us (Felman, 1983).

I believe that to bear witness is the final aim of the therapeutic work, and that it is through the process of testimony – through the empathic presence and listening of the "benevolent and committed other", as Ferenczi would say – that the survivor can not only "Abreact" his pain, but also inscribe in the self a new restorative experience, a renewal and reconnection with a human other, which gradually becomes internal as well. This process requires the full commitment of mind, body and brain, and it occurs primarily via right brain communication. It is therefore reinscribed at all levels, conscious and unconscious, explicit and implicit. Two mind-body-brain systems are working together for the reestablishment of certain truths in the world: the truths are spoken in the voice of the survivor, but they are also testified by his or her liberated body: a body that has become free from pain, from symptoms, from feelings of revenge and retaliation.

Mitchel

I imagine my adult patient as a 10 year old girl. She has been raped by family members and friends and hope is in complete shambles. Endless layers of shame and hate crumble her soul. And in the midst of the horror, a beautiful cat enters her life. Their eyes meet and the little girl senses for the first time in her life a True Other. The cat becomes her soul mate. Instinctively the cat responds to every pain and every tear of hers, without any hidden agenda. The girl gives her testimony and the cat purrs and licks and cuddles in perfect attunement to the girl's sorrow. No creature could have done as good a job as this sacred cat. Now, 12 years later, I am witnessing my patient's mourning for her only true friend, the beautiful cat who met her eyes and saved her soul.

Clara discusses with us how the soul can possibly manage when truth threatens the very foundation of one's relational world. When an individual's soul is raped by an Other, the individual is thrown into a hopeless turmoil. Believing in the truth means the downfall of humanity in the survivor's eyes. Absolute betrayal is guaranteed, and a sense of home is decimated. In contrast, holding on to humanity means the destruction of truth in the survivor's soul. And a soul without truth lives a life as undigested series of movie frames with no story line.

As I write, I suddenly realize that the trauma is experienced as a cruel choice, hurled upon us coercively, shouting at us, "Choose! Humanity or truth!" This coercion is the basic fault (Balint 1968) of the ground we stand on. Truth must part from relations - or relations must part from truth. This is an active distortion of our psychological world. For me, this distortion is not in the monadic psyche, but rather, it is constructed in the relation. Truth is in the I-You relation, and the relation is in truth. They are one until the moment of trauma, where the psyche can not fill in the missing parts to complete the picture of union. The crack is too deep to be mended.

Using Ferenczi's trauma theory, Clara explains that the "bond of trust" that was destroyed needs to be repaired. The question that concerns me is: What is truth's part in this catastrophe? If the survivor of abuse is forced to distort truth in order to save human relations, what happens when truth reappears? What happens to truth when "right hemisphere brains" meet, when limbic system emotions meet?

I read over and over Clara's thoughts. I slowly realize that there are two artificially divided stories. The story of the ruptured bond and the story of containing the traumatic truth. How we let these two stories meet is the art of the therapy. One could postulate that an individual's coming to terms with the true narrative is the primary therapeutic element. This is important but insufficient. We need an Other to help us digest our undigested pain. Our dilemma of deciding between truth and relation is not the solution but the core of the pathology. "I will kill you if you tell", "I will hate you forever if you tell", "I will be hated by everyone if I dare remember this". Truth is the I-You relation. Both truth and relation die together when one is coerced to sacrifice one of them.

The conquered, the hostage, the persecuted, and the abused are cynically offered 'a choice'. Accepting the given choice as reality is the destruction of truth, self, and other. Sometimes the so called rebellious survivor declares, "I do not recognize you and your power as a legitimate authority". In essence, this is a first step of the survivor in their quest to restore the natural co-existence of truth and relation.

And what does the therapist who witnesses the testimony provide?

Every soul bears, in certain places and times, the uncontainable. I believe that this very basic fact is the true covenant between therapist and patient. Their therapeutic alliance's bedrock is from a common psychic essence that the uncontainable lives in us in a dialectic tension with the contained. The essence of the empathic response begins with the inner feeling of the unfathomable. The therapist brings with him the capacity to accept that he is always possessed by the uncontainable, hopefully with a minimal sense of dread.

But some dread is in the soul of every individual, community and society. Is it possible that as a society we are ambivalent towards victimss because they trigger our collective trauma? That the pains of our communal selves are channelled into the drama of the private victims? In this scenario, the survivor's difficulty accepting the truth exacerbates the community's similar wish to deny the scars of the community. In contrast, the survivor's capacity to directly face the truth, may some day, some way, allow the community to confront previously unbearable feelings. As Clara beautifully states, "...giving a voice to the testimonial process and to rescue levels of truth – even if just for one individual's life – means to rescue a piece of truth within the canvas of collective history. Therefore, it mends not only the individual, but human collectivity as such."

Michal

"Truth is in the I-You relation, and the relation is in truth. They are one until the moment of trauma, where the psyche can not fill in the missing parts to complete the picture of union. The crack is too deep to be mended."

From these words by Mitchel, a new angle on the definition of trauma caused by human agency, as Clara distinguished from other kinds of trauma, arises: interpersonal trauma entails a schism between truth and relation, too deep to negotiate or bridge or reconcile. Healing, therefore, involves their reunion. Neither the healing nor the reunion should be thought of in naïve, ideal terms; but rather, as a dynamic relation of non-exclusion, of co-existence and co-creation that is reinstituted or reclaimed. And in the worst cases, perhaps even truly instituted for the first time ever.

Realizing truth requires sufficient trust and surrender, according to Buddhist thought. The same applies for truly meeting and being with an other, if we follow Buber (1923) or Ghent (1990) or Benjamin (2004) and other relational thinkers. Truth and trust are linked, and they are the links. This doesn't mean that there isn't any fear, even tremendous fear; but that some level of connection and trust is needed in order to see the truth of it. Truth and trust go hand in hand, and if they are separated – severely, extremely, all the way through vast territories of the personality, in catastrophic cases; or just here and there, only partly, as it is for us all – it is our role as therapists to attend to this separation. To switch between offering one hand or the other. Or to be a whole other human being walking in between, holding each hand on each side, passing all kinds of communications and tactile experiences. Or to accompany the hands' reaching or recoiling movements. Or just to be the atmosphere around, sensitive to truth, sensitive to love.

Clara

Mitchel writes: "I slowly realize that there are two artificially divided stories. *The story of the ruptured bond and the story of containing the traumatic truth.* How we let these two stories meet is the art of the therapy".

The nature of interpersonal trauma resides in this dual rupture: between self and other (what Mitchel terms, I suppose, the "ruptured bond"), and between displacement of truth and truth itself. And until some healing takes place, the traumatized self abides in a place of non-belonging, a zone of disconnection and displacement, sometimes even without memory. For Bromberg (1998), these are the "not-me" areas.

It is as though the truth – that is, the reality of what happened – abides in an impossible realm, which the self is sometimes capable of visiting; or in "not-me" areas, where the uncontainable or unfathomable resides, and which it may sometimes enter and touch. In the course of therapy, the veil of disconnection from truth and the covering of unacceptable reality are pierced through. In those moments, unknown areas of the self and zones of the personality emerge, perhaps incomprehensible to others and even to oneself. Sometimes they are evoked by a certain kind of light, a certain smell, a particular somatic stimulus that arouses and brings back an emotion and a memory – but then the memory itself fades and is buried deep down under other layers of experience and consciousness. The truth coincides with the unfathomable, which remains embodied, residing within bodily experience.

To some extent, the way the therapist emotionally and empathically resonates with this zone of the unfathomable and uncontainable – non verbally, through deep right brain connection – allows for **a momentary reconnection and embodiment of the traumatic truth while in a temporary deep reconnection with the other.** Of course, this is not the historical other who was involved in creating the original rupture. It is now the therapist as an other and as a witness that offers the right conditions for self-other-truth reconnection.

The healing and reconnection must come through a relationship, through reestablishing the possibility of bond with the other as human. In fact, it is when the other becomes inhuman that one's own ability to remain human is anihilated; and the return of human to human interaction in the face of the traumatic truth is precisely what Dori Laub refered to as the possibility of an internal witness, and I add – almost a basic precondition for one's own human emotional survival. The inhumanity of the other erases one's firm stance towards one's own truth, as well as one's very possibility of remaining the vital human being he or she were supposed to be, alive psychically. This vitality is compromised since, as aforementioned, in order to survive, the traumatized subject has had to renounce a piece of truth, a piece of self; and this piece, as Mitchel reminds us, is very substantial: it is bound to the traumatic relationship, especially when that relationship is an attachment relationship with family members, as often happens in incest trauma.

Freud (1914) argued that only through remembering can we regain the terrain that we have lost in the traumatic process, and that the loss of memory is a loss not only of truth but of identity and persistence of our interrelated humanity. This is still the core of what happens in therapy. But what Freud disavowed in his dismissal of the dissociative process has nowadays come to the fore in the current understanding of the traumatic process. According to this, the recovery of the lost pieces of memory goes hand in hand with the regaining and reconquering of a realm of truth, which is as individual and intrapsychic as it is interpersonal and collective; and this interconnecting position is enabled by the interaction with the therapist as thirdness – both as symbolic otherness and as embodied, unmediated presence.

Therapy reenacts, through the dual relationship that is established, the repetition of the interpersonal story between self and other. Working at the edges of emotional disconnection or through the affect dysregulation created by repetition, the new therapist-patient couple digests the old story by emotionally remembering in co-created moments of enactments, while forming a new possible re-inscription. Following a famous Shakesperean critic, Joel Fineman (1988), we can say that therapy allows for "a repetition with a difference" (p. 101). The difference lies in the restoration of unintegrated, not-me parts, and in renewed awareness to what had sunk into unconsciousness or into irretrievable dissociative memories. As a result, fragmentation, stiffness and deadly repetition are replaced by increasing vitality, strength and originality. Symbolic reconnection becomes a bodily and mental restoration.

This transition reflects, in my opinion, the re-emergence of a space of truth and grace for the individual.

Moreover, as Mitchel wrote: "Truth is in the I/You relation, and the relation is truth". And it is indeed the rupture of a bond of trust that needs to be repaired or restored or re-inscribed.

Ultimately, it is a bond of love. For Ferenczi (1932), it is a matter, again, of "difference" or "repetition with a difference": "The situation must be different from the actually traumatic one in order to make possible a different, favorable outcome" (p. 108). And, as he points out, "…not only explanations but also passionate tenderness and love should be dispensed as an antidote to the pain (genuine compassion only, not feigned)" (p. 137).

The cat in Mitchel's vignette is a medium of love for the patient as a child: a bond of unconditional love from a feeling being. It is not the intellect or the interpretation alone (the restored content of the story) that can heal: it is actually the body, the presence, the warmth and the love of another that restores the tenderness of the love bond which has been broken.

Ferenczi (1932) wrote: "What is traumatic is the unforeseen, the unfathomable, the incalculable" (p. 171). The therapist helps the survivor to restore that kind of measureless lost area, through his or her own emotional closeness. The rupture and the broken pieces can be glued only by some measures of love: "The presence of someone with whom one can share and communicate joy and sorrow (love and understanding) can HEAL the trauma. Personality is reassembled 'healed' (like 'glue')" (p. 201).

The restoration of hope and trust leads the subject to a new place, where the position of the truth is renegotiated and rehearsed from a different angle. Hope and trust are a sign that a long term link between self and other has allowed the rebirth and reawakening of a certain state that, for lack of a better word, I call "forgiveness". Forgiveness cannot be enforced, nor should it be searched for – it is grace emerging on its own. And when it does, it means that intrapsychically and therefore interpersonally (and *vice versa* – interpersonally and therefore intrapsychically), a disentanglement of the positions of both victim and persecutor has been brought about.

Individually and collectively, it is in the presence of an other that a real working through, within the transitional area of therapeutic elaboration, becomes possible; and it is there that the dreads of the individual soul belonging to a community also abide and are met. Any place of truth, I-You relation, real recognition and reclaiming, becomes a place of We. Any mending of the relation to one's own story and one's own truth becomes a "mending of the world" (*tikkun olam*).

References

Auerhahn, N. & Laub, D. & (1998). The Primal Scene of Atrocity: the Dynamic Interplay between Knowledge and Fantasy in the Holocaust in Children of Survivors. *Psychoanalytic Psychology* 15(3): 360–377.

Benjamin, J. (2004). Beyond Doer and Done to. *Psychoanalytic Quarterly*, 73:5–46.

Bromberg, P. (1998). *Standing in the Spaces: Essays on Clinical Process, Trauma and Dissociation*. Hillsdale, NJ: The Analytic Press.

Buber, M. (1923). *I and Thou*. Translated by W. Kaufman. New York: Charles Scribner's Sons, 1970.

Cozolino, L. (2002). *The Neuroscience of Psychotherapy: Building and Rebuilding the Human Brain* (Norton Series on Interpersonal Neurobiology). New York: WW Norton.

Felman, S. (1983). *Beyond Oedipus: The Specimen Story of Psychoanalysis*. Comparative Literature 98(5): 1021–1053.

Ferenczi, S. (1932) *The Clinical Diary of Sandor Ferenczi* (E. Dupont, Ed.). Cambridge and London: Harvard University Press, 1988.

Fineman, J. (1988). "The Pais De Calais": Freud, the Transference and the Sense of woman's Humor. In: J. Culler (Ed.), *On Puns: The Foundation of Letters* (pp. 100–114). Oxford and New York: Basil Blackwell.

Freud, S. (1914). Remembering Repeating and Working Through. (Further Recommendations on the Technique of psycho-Analysis II. *SE Volume XII (1911-1913): The Case of Schreber, Papers on Technique and Other Works*, 145–156.

Galin, D. & (1974). Implications for Psychiatry of Left and Right Cerebral Specialization: A Neurophysiological Context for Unconscious Processes. *Archives of General Psychiatry 31*(4): 572–583.

Ghent, E. & (1990). Masochism, Submission, Surrender: Masochism as a Perversion of Surrender. *Contemporary Psychoanalysis* 26(1): 108–136.

Hoffmann, R.F. (1978). Developmental Changes in Human Infant Visual-Evoked Potentials to Patterned Stimuli Recorded at Different Scalp Locations. *Child Development, 49*, 110–118.

Hugdahl, K. (1995). *Psychophysiology: The Mind–Body Perspective*. Cambridge, MA: Harvard University Press.

Katz, R.J. (1988). Endorphins, Exploration and Activity. In: R.J. Rodgers & S.J. Cooper (Eds.), *Endorphins, Opiates and Behavioral Processes* (pp. 249–267). New York, NY: Wiley.

Laub, D. (1992). Bearing Witness, or the Vicissitudes Od Listening. In: S. Felmans & D. Laub (Eds.), Testimony. *Crisis of Witnessing in Literature, Psychoanalysis, and History* (pp. 57–74). New York and London: Routledge.

Laub, D. & (2005). From Speechlessness to Narrative: The Cases of the Holocaust Historians and of Psychiatrically Hospitalized Survivors. *Literature and Medicine* 24(Fall): 253–265.

Liotti, G. (2014). Disorganized Attachment in the Pathogenesis and the Psychotherapy of Borderline Personality Disorder. In: A.N. Danquah & K. Berry (Eds.), *Attachment Theory in Adult Mental Health: A Guide to Clinical Practice* (pp. 113–128). New York, NY: Routledge.

Mucci, C. (2018). *Borderline Bodies. Affect Regulation Therapy for Personality Disorders*. New York: WW. Norton.

Panksepp, J., Siviy, S. & Normansell, L. & (1985). The Psychobiology of Play: Theoretical and Methodological Perspectives. *Neuroscience & Biobehavioral Reviews 8*(4): 465–492.

Schore, A.N. (1994). *Affect Regulation and the Origin of the Self: The Neurobiology of Emotional Development*. Mahwah, NJ: Erlbaum.

Schore, A.N. (2019). *The Development of the Unconscious*. New York: WW Norton.

Schore, A.N. (2003). *Affect Dysregulation and Disorders of the Self*. New York: WW Norton.

Steele, H. & Steele, M.(Eds.) ((2019). *Handbook of Attachment-Based Interventions*. New York: Guilford Press.

Steklis, H.D. & Kling, A. (1985). Neurobiology of Affiliative Behavior in Nonhuman Primates. In: M. Reite & T. Field (Eds.), *The Psychobiology of Attachment and Separation* (pp. 93–134). New York: Academic Press.

Ziabreva, I., Poeggel, G., Schnabel, R. & Braun, K. & (2003). Separation-Induced Receptor Changes in the Hippocampus and Amygdala of *Octodon Degus*: Influence of Maternal Vocalizations. *Journal of Neuroscience 23*(12): 5329–5336.

Thinking Further

Trauma and Witnessing in the Context of the Verbal and Non-verbal Messages of Society, and the Relational Nature of the World

Paul R. Fleischman, Mitchel Becker and Michal Barnea-Astrog

The three of us, Paul, Michal and Mitchel, are having a zoom meeting to discuss Clara's paper[1]. We introduce each other and almost immediately talk about the prevalent sense of social isolation, and about the difficulty in creating true dialogue.

PAUL: I think this difficulty is happening all over the world. It is certainly happening in the United States, caused by multiple dimensions. Many conversations are rancorous and divisive, and it's hard to have a dialogue. Every individual and group feel embattled, and it's very unsettling. America is politically highly contentious, and when it comes to psychotherapy, patients are increasingly looking for someone exactly like themselves in terms of gender, race, religion, etc. Pretty soon the only person one can relate to is oneself! This is the Individualistic Tradition: "I can't relate to anyone except myself and I shouldn't even try. I should just do everything on my own. Why waste my time talking to anyone else at all?"

So when a patient says "I need a therapist with this color, this age, and this background," I find myself thinking: "What you need is a good therapist. A good therapist may provide the understanding that you imagine can come only from someone who is demographically identical to you."

MITCHEL: I guess this is our way of starting our conversation with a keen awareness of our inherent aloneness, our difficulty to appreciate difference, and the sad understanding that achieving true dialogue is a rare and precious event. This takes Clara's article to a new level. If a genuine meeting is so difficult, how is one to allow an other to witness one's trauma?

DOI: 10.4324/9781003325499-14

PAUL: Yes, when I think of Clara's paper it seems that the main theme is how you preserve and digest memories, and the other's role in doing this; how you lose and gain memories through the presence of the other person; and how memories are preserved through culture, although the preservation through culture is limited, just as it is limited in the space of the isolated mind. We are dealing here with the ambiguity of the preservation and re-exhumation of traumatic memories. What are the optimal conditions under which this should happen?

MICHAL: I am thinking about Clara's point on how redeeming pieces of individual truth requires this empathic attuned witness, and how, when this is done, it is redeeming universally human truth, and not just the individual's.

PAUL: When little children come home from kindergarten, the first thing they need to do is pour out everything that has happened to them while they were away from home. They need to describe all the interactions between themselves and other children, and whose mud castle was knocked down by who. If there is no witness, if there is no mother, the child will have difficulty integrating his experiences. And this of course is not even about the traumatic level of experience. So I think that beyond the role of witnessing in the healing of trauma, feeling known and understood is essentially a basic human process. I may not know what I am feeling until I discuss it with you, go over it with you, and until you listen to me and go over it with me. I have that depth of connection with my wife, and I hope with some friends. I seek it out with colleagues. I share with them stories, sometimes humorously and sometimes with anguish, over what I have done or what I haven't done, and what has happened to me.

MITCHEL: At the end of Clara's paper, she speaks of Dori Laub's collecting testimonials of holocaust survivors. When the survivor recalls and the witness listens – what is your "Buddhist" understanding of what is the real?

PAUL: When the Buddha is talking about Dhamma – the nature of things and the path for realization and liberation – he is talking about the ideal way of life, but he is also talking about the reality of life. It's interesting that the Buddha felt that reality is the ideal. This is not intuitively obvious; in fact, most people feel that the ideal is fantasy, an escape from reality, something that is an improvement upon reality. But in the case of the Buddha, this formula was the basis for his vision and realization: that living in reality is the ideal that we should attain. The most idealistic human life is the one that is most realistic.

MITCHEL: I'd like to focus on this conceptualization of reality with regard to trauma. What happens when reality just seems too much to contain?

PAUL: It's important to understand that the teaching of the Buddha deviates from psychotherapeutic teaching. We wouldn't want to try to force a common ground between two agendas that share some commonalities, but also don't share many of their purposes. So, when we're talking about reality in terms of the Buddha, and I say that the Buddha says reality is to be embraced rather than avoided or transformed – the reality that the Buddha is referring to would be the existential, cosmological reality. He means the reality of cosmic time and place that obliterates individuality. And that's not a therapeutic agenda at all. I don't want to say it's a Buddhist agenda; it's an agenda of human beings encountering physics and cosmology in their own body.

The goal of Vipassana is not to overcome trauma. In fact, why would a severely or acutely traumatized person be practicing Vipassana, when there's something more urgent for her to do? It's as if you have a thorn in your foot, and someone says, "Here is a delicious meal," and you would say, "Just a second, I got to get this thorn out of my foot." The delicious meal is not too relevant in that moment of acute pain. I think it would be an error to try to turn Buddhist practice into a trauma therapy.

MITCHEL: Paul, while I was thinking about Clara's work, I was thinking that one of the unique features of trauma is that the traumatized person is often forced or coerced into distorting or denying his or her truth. The person seems to feel, "In order for me to hold onto my basic sense of humanity, I will forfeit my capacity to perceive truth." And in that sense, there is a major intersubjective transformation regarding the testimony.

PAUL: You've made a very important point. I wonder whether the five year old coming from kindergarten, in some insignificant way, at a subtle level, goes through the same process, whether in order to get along with his mother, instead of saying, "I wanted to kick the shit out of that other little kid," he'll say: "OK, well, he'll be my friend tomorrow," and thus sacrifice a part of his need for witnessing, in order to get reintegrated with his need for an approval system, namely his mother.

MICHAL: Something inherently good and essential may be gained by sharing experience with a meaningful other, and something may be lost. The possible goodness depends on the other's attentional attitude, as well as on the person's abilities to communicate and to absorb. The possible loss has to do, in the context of our current discussion, with a distortion of one's "reality" or "truth."

Is something unavoidably lost? Is something inevitably forsaken when we put a non-verbal experience into words, or when we let some delicate feeling leave our inner space and take its chances out there, in the relational world? Also, does the shared content become more real, gains depths of truth, thanks to new links formed through the acts of articulation and communication, or does it lose its realness and vitality due to exaggerated "false self" functions? These are the questions to ask, I think, when we look at the qualities of a witnessing encounter or of a dialogue.

Buber, the Buddha's Teaching and Relatedness

MITCHEL: I have to ask a question, which is a bit of a leap here but relates closely to other angles of the matters we're discussing, and I'm just too curious about it: has Martin Buber's work "I and Thou" been important to you? And if so, how do you put it together with your other thinking?

PAUL: I went to college during the 1960s at the University of Chicago, which has a major divinity school. Many people at that university were associated with it. So there was something of a religious tendency to the university. There was a famous ironic quote that the most renowned and important Protestant theologian of the 20th century was Martin Buber. In other words, Buber was held in such awe by Protestant theologians that they seemed to imagine that he was one of them.

He was very influential in American intellectual circles in the 1960s. He was reinterpreted as an interpersonal, culturally psychotherapeutic presence. He was held in esteem as a thinker who had to be reckoned with by everyone. Meaning, if you were a rigorous Lutheran minister, you shouldn't get your degree unless you had written a paper about Martin Buber. Paul Tillich was a Lutheran theologian, and a preeminent religious scholar at the University of Chicago, and he was very influenced by Martin Buber. In Buddhism also, D.T. Suzuki, the famous Japanese Zen Buddhist writer, was also very aware of Martin Buber's writing.

And on the other side of things, one of my American heroes is William James, the famous Harvard psychologist, Pragmatist philosopher and writer, whose most aggressive critic was Martin Buber. I'm a big fan of William James, whom I've been reading my whole life, starting from my first year of college. His book, *The Varieties of Religious Experience* (James 2012), is in the sacred inner circle of the most important books that I have read during my life. I also love the antipathy between these two great writers. It creates moments where I find myself deferring to the great masters sequentially, thinking: "He's got to be right, it's so brilliant. Wait! He's right, **that**'s brilliant!"

The main zone of contention between them was that for William James, internal aloneness experiences are the ultimate: a person encounters ultimate reality in some deep, spiritual, religious, psychological internal way. Whereas for Martin Buber, as you know, there's no way an individual alone experiences anything. In his view, all experience is interconnected, and influenced by relationships that start at birth and continue through life. I would say that on this point, I think Martin Buber was more correct. When William James was an older, ageing adult, he read Freud, and he admired him and was positive towards his ideas. But most of his previous development was in an environment where individualism was the supreme value, the American value. And while I echo with that and find it a part of my own culture, I feel it's slightly naïve. I feel that James underestimated how an individual's religious experiences are actually not individual at all. So to answer your question: yes, Martin Buber was hugely influential on me.

MITCHEL: In your book, *Wonder* (Fleishman 2013), you write that everything that exists in the universe is composed of matter, energy and communication. If I put it together with what you've said now, would you say that all three of those are relational? Do you think that it would be right to say that matter is relational, energy is relational and information is relational?

PAUL: I think so, yes. I think the message of modern science is to affirm the fact that nothing is static or isolated anywhere in the universe. Everything is influenced by its interactions and its environment. Even fundamental particles of matter exist only because other fundamental particles exist. There's no reduction down to the finest level of existence, where you wouldn't find relationships as the core phenomena. So I think that that's a fair interpretation of science, although many scientists I'm sure will disagree, and I think that that's a fair understanding of what the Buddha was trying to teach, although the language was different. I would also add that a limitation of the Buddhist teaching is its understanding of interpersonal relationships.

Standard Theravada Buddhism puts a premium on individual efforts to overcome one's own saṅkhāras and attain nibbāna (to perfect one's virtues, to eliminate one's failings, and so to become perfect in love, compassion and joy). And it seems that most people read Theravada Buddhism and understand it as an individualistic effort towards an individualistic goal: "I'm suffering, I want to come out of suffering, I have to do certain meditative, psychological, psychosocial processes to come out of my suffering." Goenkaji (Satya Narayan Goenka), who was the Vipassana teacher with whom both Michal and I studied, reinterpreted the Buddha's teaching or correctly interpreted its original meaning, as a more communitarian process. So modern Vipassana practice is highly social in its intentions. And in this context, Mettā ("loving kindness" or selfless love. See "The echo chamber is not empty," p. 101) is generated as a social connection.

As I see it, in the basis of the teaching of the Dhamma, there is a recognition that we're not isolated individuals, that we don't have any core, independent individuality, that our attempts to rescue ourselves are futile and will never work, and that we need another dimension. This other dimension is the communitarian, the psychosocial, the familial dimension. And therefore, Mettā is transferring the work that gets done on the individual level into its partner – its psychic partner – the social, communal level. And that's an essential in Goenkaji's teaching. You're not practicing properly unless you're generating Mettā. Love and caring for others are essential components of the path to nibbāna, and they are not an afterthought or a self-deceptive narcissistic inflation.

The Non-verbal

MITCHEL: I have so many different thoughts regarding this interpersonal transmission. There seems to be a basic dialectic between what we can describe, know and understand and between the mysterious or unknown.

I want to tell you a short clinical story. I have this patient, who came to therapy a few years ago, when he was about ten years old. He's very intelligent, but he had some bizarre behaviours – sometimes of a two year old. He would, for instance, go on all fours in the middle of the classroom and start licking the floor. In time, we found together an amazing form of dialogue. We started writing poetry together. I would write a sentence, and then he would write a sentence and then I would write a sentence, and something magical would turn out. Gradually, we got to a point where we would "compose" a wordless poem, a song made out of musical notes. I would make a sound, and then he would make his own sound in response. The energies in the room were totally therapeutic. We are now very close to ending therapy. How do you see that? What is actually happening there?

PAUL: Well, I wouldn't know. I think it would be multilayered. It's about a feeling of friendship and trust. You're both trusting each other to do something that's eccentric and not socially acceptable, but neither of you will humiliate nor make fun of the other. So you're bonding as friends; or as patient and therapist, but in a friendly way. **Trust** is the key word. At the same time, you're making an audible sound, so you're literally creating vibrations that enter each other's brains. And the vibrations carry a meaning. It may not be a meaning reduced to "I like you"; it may be a non-reducible meaning. It is like a poem or an orchestral piece having a meaning, but it's not a meaning we can state in language. So there is trust and communication, and there's some vibrational impact at another level. What did you feel you were putting into that sound? What did he feel he was putting into it, if he could name that? Is it humour? Is it affection? Is it anger? Certain affects must have been conveyed through the sounds. I would consider all these layers when I try to think of what was going on.

It was very creative, because it sidestepped the need for cognitive articulation and gave direct affectional and vibrational contact. That's pretty good.

MICHAL: This is, in a way, what we do in Hakomi. We access the relational unconscious through its non-verbal indicators. The way one holds and moves her body, the way and feel of her glance, her tone of voice, typical facial expressions, style of relating and other habits of organizing experience and expressing it – all of these point to some meaningful unconscious material. We do not presume to know or understand it, but instead, try to create opportunities to explore it together. And the conditions that support this exploration and the consequent "healing" or natural, beneficial transformation, have to do with positive, attuned messages. These messages are largely non-verbally communicated, like you said, Paul, with regard to Mitchel's inspiring clinical example.

Clara too stresses the importance of non-verbal, right brain to right-brain communication. This is the realm from which the relational unconscious picks up the clues and evidence that it is safe to be revealed and to hand out lost pieces of truth.

And as for Moving between the Individual, the Culturally Dependent and the Collective Levels

PAUL: What about what Clara wrote that we are collecting traumatic memories for human kind?

MICHAL: I think that in a deeper sense, this is not about the specific details of memory, but rather about the act of witnessing, of saving pieces of human experience instead of denying and turning a blind eye.

PAUL: I have my doubts about that, though it feels true in my heart. After all, emotional expression is a cultural value. In China, Japan or England, do people think that recovering and expressing emotion is something good or desirable? I think if we take the most basic psychoanalytic values, which are common to all the psychoanalytic schools and emerged into a dominant world culture through Freud – that is, self-examination, access to emotions and some degree of interpersonal trust in authority figures like doctors – we can see that these values are not necessarily shared everywhere in the world.

And regarding preservation in the cultural context, I think that things – memories, individual "truths," modes of being – can get lost. For example, I was brought up in a culture that believes that everything should be questioned. But suppose we observe a culture that demands obedience to authority, where a child should not question a teacher or a parent or a leader. I think that a person can be brought up in a manner that may lead them to lose capacities for certain kinds of thought, feeling and relatedness. This may have happened to the three of us also, but it may only be observable by someone who has cultured different modes of being a person, and we may not be able to self-observe it, or even observe it in each other. Some capacity is gone because it was never developed. Some things are universal and others are not. And the dialogical treatment, the talking cure that Freud created, is not a universal idea. It is culturally bound.

We are creating a chaotic, non-linear, multi-factoral attitude to the question about the role of the significant other in healing trauma. And we are coming up with a nest of influences that are very different in their saliences and in their presence in any dyadic therapeutic relationship.

MITCHEL: So let's go back to the statement about helping human kind via containing an other's testimony.

Imagine someone severely suffering from trauma, who is literally a walking time bomb. When he lives amongst others, those trauma-filled energies are absorbed by his community and society. So when society tries to find a process of healing these charges, it is also healing itself. I think that this is part of Clara's idea.

MICHAL: Yes. And it also relates to what you described, Paul, about the transmission from the individual to the communal level in the practice of Mettā and Vipassanā.

We transmit so much pain, in all its diverse forms, into others: through projective identification or transference or intergenerational transmission; through mirror neurons, limbic resonance or other sorts of right-brain circuits and communication; or through vibration or oscillation passing via the interlinks of all particles of the universe – or, however, one with actual knowledge of physics may more accurately call it. We are constantly, unknowingly, affecting and are being affected (Barnea-Astrog, 2017). This affect may be charging or discharging, toxic or nourishing, bluntly blocking or benevolently inviting. It may repeat hurtful circumstances, or create new and this time good conditions, in the context of which the traumatic or not so traumatic truths may arise and be communicated and integrated. The disentangling of the individual's misery depends on a positive "attentional environment," internal and interpersonal (Barnea-Astrog, 2019). And just like we spread pain all around, we may spread the positive attentional environment and the love that automatically springs when misery is dissolved. Things are relational, co-dependent. This is why any individual hurt, truth and healing can never remain solely individual. They filter through.

Note

1   This text is the result of two online meetings between the three of us: Paul R. Fleischman, Mitchel Becker and Michal Barnea-Astrog. It is an edited text: some remarks and lines of thought, perhaps no less valuable, were left out. Some words or sentences were changed or added for the sake of clarity, coherence and integration.

References

Barnea-Astrog, M. (2017). *Carved by Experience: Vipassana, Psychoanalysis, and the Mind Investigating Itself*. London: Karnac.

Barnea-Astrog, M. (2019). *Psychoanalytic and Buddhist Reflections on Gentleness: Sensitivity, Fear, and the Drive towards Truth*. London: Routledge.

Fleischman, P.R. (2013). *Wonder: When and Why the World Appears Radiant*. Amherst: Small Batch Books.

James, W. (2012). *The Varieties of Religious Experience: A Study in Human Nature*. Oxford: Oxford University Press.

Mucci, C. (2023). *Is Truth a Testimonial Process? The Need for a Testimonial Other for the Reestablishment of Truth and for Healing* In: M. Barnea-Astrog & M. Becker (Ed.), Relational Conversations on Meeting and Becoming: The Birth of a True Other. London: Routledge.

Part III

Third Dialogue

The Haiku Interpretation and the Chain of Caesuras

Hilit Erel-Brodsky and Hagit Aharoni

Chapter 7

In the Blink of an Eye

The Minimalist Interpretation

Hilit Erel-Brodsky

In this article, I will be discussing what I term "the minimalist interpretation," whereby the analyst proposes a brief, succinct interpretation. As the psychic truth is elusive and is a retrospective formulation of past experiences, I suggest that the required interpretation frequently occurs in the blink of an eye, akin to a Haiku poem. I will be examining the possibility of experiencing the psychic truth from a Bionian perspective, with an affinity to Haiku poetry and with references to Freud's and Bion's respective concepts of the caesura. This directly relates to the immanent "cleft tongue" (Amir, 2013) which opens up in therapy at the moment when truth is formulated into words and an interpretation. It is the analyst's ability to process psychic experiences into alpha elements that enables the patient to experience a truthful encounter with himself together with the return of the psychic movement. This encounter, much like a Haiku poem, encapsulates the existing and the absent, summoning a humbling and momentary encounter with the psychic truth and its ever-changing essence.

The Israeli novelist Eshkol Nevo recalls the renowned novelist Amos Oz saying, at the beginning of a writing workshop that he can't teach how to write, but he can teach how to erase (Gretz, 2020)[1]. I tend to think in a similar manner about the psychoanalytic technique and about the over-interpretation, which as I see it, contrasts the interpretation the psyche yearns for – that is, a refined, delicate, contoured interpretation that captures the truth in the blink of an eye. To learn how to erase means to listen attentively to that which takes place between the words, namely, to the caesura.

Bion maintains that in order for us to hear what is actually taking place, one has to listen beyond the cacophony of the articulated words

DOI: 10.4324/9781003325499-16

(Bion, 1977). The kind of attentiveness he refers to is similar to the attentiveness known in music as the "upper tones" (Amir, 2013). This attentiveness identifies something not merely beyond sound, but also beyond tonality, beyond the musical scale altogether, although derived from it and associated with it. It is an attentiveness which identifies that which is hidden inside the tonality without encapsulating a formal representation. This ability to listen to the floating elements, found in different frequencies, requires an entirely different quality of listening (Amir, 2016). This frequency, existing slightly beyond the signifying frequency, deviates from the regular scope of everyday language and becomes a kind of a "life momentum" (Bachelard, 1964). The resonance required by this attentiveness includes an interpretation that enables the hidden to be revealed partially and reductively – like in a momentary blink, or through eyes that are halfway open and halfway closed.

Seeking an encounter with the truth at the very moment of its occurrence – in the blink of an eye – while at the same time striving to erase and reduce the interpretation as much as possible, I turned to Haiku poetry, which cherishes the minute, humble presence. Winnicott (1984) once said: "As years go by I begin to grow smaller" (pp. 221–222). I wish to imbue my clinical work with this quality.

Haiku

Originating in Japan about five hundred years ago, the Haiku is the shortest of all the poetic styles both in the East and the West. Traditional Japanese Haiku consists of three phrases that usually contain seventeen syllables in total: in the first phrase five syllables, in the second seven and in the third five. It is acceptable to deviate from this number of syllables, and in many poems there is one longer phrase of six syllables instead of five, or eight instead of seven. The Haiku evolved from the Tanka, which contained two additional verses with seven phrases each. Both Tanka and Haiku were preceded by the Renga: a group of inter-related Tanka poems. In addition to traditional Haiku, there is also a free rhythm Haiku. The free Haiku superseded the traditional form-content rules favouring a spontaneous expression of thoughts and feelings in the spirit of the Haiku. The three-phase structure is no longer used, and the number of syllables is generally arbitrary (Arntzen, 2007).

Haiku captures the moment when perceived nature meets the psychic experience (Reichhold, 2013). There is no rhythm, and oftentimes the traditional Haiku incorporates a so-called season word, implying the time of year in which the poetic scene occurs. When the poem depicts a seasonal image, a rapport is formed between parts of the poem, creating an unexpected interval between the images of nature and the inner psyche, leading to a moment of revelation, a sense of truth.

> My childhood home
> Crying, I hold my umbilical cord
> The year ends
> (Matsuo Bashō)[2]

Haiku poetry is a clear, lucid expression of an experience, which does not employ a complex metaphoric. It directly evokes a lively moment with all its "suchness" (Raz, 2011). Similar to Japanese Zen paintings, the Haiku poem leaves an empty space where one does not think about the poem, but experiences it with the senses. The secret lies in the charged balance between the stated and the unstated, and in the ability to create a space from which the form, the sound and the word emerge (Elitzur, 2017).

In Haiku poetry, the charged space is the unstated, the caesura, and it is often as important, perhaps even more so, than the stated. The aesthetic value is embedded in the charged absence. Poetry, in general, and Haiku, in particular, can teach us a great deal about the power of silence and the immanent tension between the stated and the unstated: "To erase requires courage not because it lacks validity, but because you want the patient to complete it by himself. Too much talk weakens the spoken and does not leave space for resonance in the other thereby limiting his ability to participate with his own rhythm and language" (Elitzur, 2017).

Caesura

The Latin term caesura means "to cut." In music and poetry, it signifies a musical break. Bion (1975), in his article on the caesura, begins by quoting Freud (1926): "Between life in the womb and early infancy, there is a greater continuance than the impressive caesura of the birth event allows us to believe" (p. 37). Freud (1926) notes that during the birth process, the infant experiences a real life-threatening, earth shattering event that affects his life thereafter: "One can easily say that the newborn will relive the anxiety in every situation that reminds him of the birth event" (p. 138). Thus, Freud provides a glimpse into his hypothesis regarding the records existing in the psyche from the life in the womb. He allows us to comprehend that even when we are determined to unequivocally recognize that one thing is separate from the other, the notion of disconnection prevents us from seeing the ever-present buzzing of continuity.

Bion (1975) turned this notion into a thinking paradigm denoting the movement of continuity and connection whenever everything appears to be disconnected. In this sense, the term "caesura" encapsulates the notion that stillness, although cutting, is part of a continuous sequence. The challenge of the caesura becomes clear only when we are placed in stillness, and a connection or bridge appears impossible in the face of separation. The caesura is at the same time the reality of infinite breaks within the self, and the possibility that this break envelops the continuity of being.

The Minimalist Interpretation

In the chapter entitled "Less is more: Interpretation and Over-Interpretation," Dana Amir (2013) deals with the art of interpretation and the difference between an over-interpretation and a reduced interpretation. She argues that the strength of interpretation lies in its form rather than in its content, and in the delicate balance it offers in the manner of "laying out the thing to be looked at" (p. 157), instead of seeing the phenomenon itself or naming it. It is an act full of wonder, not words.

The difference between reduced interpretation and over-interpretation does not derive from the accuracy or inaccuracy of the interpretation itself, rather from the measure. It is for the analyst to hold the truth which becomes clearer during the analytic process and to avoid the urge to both describe and assess it in its entirety. It is a paradox that generates the tension between the revealing language and the concealing language (Bergstein, 2020). The stance we need to take is one that Freud (1912) referred to as "hovering, floating attentiveness," which neither clings to the words nor to the urge to comprehend or remember it all. Word usage is a retrospective depiction of the truth, one that was true at a particular moment. Once truth penetrates into language, it oftentimes becomes a distorted version of the truth.

The concept of Cleft Tongue by Amir deals with the complexity encompasses grief work in relation to the experience of partiality and separation, as the motivation to talk requires the recognition that the I is separate from the other, and that the I needs to communicate with the other in order to be understood by him. Amir (2013) maintains that language does not signify that which exists, but rather, that which is unattainable. Language is not the thing in itself; in fact, it is the space created around the thing it signifies. In this sense, language does not reveal the truthfulness of the existing thing; instead, it exposes its inherent inability to capture the existing. Paradoxically, it exposes or represents, its "caesurality."

Capturing the sense of a psychic truth was termed by Bion (1970) "becoming O." The O signifies the truth, which is impossible to know; it is, nevertheless, possible "to become it" and to encounter all of its transfigurations. As it is transient and ever-changing, there is a need to seek a delicate balance between the conceptualization of the sense of truth as in a psychoanalytic interpretation, and the possibility of containing the emerging sense within us without any verbal formulation of it. It means maintaining the tension or the magic between the revealed and the concealed (Bion, 1976).

It is preferable that an interpretation that comes from the analyst and enters the patient's heart includes this moment of proximity to O, to the truth in its suchness. This is a moment of psychic transformation. Transformations – poetic, artistic, scientific and psychoanalytic – are all constructs created by the psyche in order to represent O. They are not the thing in itself, but a transformation of O. The visual image is transformed into an abstract, more flexible mode of representation; thus, it will forever lack the intensity of the thing itself (Symington & Symington, 1996). Therefore, there is always a gap between the spoken or the represented and the O, both in Haiku and the psychoanalytic interpretation.

Clinical Illustration

Yael came to therapy as a result of workplace turmoil. She had quar-
relled with her supervisors in all her jobs and consequently either
was fired or resigned. Despite her academic credentials, she had not
worked in her field of studies. Yael said she was smoking drugs on
a daily basis, and talked about her frequent sexual encounters with
numerous men. She described situations where she often endangered
herself, fearlessly entering strangers' homes, feeling disconnected and
alienated. It was I who was holding the shock and panic at that time.
I felt that Yael was moving from one abusive relationship to another
and was afraid she might be raped or even killed. Once, before she
was to meet with one of these random men, I told her that she was
putting herself in danger, and that it could end in disaster. She dismissed me by saying: "Why would a man rape me? I'm sleeping with
him anyway." Later, I learned that her brother, five years her senior,
had molested her throughout her childhood, since she was five years
old. In addition, she was subjected to severe physical violence perpe-
trated by her parents.

Yael recalled a time when her brother was molesting her and their
mother caught them in the act. Their mother yelled at her brother, but
that was it. Yael anticipated that her mother would talk with her, but
it never happened. In retrospect, I wondered if she had hoped that her
mother would save her, or rather, that she would punish her for her
"misdeeds." Yael was left with great disappointment and pain and without an attentive ear. It appears that this was her most painful moment.

In the fourth year of analysis, we experienced numerous disasso-
ciations while in the room. In one of the meetings, she recounted "I
recall images of my brother rubbing against me from behind. I can
see the room, the mirror opposite the bed. I feel only the rubbing,
not what I feel on the inside, but only what I feel on the outside."
She experienced fear from the memory and the physical events. She
held her breath (as she did in her childhood), keeping her legs tightly
pressed together. There were no words, there was no face.

Yael: "I see my physical position in the mirror, but not my face. I
don't see my face."

I finally managed to extricate myself from this dissociative, disaster-
stricken zone and find the words – the words that were needed to
bridge the gap, the caesural space between us. After a few minutes

our breaths synchronized, and I, alert and as horrified as she was, said: "You're searching for the face and the inner inter-face."

In retrospect, I think this was a critical and pivotal moment. I was attempting to be part of the little girl's cry, her silence, feeling the dread in the room, and offering an interpretation that came from me and from her. The minimalist interpretation that emerged exemplifies my intuition that what we most needed at that particular moment was less, not more. During our encounter, with the excess and awfulness of the traumatic experience exposed, the emerging moment of truth and the modest interpretation offered suited the measures of the moment.

Pre-verbal Communication

According to Bion (1975), the analyst's role inevitably utilizes transitive ideas. He depicts a situation where the analyst is uncertain about the thing making itself present and has to intuit without having a concrete idea, using "blind intuition" (p. 45). Moreover, Bion (1975) maintains that intuition without conceptualization is blind, whereas conceptualization without intuition is empty. The analyst's problem in such a situation is how to connect between her intuition and a verbal formulation. This should be done **before** offering an interpretation. All the while, the patient is attempting to formulate into words an experience using his free associations. Bion further argues that the problem facing analysts is how to express something in a rational, conscious language so that the source of the feelings can still be identified. The focal issue of our work is to find the best way to communicate those primal psychic layers, the subcutaneous fears, when interpretation is the only thing that is available (Aharoni & Bergstein, 2012).

In the psychoanalytic experience, as with a mother's devoted care of her baby, we have to manage both the processing of the patient's intolerable, shapeless, nameless experiences, as well as the act of giving them shapes and names. We deal, in fact, with the translation or transformation of what we do not know into something we do know and can communicate. Furthermore, we deal with translating what we know and can communicate into something which we do not know and are unaware of, since it is unconscious and may pre-date the birth of the psyche and mental life (Bion, 1975). Thus, the analyst's main challenge is to endure the caesura between language and those areas which are untranslatable into language. Nevertheless, it is present, hurtful, fills us with dread, and requires naming and transformation in order to become processable and containable (Aharoni, 2012). The French psychoanalyst Piera Aulagnier (2001) stresses the mother's role as the "word bearer" (p. 10) – the one who gives the child the tools (words) for thinking and represents the laws of the external world. She thereby enables him to establish a sense of reality. Her role includes reality regulation through her psychic activity, thus creating a space which enables the baby to give meaning to his experiences rather than experiencing them as a meaningless assault. The baby's psyche is in close contact with the mother's psyche; therefore, it is replete with her words and actions. Aulagnier refers to a certain aspect of the mother's influence on the baby's psyche as "primal violence." It marks each psychic act where the mother forces a thought, an emotion or an act on the baby's psyche. The baby's psyche is compelled, in turn, to respond to them. Aulagnier further maintains that a certain degree of primal violence is normal and is even necessary for the purpose of constructing meaning. However, the imposition of the mother's psyche on the baby's psyche ultimately hinders his ability to give meaning to his own to experiences (Amir, 2016).

In what sense does the mother/word-bearer inflict violence upon the infant? This necessary, "primal" violence is violence nonetheless, in that the infant feels the imposition of the word-bearer's interpretations of the world. As Aulagnier (2001) explained, the mother maintains a "spoken shadow" relationship with the infant, but the infant never completely coincides with this shadow that preexists it. The violence is linked to the need to create and hold a subject-place (the spoken shadow) where there are as yet only potentialities. Accordingly, the future subject, the I, will come into being in a space preformed by expectations that are not its own. This is the necessary violence of maternal interpretation. But just as there is no such thing as a developmental *tabula rasa*, there can be no human subject without this preform. It is the discrepancy between the infant and shadow that makes it possible to situate a violence that will only really be violent (secondary violence) if the mother imposes it no longer upon the infant, but upon the I of the child (Aulagnier, 2001).

***

In our analytic work, we strive to give meaning to and conceptualize the patient's life events. This conceptualization incorporates an immanent tension between the epistemological urge to know and the painful experience of an absence and dependency. The process which takes place in therapy is based on the presence of the other (the analyst) and at the same time on the absence. Words constitute a substitute for "things-in-themselves." This inner struggle is overwhelming due to forces which pull the psyche in opposing directions: the attempt to fill in what is missing vis-à-vis the need to become reconciled with what is missing. The language of the analyst must contain the dialectics of the present and the absent, the possibility and impossibility of knowing. Words represent what is missing while also replacing it.

The minimalist interpretation contains the word and the absence of the word, the sound and the absence of the sound, the connected and the separate, the continuity and the caesurality. A revelation may take place in the interval between the words and the experience. It may be partly interpreted and symbolized (words) and is partly dependent on the analyst's blind intuition, a blind zone from which the word that unearths meaning emerges.

The moment of interpretation is a moment of profound presence, an encounter between two psyches whereby the words hold only some of its truth. At such a moment, a saturated interpretation might be experienced by the patient much like primal maternal violence. As the encounter with Yael demonstrates, I was required to offer a minimalist interpretation that would contain her trauma while at the same time hold it in a manner that both identified it without excessively reliving it. We worked together for many years and have oftentimes experienced similarly close, lucid moments as the one I've described. I view these moments as generating a transformation of the O, enabling Yael to explore her world and become more attuned to her psychic truth as well as to her environment.

Thus, Haiku poetry for me is a delicate model of the act of unearthing and enveloping what might be rendered into words and what hides among them, between the continuity of the psyche and the caesurality of the experience. A good Haiku poem clearly illuminates and displaying things in their "suchness," all the while presenting us with an absence. Much like an analyst at his best, a Haiku can capture the moment and the truth of the moment, or at least the moment in retrospect, that is, the transfiguration of O.

The Haiku poet surrenders himself to the moment, both to the emerging image and to the written word. The analyst surrenders to the projective identification at the moment within the hour. During both the writing process and the analytic encounter, the Haiku poet and the analyst become almost invisible as they penetrate the event which they experience or witness. From that point, the poem or the interpretation grow and develop with barely any mediation (Raz, 2011). This is an analytic stance that invites both the analyst and the patient to engage with daily events in a new analytic manner, "without memory and without desire" (Bion, 1962). This is not an overly wordy interpretation; it is an encounter with the present moment, rather than with history. This approach demands a quiet anticipation of the O performances that touch us in the here and now if we are open to them.

Notes

1 Thanks to Yael Magel who brought this anecdote in Nurit Gretz's book (2020) to my attention.
2 From Japanese: Eitan Bolokan.

References

Aharoni, H. (2012). *Covenant of the Pieces: The Caesura as a Model of Movement and Paradox*. In: W.R. Bion (Ed.), *Caesura* (pp. 99–145). An annotated translation and other papers by Hagit Aharoni & Avner Bergstein. Tel Aviv: Tolaat Sfarim [Hebrew].

Aharoni, H. & Bergstein, A. (2012). *On the Caesura and Other Caesuras*. In: W.R. Bion (Ed.), *Caesura* (pp. 7–24). An annotated translation and other papers by Hagit Aharoni & Avner Bergstein). Tel Aviv: Tolaat Sfarim [Hebrew].

Amir, D. (2013). *Cleft Tongue: The Language of Psychic Structures*. (pp. 1–30). London: Routledge.

Amir, D. (2016). *When Language Meets Traumatic Lacuna: The Metaphoric, the Metonymic, and the Psychotic Modes of Testimony*. Psychoanalytic Inquiry, 36: 630–632.

Arntzen, S. (2007). Haiku, Haikai and Renga: Communal Poetry Practice. *Simply Haiku: A Quarterly Journal of Japanese Short Form Poetry* (pp. 1–5). Spring.

Aulagnier, P. (2001). *The Violence of Interpretation: From Pictogram to Statement*. Philadelphia: Brunner-Routledge.

Bachelard, G. (1964). Chapter Two: Home and Universe. *On Poetic Imagination and Reverie: Selections from the Works of Gaston Bachelard* (pp. 81–124). London: Penguin.

Bergstein, A. (2020). From Man's Tongue to God's Tongue and Back. *Sihot* 35(1):4–10. [Hebrew].

Bion, W.R. (1962). *Learning from Experience*. London: Karnac Books, 1984.

Bion, W.R. (1970). *Attention and Interpretation*. London: Karnac Books, 1984.

Bion, W.R. (1975). *A Memoir of the Future*. London: Karnac Books, 1991.

Bion, W.R. (1976). *Four Discussions. In Clinical Seminars and Other Works*. London: Karnac Books, 1994.

Bion, W.R. (1977). *Two Papers: The Grid and Caesura*. Rio de Janeiro: Imago Editora. [Reprinted London: Karnac Books, 1989].

Elitzur, A. (2017). Coming Out of the Well, or Haiku for Breakfast: Recommendation for Therapists. From: https://pdharma.wordpress.com/261-2/238-2/. Accessed January 14, 2022. [Hebrew].

Freud, S. (1912). Recommendations to Physicians Practising Psycho-Analysis. In: R. Langs (Ed.), (1981). *Classics in Psychoanalytic Technique* (pp. 391–396). Oxford: Jason Aronson.

Freud, S. (1926). *Inhibitions, Symptoms and Anxiety*. SE, (Vol. 20, pp. 75–176). London: Hogarth.

Gretz, N. (2020). *What Was Lost in Time: A Biography of Friendship*. Modiin: Kinneret Zmora-Bitan Dvir [Hebrew].

Raz, J. (2011). A mirror to the Zen tradition. In: E. Bolokan (Ed.), *Within the Thin Snow: The Zen Poetry of Dogen and Ryokan* (pp. 95–100). Tel Aviv: Keshev Leshira [Hebrew].

Reichhold, J. (2013). *A Dictionary of Haiku*. Dallas: AHA Books.

Symington, J. & Symington, N. (1996). *The Clinical Thinking of Wilfred Bion*. London: Routledge.

Winnicott, D.W. (1984). Children under Stress Wartime Experience. In: C. Winnicott, R. Shepherd & M. Davies (Eds.) *Deprivation and Delinquency* (pp. 6–69). London: Tavistock.

Chapter 8

And You Said Mmhmm[1]

Hagit Aharoni

"I remember you sighed," my patient told me, "this was one of the most significant moments for me." It was in one of our final sessions before ending his analysis, a final note after many, meaningful years. My sigh resonated between us and we both knew what it meant, what was sighed. I recalled this particular sigh while reading Hilit's thoughts regarding the minimalist interpretation, and I will keep it in mind in my discussion of her ideas.

Freud (1900) consistently dated his book *The Interpretation of Dreams* to the year 1900, although it had been printed a year before. Thus, he established the beginning of psychoanalysis, and psychoanalysis, in turn, provided the opening note for the twentieth century. With this in mind, his book *Studies on Hysteria* (1895), published a few years earlier, constitutes the prologue, the exposition. In this book, Freud introduced his preliminary theory of psychoanalysis and its clinical application. He described a number of clinical cases from which he derived a radical theoretical notion; or perhaps, an idea that had been waiting to be discovered germinated and was retrieved in his clinical encounters. Hence, the connection between theory and clinical practice is cyclical in its very essence and does not require – perhaps does not even permit – the differentiation between cause and effect, rendering it almost impossible to determine what preceded what and what gave birth to what. The theory and clinical practice mutually co-create and co-establish one another.

In light of these ideas, Hilit proposes a theoretical notion with a technical-clinical implication and supports it with a clinical illustration; by contrast, she experienced a meaningful clinical occurrence out of which an idea emerged. Or possibly, as previously mentioned,

DOI: 10.4324/9781003325499-17

it is impossible to separate the two. There is no causal directionality, but rather two converging parallel lines.

In her paper, Hilit discusses the analyst's modality of response which she terms "the minimalist interpretation," whereby the analyst offers a breath-long response, a brief and succinct interpretation which she likens to the Haiku poem. She explores the possibility of encountering the psychic truth from a Bionian perspective while referring to the immanent "cleft tongue" that expands during therapy at the precise moment this truth seeks to be articulated. The clinical illustration she presents relating to this topic is both moving and thought-provoking.

I view the relationship between theory and clinical practice, a notion and an exemplification – between K and O – as a space containing simultaneous and bi- or multi-directional mutual infiltrations. However, language compels us to choose sequence and order over concurrent events. I choose, therefore, to discuss Hilit's line of thought from the clinical perspective and to proceed from there to the theoretical notion. I will consider her clinical vignette in the light of my personal association of a sigh followed by a clinical reverberation as reflected in a poem by the Israeli poet Anna Herman.

The psychic truth, as Hilit maintains, is elusive, transformative and in constant motion; we do not have direct contact with it, merely with its evolving revelations. Thus, some may conclude that any contact with it must be brief and minimalist. Yet, I propose that every a priori attempt to attain any particular modality of interpretation, any pre-planned construction and search for a formula, narrows and shuts down the psychic openness, receptiveness, movement and intuition. An informed search for a brief and concise interpretation might, as with any other construction, become a saturated and diminishing intention, imbued with memory and desire (Bion, 1967).

I believe, therefore, that an encounter with both psychic truth and the ability to formulate a meaningful, resonating interpretation, should by no means be pre-constructed, whether it be form, shape, length, rhythm or temperature. I will illustrate my line of thought by means of a clinical vignette and a poem. They both present a minimalist response, though one generates an affective and linking vibration, imbued with an emotional resonance; while the other is remote and distancing, isolating and tormenting.

From the Analyst's Consulting Room

Hilit reflects on her patient who was experiencing an emotional over-flow due to the reactivation of a sexual assault and traumatic childhood memories. Lying on the couch, in the safe analytic lap provided by her analyst, her deeply ingrained and unrepresented traumatic traces within her body and mind were both triggered and overflowed. Hilit, together with her patient, or at least very close to her, was situated in a wordless, breathless "disaster-stricken zone." She was terrified, and albeit to a lesser degree, endured some aspect of the traumatic event. She did not merely listen or comprehend, but literally experienced a hint of the trauma, maybe an echo of it, within her own body and mind. She was in close and profound contact with her patient's psychic truth.

As aforementioned, Bion (1970) claims that it is impossible to know the ultimate psychic reality or O, with which one can only get in touch through becoming. The "Haiku interpretation" that Hilit proposed to her suffering patient indeed emerged only after "becoming." Only after the shattering experience, and the mutual regulating and syn-chronizing of their breaths, did she find words that rendered the expe-rience into an interpretation: "You are looking for the face, for the inner inter-face." She then writes:

> "The minimalist interpretation that emerged exemplifies my intu-ition that what we most needed at that particular moment was less and not more. During our encounter, with the excess and awful-ness of the exposed traumatic experience, the emerging moment of truth, and the modest interpretation offered, suited the meas-ures of the moment."

She further states: "As psychic truth is elusive and is a retrospective formulation of past experiences, I suggest that the required interpre-tation frequently occurs in the blink of an eye."

The verbal interpretation that emerged was indeed brief, though it had additional characteristics other than its length and content. It is based on a pun in Hebrew where two homographic words having the exact same spelling but a slightly different pronunciation: panim (face) and pnim (inner) are used. This resonance of similarity and difference imbues this statement with a poetic quality and meaning. Hilit presents it as an example of a "Haiku interpretation."

Robert Frost once remarked that poetry is that which gets lost in translation[2]; Hilit's poetic statement is indeed both translatable and untranslatable at the same time. Its content, the verbal meaning, can be translated; yet the alliteration and poetic component are lost in translation and with them a significant part of the interpretation. In fact, this happens not only with translation. Every time we recount a clinical event, something essential is omitted and lost. We are able to **tell** something, to **tell about** something that happened, and at times we are able to evoke an emotional response in the listener or reader; however, we are unable to have the real contact with the past experience, to be in touch with the concrete emotional encounter, with O, the precise moment of being.

From Poetry

In her thoughts about Haiku, Hilit directs our attention to poetry. Poets, after all, essentially strive to create contact with mental and emotional states. Therefore, I, too, turn to poetry as a clinical illustration, specifically, to the following poem by Anna Herman (2006), translated by Adriana Jacobs (2013).

Mmhmm

I said I am really bleeding, and you said mmhmm
Every orifice is seeping, and you said mmhmm
I said my death is nearing, and you said mmhmm
I heard a raven shrieking, and you said mmhmm
I said: in a bit, I'll be dead, and you said mmhmm
My mind is hanging by a thread, and you said mmhmm
Misery consumed me, and you said mmhmm
Death hums like a flea, and when you said mmhmm
it came back and drained me, and you said mmhmm
but mmhmm doesn't rhyme with a single thing
The waters come unto my soul and neck
but mmhmm doesn't rhyme with anything only
mmhmm
with mmhmm
(I said it's my birthday
and you didn't say good luck
but you didn't give me pills
or an electric shock,
and that's good too.)

It seems there is no need to interpret this poem. It presents its meaning in an unequivocal, powerful and unsettling way. Nevertheless, the key word in the poem is "mmhmm," if one can characterize this vocalization as a word. This vocal articulation may signify various states of mind: it can represent a consent equivalent to saying "yes"; it can express encouragement ("I'm listening, go on"); it may express impatience or reluctance to respond; and it can additionally express incomprehension or disagreement. The difference between these possibilities is made evident by the melody, emotional intensity, the psychic perspective of both the "mmhmming" one and the "mmhmmed" one, and, of course, the particular context. In Herman's poem, the recurring "mmhmm" is the analyst's response to the tormented account of the patient. It is a brief, repetitive response which is experienced as cold, detached and indifferent.

Jacobs (2013), who translated this poem into English, wrote about the translation process where in an earlier draft she had translated the title "Mmmhmmm"; however, later she realized that the repetition of the "mmmhmmm" is laconic and disrespectful, perhaps even ridiculing, hence she chose to shorten it to "mmhmm." Jacobs perceived the way in which the narrator in the poem ridicules, although with great pain, her analyst's response. The translator sensed the emotional melody of the hum, as experienced by the lyrical patient, and attempted to convey it by shortening the sound. A hum, either long or short, may also represent an emotional detachment, rather than closeness.

***

These three illustrations of clinical interventions: Hilit's interpretation, my sigh, and Herman's hum, open a porthole to a discussion about the concept of the minimalist or Haiku interpretation. They are all brief, yet constitute different types of interventions. Two are touching and transformative, one is remote and hurtful; two are non-verbal and emotional-tonal expressions; two, specifically the more emotionally in tune, do not easily surrender to communication and translation. Let us examine these illustrations in light of the notion of the minimalist interpretation.

Hilit's verbal interpretation, presented as an example of a Haiku interpretation, presumably was moving and transformative. As she mentioned, Haiku poetry originated from the Tanka. In this ancient poetry, a 17 syllable (5-7-5) stanza is followed by a 14 syllable stanza (7-7). The first is considered to be an invitation, often a courting, and the second is the response. Raz (2006) writes: "A good Haiku poem forms a kind of invitation, a stone cast into a pool, creating ripples of waves." Hilit does not tell us what her patient's response was, in fact, we do not know if she said anything at all, but all the while it is evident that an emotional transformation did take place, and that there was a relieving and easing of the sense of dread. They were both extricated from the disaster zone. What made it possible?

Hilit's interpretation is indeed brief, but as mentioned it has additional qualities such as the content and alliteration, the melody and the tone of voice. Furthermore, this interpretation was offered in a specific context as part of an ongoing emotional process. The patient evidently perceived her analyst's pre-verbal emotional response, "her emotional participation in the dread," and the momentary cessation of breathing. Although the verbal interpretation is akin to a breath, the entire event constitutes a mutual process which is both fleeting and eternal. As Hilit herself points out, beyond the minimalist statement there was a close encounter and a moment of truth.

Turning again to my clinical breath-long moment, although my sigh was not an articulated statement, it could be perceived, nonetheless, as an interpretation. In this particular emotional context, my sigh was a form of communication which conveyed to my patient profound meaning. Jacobs (2013) quotes the poet Marina Tsvetaeva saying that she attempts, in her poetry, to use words (that is, meaning) in order to express a sigh: "Ahh." She attempts to express a sound, or in fact to convey an emotion or a state of mind through words, so that ultimately the reader experiences the sigh; so that the only thing that remains in the ear is Ahh. I am not a poet myself and have no way of describing the occurrence other than by saying that I sighed and that my sigh touched my patient profoundly.

The therapeutic experience described in Herman's poem is harsh, in fact, unbearable. The analyst's response is brief, but by no means is it a Haiku. Haiku is not examined merely by its length; it is a mind-set, a glance, a modality of being. It seeks to be in contact with the here and the now. Raz (2006) writes: "In the emptiness of the Haiku lies a great depth as it evokes waves of images, thoughts, memories and unpredictable emotions..." (p. 129). He further argues that "its length, which is akin to the length of a breath or a brushstroke, forms the place where language is careful not to harm the sacredness of the omnipresent...|" (p. 132). Herman's "mmhmm" does not meet these criteria. It is short, yet laconic and remote. An important point must be added: Herman's poem, of course, is not a Haiku. It's meaning and emotional impact derives from the repetition of the mmhmm, from the ongoing devastating reaction.

I return to Hilit's proposal which favours a minimalist interpretation, specifically in the Haiku form: "While striving to erase and reduce the interpretation as much as possible, I turned to Haiku poetry." The clinical situation she presents was indeed transformative. Both the patient and the analyst shared a shattering emotional process. The reader was also rendered breathless vis-à-vis the horror and have their breath retrieved together with the patient and the analyst. Hilit offered her patient a brief interpretation; however, as I wish to demonstrate through Herman's poem, the strength of the process was not connected to the brevity of the interpretation. Minimalism does not guarantee emotional contact.

The psyche, Hilit argues, requires an unsaturated interpretation that captures the truth in the blink of an eye. While this idea is well formulated and true, the psyche needs many different things that should not be limited to a single pre-dictated modality of reference. Oftentimes in analysis, the psyche needs an organizing and holding interpretation or intervention. At times, on the other hand, it needs friction rather than a subtle response; a closing rather than an opening; a more in-depth rather than a brief interpretation...

Hilit employs the Haiku as a model and metaphor for the unsaturated, minimalist interpretation. Evidently, she relates to the spirit of Haiku, to the attempt at capturing truth at a breath-long moment, the here and now in its deepest sense. At the same time, however, one should remember that Haiku is one of the most rigid forms of poetic expression, both thematically and structurally, and in this sense is not merely emotional and psychic, but is also highly rational. In contrast, the analytic interpretation should be neither restricted in structure nor overly intellectually engineered. Furthermore, Hilit's suggestion might raise questions, as she often uses the word "desire" expressing a conscious desire or wish to erase and reduce the interpretation. To paraphrase Bion, on whose thoughts she relies – memory, desire and a priori intention are saturated and restrictive. As I suggested above, a search for a concise interpretation might be reduced to saturated intention, memory and desire.

A Chain of Caesuras

The Haiku spirit may indeed accompany us in our long clinical journeys. In the early stages of the development of the Haiku, poems were linked to a chain. Thus, dozens of linked Haiku verses were intertwined to form one lyrical poem. Much in the same manner, analysis is a series of links in a chain, a long process with numerous stages punctuated by infinite caesuras. An interpretation is a way-station along the journey, and each analytic session has infinite way-stations. We aspire to attain an interpretation which is open and is opening as opposed to a closed and a closing interpretation. However, due to the fact that we respond – mostly with words, often with gestures – we move from O to K, from the infinite to the finite, from the open to the closed, and vis-versa, again and again. This movement is the very essence of analysis: Open-Closed-Open, as Hilit quotes Amichai.

Dan Daor (2010), a sinologist, translator and a great traveller, ends his book *A Feast for One* with an assemblage of Haiku poems. He recounts that they came to his mind during a ten-hour bumpy bus ride in India. As Haiku consists of 17 syllables, Daor proposes this assemblage which includes 17 interconnected Haiku poems which share a thematic development, a kind of a plot. A diagonal pattern running through the poem is a further requirement that is imposed on the rigid structure of each poem. The first syllable of the first Haiku, the second syllable of the second, the third of the third and so forth are all connected into 17 syllables from the 17-poem assemblage, thus forming a new Haiku poem made of layered layers.

I find it difficult to embrace both the structural and thematic rigidness of Haiku and the exclusivity of minimalism in the context of the analytical interpretation. Nonetheless, I do embrace the mindset of Haiku and, metaphorically, the structure of the multiple links that evolve into a chain, an ongoing infinite process. We may perceive the analytic process as a lyrical chain: each encounter, each interpretation, every gesture, is in itself an independent link, while together they form a caesural evolution, infinite, transformative chain.

Notes

1   This title is taken from "Mmhmm", a poem by Anna Herman. In: Herman, A. (2006). *A Book of Simple Medicines*. Tel Aviv: Hakibbutz Hameuhad, p. 47.
2   This remark, referred to Frost, appears in variant forms and often quoted, though it appears not to have a source in his published writings.

References

Bion, W.R. (1967). Notes on Memory and Desire. In: *Cogitations* (pp. 380–385). London: Karnac 1992.

Bion, W.R. (1970). *Attention and Interpretation*. London: Tavistock.

Daor, D. (2010). *A Feast for One*. Tel Aviv: Xargol.

Freud, S. ([1895] 1955). *Studies on Hysteria. SE, 2*. London: Hogarth.

Freud, S. ([1900] 1913). *The Interpretation of Dreams. SE, 4*. London: Hogarth.

Herman, A. (2006). And You Said Mmhmm. In: *A Book of Simple Medicines* (p. 47). Tel Aviv: Hakibbutz Hameuhad.

Jacobs, A. (2013). Mmhmm. *Michigan Quarterly Review* 52: 2.

Raz, J. (2006). *The Narrow Road to Oku*. Translation to Hebrew from Japanese by Jacob Raz. Tel Aviv: Xargol.

Chapter 9

In a Few Words

Hilit Erel-Brodsky

Hagit concludes her thoughts with the following words:

> I do embrace the mindset of the Haiku and, metaphorically, the
> structure of the multiple links that evolve into a chain, an ongoing
> process. We may perceive the analytic process as a lyrical chain:
> each encounter, each interpretation, every gesture, is in itself an
> independent link, while together they form a caesural evolvement,
> becoming one transformative chain.

My response to her is both a link in the thought-chain and a caesural
moment of encounter, a break, followed by another encounter.

Hagit's writing makes me pleasantly contemplative. In her delicate,
non-saturated manner, she causes me to reevaluate my thoughts,
search within them for the lucid, elusive and ever-changing truth,
perhaps even agree to become smaller. I think about the way in which
Hagit's beneficial presence as a thinker, a reader and a witness enables me to reflect upon my thoughts. She wonders what my patient's
reaction was

> we do not know if she said anything at all, but all the while it is
> evident that an emotional transformation did take place, and that
> there was a relieving and easing of the sense of dread. They were
> both extricated from the disaster zone.

Indeed, the patient's reaction described the fear of falling apart and
the possibility of being extricated from the disaster zone.

DOI: 10.4324/9781003325499-18

Yael recounted a dream: "I was going up the elevator with several people when suddenly a woman began falling about twelve stories, but when she finally landed she was uninjured. I was very surprised. And then there was a part when I cried a lot, but my face didn't reveal that I was crying. I looked at my face in the mirror but it was frozen and you couldn't tell that I had been crying. I sensed that I wanted to hold on to an impossible love, that I wanted to fix something that was unfixable."

I thought the dream might have originated from the context of the minimalist interpretation in our previous session. Yael was expressing, through the dream, the connection and the disconnection between what was seen and what was actually occurring, between the [sur]face and the inside (in Hebrew: Between the *panim* and the *pnim*). Perhaps Yael described a kind of a breakdown, which I myself experienced during analysis; perhaps that breakdown had already taken place but had not yet been processed. She was crying when she said: "I was there all alone, so alone."

I continued her words saying: "How would you know if anything had happened to you, how would you be able to identify your pain? There are no visible signs that something happened to you, but still, there is a feeling within that something is broken and you want to know if it can be repaired."

Yael: "But what is it that was broken? How can you tell what was broken?"

The dream she recalled in the wake of the minimalist interpretation recounts the primal trauma and the incest (that ended at age twelve), while at the same time presents the possibility of repair and renewal. In my view, the minimalist interpretation encapsulated my words and perhaps my thoughts; but to an even greater extent, it contained my presence and the sincere interpersonal encounter in its suchness.

My suggestion to both the reader and the analyst to become smaller is indeed complex. It might not necessarily be derived from clinical practice; but rather from a deep understanding that whatever truly extends from one psyche to another and creates the O is the analyst's profound presencing (Eshel, 2004).

I am reminded of Winnicott's idea (1954) regarding the mother-environment, that due to the infant's excessive dependency, the mother's presence must be non-saturated and non-intrusive, much like the air the new born breathes (Balint, 1987). This also brings to mind the thought of Aulagnier, that when the mother's presence is excessive, she might be experienced as a violent object, thereby laying the foundation for potential trauma in the baby's psyche.

Hagit is right. A small interpretation can oftentimes be highly beneficial for the patient, while at other times an elaborated interpretation can be far better. However, since Freud and the early days of psychoanalysis, we have grown accustomed to expanded, elaborated interpretations. This analytic interpretation can be overly lengthy and tedious. Therefore, I strive to reduce, or at least ask myself when it is best to provide a minimalist interpretation.

Hagit assists me in further focusing my thoughts. I think that a reduction in interpretation is required to a greater extent in trauma cases, when emotional overflow is inevitable and the analyst must constantly assess the patient's capacity to contain and endure the analyst's words. When do the analyst's words envelop the patient and become a kind of a sonorous bath, and when do they remind the patient of the analyst's painful otherness and separateness? These distinctions may aid us in discerning when it is suitable to employ the minimalist interpretation.

In light of Hagit's thoughts, I would like to emphasize that it is most important for us to adjust ourselves to our patients and thus become an adjusted container for them, attuned to the particular moment in time and space.

I wish to conclude with a poem by the Israeli poet Moiz Benharroch (2010), a poetic response to the poem "Mmhmm":

Grateful Silence

I wanted so much to be silent with you
And you wanted so much to talk with me

And you talked to me about
Me wanting to be silent with you

And I talked about
Me wanting you to be silent with me
And I didn't know how to talk with you
As much as you didn't know how to be silent with me (p. 28.
From Hebrew: Nili Evron Rothenberg).

References

Balint, M. (1987). *The Basic Fault*. London: Tavistock.

Benharroch, M. (2010). Silence as Gratefulness. In: *Not Going Anywhere* (p. 28). Beersheba: Resis Nehara.

Eshel, O. (2004). Let It Be and Become Me: Notes on Containing, Identification, and the Possibility of Being. *Contemporary Psychoanalysis* 40: 323–351.

Winnicott, D.W. (1955). Metapsychological and Clinical Aspects of Regression within the Psychoanalytical Set-up. In: *Through Paediatrics to Psychoanalysis: Collected Papers* (pp. 278–294). London: Karnac, 1992.

Third Associative Trialogue

On "No Experience" with All My Heart and Soul

Mitchel Becker, Michal Barnea-Astrog, and Paul R. Fleischman

Mitchel

Imagine saying something every day and never really "getting it."

Not because it is trivial and not even because it is too awesome but rather because the heart and soul are incapable of letting go of the concept "experience."

After all, what do we have left if we have no experience.

It is Martin Buber's contention that our most natural instinct to "grasp" or "hold onto" our experience is the way we leave the other as an "it," as an object to be possessed.

Those who are fond of Buber's "I and Thou" (really should be "I and You") may protest that I am misreading Buber. And here I claim, dear reader, "Imagine knowing something and yet not surrendering."

Buber writes, "Those who experience do not participate in the world. For the experience is 'in them' and not between them and the world. .... The world as experience belongs to the basic word I-It. The basic word I-you establishes the world of relation" (p. 56).

"If you love someone let them free."

The natural interpretation is usually centred on letting the bird free. Letting go.

But how does one fathom what happens next?

Or what happens after de-possession?

Let me start with a sort of poem:

> He knew how to close gates of his heart like he knew how to put
> on a pair of pants.
> Effortlessly sealing off the silent screams of alienation.
> Any hint of rejection could retroactively undo the link.

DOI: 10.4324/9781003325499-20

And then the chorus begins:

"Never was real.
She never loved me.
I don't know what I was thinking.
Who cares.
Forget it."

Until now.
"Now" (also known as feeling present in the present) looked up
    at me and said "speak your truth."
I sensed the walls of concealment crumble.
And then last pangs of anxiety looked at me as if betrayed.
As if the anxiety said, "but we are loyal friends"
And tranquility hugged me.
And I was left with the naked truth
"I love you"
The "loyal friend" anxiety is truly loyal. Loyal to the real world
    of I-it.

We are anxious when we sense an imminent loss and destruction of
the current I-it that we possess. This possession is any part of this
world that we treasure in our psychological treasure house.

And the naked truth? It seems naked of experience, naked of perception and even naked of thought? We are exploring moments and
not any fixed mode of being. No one is capable of non-stop I-you.
But the non-experience can make us weary. So is that psychotic? Or
perhaps dissociated?

The non-experience moment or mode is being so present that no
mirror or contemplation or intervention occurs. What does occur is
pure heart soul and truth.

It is a dreaming without a narrator. When Grotstein asks who is the
dreamer dreaming, there is already a cognizance of a narration. The
I-you non-experience is a meeting with no memory, no understanding
and no desire. A meeting of soul's hearts and truths.

Michal

As I meet these words, I can feel myself moving between two modes. At times my thoughts arise as opposed to or otherwise relatively to the words and to what they evoke in me. In this mode, some parts of me make it their first priority to assert me and not-me, mine and not-mine, identification and dis-identification. A kind of "boundary-setting function" (Sandler, 1993, p. 1102) operates there. The product of old habits, it is a manifestation of a self that wants to feel and appreciate itself, and then sometimes to also be expressed, so that it can be felt and appreciated by others. These parts are quite pushy, and the overall state that comes along involves a somewhat boxed, solid-ified, confining-confined experience. It is accompanied by increased physical and psychic tension: the tension of comparing, the tension of self-identity views[1], the tension of holding on (to an idea, to the idea of self, to the illusion of independence and separateness). It can grow and accumulate, causing restlessness and strain, or it can be very sub-tle and the tension hardly noticeable.

Then this state fades or moves to the back and gives way to a sense of an intricate, living stream. Here, whatever mental content that appears as a result of meeting the text is experienced as a conditioned phenomenon triggered by other conditioned phenomena, arising from and passing into a beginningless, multi-layered, multi-dimensional flow of mind and matter events, linked to each other and to the rest of the world through various relations.

Some relations are thick and highly influential. Some electric and some stagnated. Some visible and others invisible. Some are demand-ing or constraining or suffocating, and others are nourishing and pro-moting growth. Some are so thin, so remote, hardly there at all – but a closer, more sensitive look reveals that in fact they exist, forgotten almost as soon as they show.

This second state is accompanied by curiosity and awe, by a chang-ing motion – sometimes rapid, sometimes slow – through currents of joy and excitements, of careful examination and foggy misunder-standing; through ponds of feeling and lingering, through darker zones of the unknown. In this state, the "I-experience" is much less concrete or framed. Creator and created dance together, switching roles depending on the stand point. Duality between observer and observed doesn't make much sense, although they are not confused or merged.

Rarely (not today anyway), a third state appears, where there isn't even this; where the I-experience is temporarily suspended or gone. The senses are working, sensation and perception occur – but the feeling "I" is not there. There aren't any contours around any kind of self. Nothing is me or mine to hold on to, yet reality, internal and external, is very much alive and there. Let's call the first state "conventional-confined"; the second – "streaming" and the third – "temporarily self-less."

I go back to Mitchel's words:

> The non-experience moment or mode is being so present that no mirror or contemplation or intervention occurs. What does occur is pure heart soul and truth. It is a dreaming without a narrator. [...] The I-you non-experience is a meeting with no memory, no understanding and no desire. A meeting of souls hearts and truths.

Where exactly does this notion, enveloping Buber's and Bion's ideas, overlap with the three modes? Does it coincide with the "streaming" or with the "temporarily self-less"? Somewhere in between? Somewhere else?

Leaving these questions aside, for the time being, I wish to point out that all three modes are **within the realm of experience**. Reality touches us, each and every moment, and as long as our sense doors, or at least one of them, are there to meet their respective slices of it – we feel. And the mind is a sense door too. We sense and we perceive and we therefore experience. Having no experience is not the same as not clinging to experience – unless the emphasis in this expression is on **having**, that is, claiming experience as a possession of one's own. Then division and contraction occur (conventional-confined mode). Then duality is switched back on, and a thicker veil is thrown over the naked truth.

Mitchel asks:

And the naked truth? It seems naked of experience, naked of perception, and even naked of thought? We are exploring moments and not any fixed mode of being. No one is capable of non-stop I-you. But the non-experience can make us weary. So is that psychotic? Or perhaps dissociated?

Meeting and experiencing can be hard work or they can be a thrill or they can just be. When we "stream" in the second mode, we are not trying to manipulate or to control. We don't need to understand. We are listening to Jazz. We are improvising along. We are not concerned with reaching back, again and again, for our safe familiar base, to size up and feel our old selves – the selves that used to exist before the present meeting-moment, a year or a week or ten minutes ago. There's a certain kind of freedom there, a certain kind of aesthetic delight. In some other mental states, which are deep and tranquil, thought may temporarily cease. In some states, the I-sense is temporarily gone and we are even more free: free of the constructs it imposes on reality and of the immense effort needed to constantly create and maintain them. In each of these cases, if we are not deluded, we can touch deeper truths. But this does not mean that we are beyond experience altogether.

Experience is a characteristic of life: it is constantly changing, always conditioned, never independent or possessing an autonomous core. It is a result of mind and matter touching mind and matter. It appears and passes. It grows and decays. What is beyond experience has to also be beyond change, and therefore beyond mind and matter, life and death. In Buddhist terms, this is "Nibbāna" (Ud 8.1; Ud 8.3). Nibbāna too is without essential self-core, and so it doesn't offer an alternative solidity to grasp or to lean against (DN 22; Ud 8.1). And anyway, we are here. We are roaming the fields of experience, of relation and of relation to experience. This is our partly charted, mostly un-charted, homeland. Some of us, led by the love of truth – by the love of true meeting, by the love of You – try to explore it eyes open: to detect delusion and dissociation wherever they occur and to undermine them or to see through.

Being With: Meeting in the Stream of Experience

Being in touch with experience is being in touch with the world of mind and matter. Since the other (or Thou or You) is a part or the world, one may say that we treat whom we meet similarly to how we treat our experience. And this is true: if we are violent towards experience or if we are numb to it, there's a good reason to assume that the violence and numbness will find one way or another into our relationships, too. But there's another angle to the matter. Some people are having a very hard time being with experience. Others are quite accustomed and even skilful in being with experience internally, but find it extremely difficult – perhaps impossible – to be with their own experience while being with others. An example:

A person can look inside and be very much aware of his mental contents and overall mental and bodily state, but is only able to describe them to the therapist after the emotion or memory or other experience are already subsided or gone. Consequently, he cannot verbally and consciously communicate his experiences to the therapist while they are foggy, raw, elusive or otherwise undefined, but only when they are more fully formed. Both the process of feeling them out, searching the chaos for meaning and coherence, as well as the moments of clarification and insight, happen privately within and are only shared after the fact.

Experience is not a steady thing. It's a flow of events, rather unpredictable and therefore unknown. Riding the waves of experience with no hands, not allowing memory and desire (and anxiety and the need to understand) pour experience into fixed, familiar templates – wished or comfortable or dreaded – requires a considerable measure of trust and surrender. It requires F in O (Bion, 1970).

The self dreads dwelling in the unknown. It feels unheld, unwrapped, unframed and uncontained. But to dwell in the unknown in the presence of another means introducing an additional complex entity into the situation. In some cases, one person relies on the other: the other is felt as a safe "known." And so her presence supplies the ground, the holding, the wrapping, the frame, the container. It therefore relieves the dread and supports one in his quest to ride the waves of experience, to surrender and to dwell – eyes open in the darkness – in the unknown. But for the person I mentioned above, the therapist is yet but another unpredictable, untrusted element. For him, staying with her while keeping close touch with experience is absolutely impossible. At least for now. The darkness and chaos accumulate and grow too big. They cannot be felt and processed into what would eventually become a meaningful, nourishing substance. Instead, this person has to alternate between being with his experience (with himself, with "his truth") and being with his therapist (with another, in a relationship). One or the other must be abandoned. At each moment, something remains isolated, something is held on to and something is lost.

Another example:

A person can enjoy a pleasurable moment only while keeping her focus inside. She has to "eat it by herself." She must dissociate from feeling it and cannot enjoy it while in contact with her therapist or with her partner. Shame and anxiety are too strong to allow pleasure and company to co-exist. The danger in being seen when enjoying something is too great – she might be condemned or persecuted for it. She might be robbed of the pleasurable object altogether. She, too, faces a painful choice: either enjoyment is forsaken or connection. But enjoyment that must be kept in isolation is deficient to begin with ("if you eat alone, you die alone," as the saying goes); and a connection that cannot tolerate sheer delight is deprived too. Intimacy is broken at the root.

Mitchel wrote: "We are anxious when we sense an imminent loss and destruction of the current I-it that we possess." Anxiety and fear result from clinging to an ever-changing, perishable phenomena misperceived as enduring and essential, or in other words, clinging to a self or an object that are bound to be lost (Dhp 212–216; MN 138). The alternative would be to de-possess, not to hold on. But not at the expense of losing touch.

Being in touch with the flow of experience and seeing it for what it is (as appose to: A. dissociating from it, and B. remaining deluded about its nature) and Being With experience while Being With another require receptivity to the fluid and to the amorphous. We cannot infer deeper truths from solid, misperceived sense impressions and ready-made concepts that we cling to. We usually cannot move directly from K to O (Bion, 1970). Some solidity must be dissolved, some of our most primitive mental habits must be recognized and in some way subverted. Some wearisome functions, originally adaptive and vital for survival, presently still necessary in certain situations but otherwise overgeneralized, compulsive, restricting and superfluous, must be carefully and compassionately examined so as to weaken their domination.

What makes us weary? Memory, in Bion's sense of the word, makes us weary. Desire, definitely, as well as trying to hold on, to understand and to control. The further we get away from these, the less restless and tired we get when we meet, and the closer we get to, in Mitchel's words, "…being so present…," to "pure heart [...] and truth." We can only imagine (or we cannot imagine) a non-state which is entirely free of "memory and desire," of delusion, of selfhood, of any type or level of rejection or possessing, of restlessness and stress. Of creating and destroying? Of life and death?

Because ultimately, creation and destruction make us weary. The whole process of becoming and decaying is marked by challenge and fatigue. At the same time, creation is vitalizing, like breath, like oxygen. It can light us up like sunrise. And truth nourishes us and makes us grow. But the sun is cancerous and oxygen ages the tissue. "Oh God! May I be alive when I die," as Winnicott (1989, p. 4) prayed and Rina quoted in the first dialogue. "Oh God! May I be alive when I'm ill," as she paraphrased. Sense impressions constantly impinge on us, our habitual mental reactions are a drag, and even the relentless stream of consciousness is exhausting (SN 12.11). They create us and they create our worlds. We cling to them, and so they wear us out. We are clinging and we are tired and we are so marvellously alive! And so are most of the beings around us. We are partners in creation and destruction. We meet and we are met. For better and for worse, we are there to be touched.

Paul

You Can Never Speak Up Too Often for the Love of All Things[2]

You can never speak too often for the love of all things.
For every living thing or natural place on earth, there is someone
   who wants to kill or destroy it;

Therefore, you can never speak too often for the love of all things.

These families of geese that I watch as I sit beside the pond,
Two pairs, four adults, with their clutches of downy goslings
    who are carefully sheltered between the
    tall-necked, attendant goose and gander,
There is a hunter who yearns to kill them,
Who feels entitled to his killing of them,
Who would be outraged if you implied he had no right
    to gun them down in season.
This pond, set like an opal in the precious ring of earth,
    wind sparkling among shaded forests of hemlock and pine,
There is someone waiting to race his motorboat across it,
    knifing the soft skin of its silence,
    leaking oil into its pearl waters;
    develop it, build beaches,
    bring in crowds with boomboxes surging across
    macadamized parking lots.
Therefore, you can never speak up too often for the love of all
    things.

All beings spring up from the same womb of life.
Sunlight strikes the earth, plants catch it, and as they hold light
    in their secret birthing place,
The embryo of life unfolds in their leaves and seeds.
This green gift of light becomes the food that feeds
    the worlds of birds and beasts and men.
All beings share the same joy that flows in the company of other
    lives.
All beings share the same tremor in the face of death.
Therefore, you can never speak up too often with the love of all
    things.

The silence found throughout the world in evening ponds,
    unbroken forests, mountain-enfolded ravines,
    hilltops at dusk,
Is not an absence of noise, but a presence.
In the company of silence, people hear more clearly the passage
    of eternity,

rustling between the cells of their own mind,
like wind through a screen.
In the calm of silence — as if its arms were folded, and a presence
were waiting,
watching, patiently devoid of impulse or haste —
People hear the common tongue of love, the universal language
of mortal things, soft, like a baby's voice,
passing from person to person, pulsing from
trees and grass and animals, connecting
existence with existence.
Through the universal silent sound of mortal joy, individual life
becomes bonded, tolerable, and touched.
Aware of this,
You can never speak up too often with the love of all things.

In the heart of every hunter, silence breaker, mass murderer, taker
of life big or small
Is static.
Due to this static, some people cannot hear the way that tall grass
stems
sing lullabies to their neighboring grass; or
the ways that birds, anxious, fretful, diligent,
chase after their new-flown fledglings with
morsels of food, or with admonitions of danger.
Those who are bedeviled by the static give it names that please
them.
They befriend and flatter the static; calling it god, praising it as
a folkway or as an heirloom.
They say the power of the static in their minds exempts them
from the laws of love.
The deer hunter feels enthroned above the animals —he has
forgotten,
lost touch with, cannot feel the way the
doe turns to nuzzle along in haste the fawn,
heart-beating, eager to spur it on towards
safety.
The terrorist, ethnic cleanser, nationalist, religionist, invokes the
names

and ideas of old books and imposing buildings.
They are deaf to the inaudible, dumb to the unspoken common
    tongue.
Listening to static and lost to love they kill the Jews of Europe, the
    Tutsis
        of East Africa, the intelligentsia of Cambodia, the
        elephants of the Congo, the orangutans of Borneo, the
        Atlantic and Pacific and Arctic whales.
Killing is indiscriminate and everywhere, the excuse changes, the
    reason
        changes, the alleged necessity changes.
Therefore, you can never speak up too often for the love of all
    things.

Here is a pond on a summer afternoon, its water iridescent green
        and blue beneath the long bright solar rays,
And here is a young man and young woman dipping into the water,
        merging their bodies with the body of the pond.
From long ago they ran from hunters; as deer they ran from men
    with
        painted faces and burning torches in the
        Pleistocene night;
As rabbits they ran from dripping dogs;
For generations, their ancestors were Jewish runners, homeless
    here and
        there across the landmass of Europe, chased by
        people with a dozen different pedigrees.
As Africans they came in chains.
As trees, they were cut down at their feet, and fell on their faces.

Today, the pond skin shimmers in ecstasy of love as the breeze
    draws
        its fingers across the water's surface.
The young man and the young woman dip into the pond's original
    and
        fathomless watery womb.
And their child, who years later comes to the pond, dives in
        all sweat and muscle, bull-necked from
        mowing in the field,

His jeans and hair are jumbled with hay stems of daisies and wild
pinks.
For each and every presence, place, person, animal, plant, on
this earth,
there is someone who wants to kill or destroy them,
And there is also a great and universal love inside them, a love and
joy entwined, like a young man after a day's
work diving into a summer pond,
Like water, green, blue, clear, murky, impenetrably old primal
element
of life, catching him, bathing him, whispering to
him unbeknownst to him himself, the secret and
universal words:
You can never speak up too often for the love of all things.

Michal

These unfathomed states and emotions that I watch as I'm sitting
here with you, in this room, with the pomelo blossom scent gently
gliding through, every now and then, whenever the north-west breeze
becomes nearly noticeable; these unfathomed states and emotions,
with the claws of self-identity holding on to them, to the flesh of the
heart, to the streams of sensation and thought; tall necked and attendant, their luxurious plumage covering still finer states and emotions
in need of shelter, whose soft organs mix up with those of their protectors, peeking out only rarely, when a sign of love appears, the perfect arch of a true embrace; when enough evidence gathers to prove
it is safe;

These unfathomed states and emotions that I watch as I sit here
with you – there's someone who wants to kill them. Who feels entitled
to do so, who feels it's his job. Who would be outraged if I implied
he had no right to do so, or that it would be a shame if he did, or
that he actually could not destroy them completely, only twist them
into something else; only temporarily bury, temporarily exile, ostensibly erase; only make their protectors grow thicker feathers for better
cover, only make self-identity's claws grow bigger, adhering to them
more tightly, more stubbornly.

As we sit here, in this room, I hear the static. It comes and goes in waves: denial, objectification, cynicism, doubt, self-loathing, conceit. Sometimes it is an undercurrent, impinging and annoying while beauty still lives. Sometimes it increases, making the creatures of the mind deaf to the inaudible, dumb to the unspoken, common tongue shared by all living things. It is capable of killing fragile creatures. It is ready and willing to kill. It cuts through good thoughts and severs lush links. It interrupts the signals of love and doesn't allow them to reach and call out the soft ones in hiding. It makes the most convincing excuses: the reasons change, the fashion and expression change – but the outcome is the same.

I shake myself from its domination, I touch it, my fingertips sensitive, while the volume of beauty increases.

Here, in this room, on an April afternoon, something ancient is awakened in you. A huge pelican casting its shade upsets the seemingly peaceful surface of your water. An octopus shuffles a pile of prehistoric pebbles that have lain untouched for years. A school of small silver fish sharply changes direction. A cold stream surges, yellow gas drifts up, the water is coloured smoke-like by ink.

Just the other week you said that you feel you are ready for life, ready for more. Just a moment ago (I could see the reflection in the pond of your gaze) you were thinking you finally reached a firm shore. Your intellect knows that change is there (that change is life; that change is the curse and the opportunity of all living things; that change is your "more"), but the claws of self-identity and of other attendant protectors clutch at the shore.

You were thinking that you were ready for more, and you were thinking you had reached solid ground, and the interface of these two currents felt smooth and pleasant and right. You felt like the best you ever! And your intellect missed the fact that logically, these two currents do not coincide. But in the sea of mind and matter, logic is just one opinion. For some it is well maintained and strong, carried around everywhere like an old tool box or lived in like an inherited house. For some it's as flimsy and dangling as an insect's limb. For some it is a form of art, for some it's a lie, for others it's the art of deceit. Either way it is not a sovereign, and different currents flow along without its permission. You thought that you were ready for more, and you thought that you were standing on a reliably firm shore, and you felt relieved and victorious; and you missed the fact of change stirring underneath and above it all. That it's coming without your permission. That this is your more.

I smile at you. I feel the dread of your grounds shifting, and I smile at you.

Once upon a time there was a man who imagined this smile to be dismissive, indifferent, almost ridiculing. His static was very loud and high pitched. He was outraged. He tried to smash my smile with sharp metal weapons. He scared off my white-tailed fondness of him, my staggering fawn legs approaching, with his blazing flames of hate. Years have passed since then, years of smiles and scare and approaching and blazing flames. Now I smile and look at you with my big brown doe eyes, gently nuzzling your frightened lost young ones, gently nuzzling mine.

With these eyes and this smile, in this room, with the curtain quietly moving, closer and away from the window that reaches down to the floor, almost entirely open – anything can become. You look back at me for clues of what's going on. I'm not offering any answers – not out of cruelty or impassivity, not because I'm not allowed to, not because I want to manipulate you into arriving at the right answers on your own – but because any answer, no matter what, would be wrong and deadening in this moment; because the window is almost entirely open, and the curtain is quietly swaying on the hardly felt breath of air, and we have nothing to do but sway along.

We now sway in the soft, citrus wind. We now drift in the wind that has grown stronger. We now fall into the water, hugging ourselves, just in time. Now we swim together in the branched tributary of mind and matter. We are immersed in the golden pond of beings capable of knowing other beings.

Now we sink into a deep well, moving in the dark groundwaters, bumping into pointy, tiny stones, blocked by harsh walls. Now we clutter in resentment, freeze in terror, turn ourselves into stones.

We are then completely fed up with being still and buried. We break open the ground, erupt like lava, blaze in flames, swirling in smoke. Then we gloomily flow down the mountain, cooled and clogged by shame and regret. Then we breathe sweet air again, sighing with relief, soaking up the warmth of the spring sun, grass and the modest yellow flowers sprouting from our feet and hands.

As we sit here, in this room, the titmice skip from branch to branch of the pomelo tree. One stops and briefly looks at me, his chatter joining your voice, the slight, scented wind, the stream of my thoughts, our heartbeats. And I feel love for you. I feel love for the finest and thickest feathers, the stubborn claws, the tender ones, hiding, the hasty protectors rushing to the front; the short-handed logic, the smooth surface that covers cross-currents, the pebbles and pointy rocks; the staggering movement, the misplaced and the misconceived, the slight and unfathomable, the all-pervasive mist. I feel love for our shared tremor, for our dread of the horrible things done to us, done by us, done to others, done but never felt. I feel love for all that is not shared

This moment of silence now, between us, is not an absence but a presence. It is suffused with ancient past coming alive, with the fumes of lucidity rising up from the golden pond of beings capable of feeling other beings. It is suffused with whatever is.

Stone walls may melt, sighing in relief as they shed away the burden of blockage and ownership, or they may remain, as if forever, tall and grey and stern. Our dark-blue groundwater may turn sweet and pure, or it may be poisoned and poison other wells. Our lava may destroy anything in its course, turning flourishing civilizations into Pompei – or it may become the most fertile soil on earth. Exotic, magnificent things can grow on it, or the most modest mould and grass, for the simplest bare feet and snails.

The stone walls are only seemingly solid, the lava only seemingly invincible, the deep, ancient caverns only seemingly beyond reach. And in this room, in this moment, all the great elements of matter and all the creatures of the mind come together, and pulse, and swim, and shift. And they wait. They wait for the unmutilated signals of love, for the long ready embrace. They have no other way of being truly seen. They have no other way of being truly met. Someone should listen and someone should sing: you can never speak up too often for the love of all things.

Paul

The poem, "You Can Never Speak Up Too Often for the Love of All Things," may have more psychological origins than I am aware of. It certainly derives partly from some frightened and objectifying experiences like a Holocaust and its echo in the hunting habits that North Americans take for granted. But the poem has its deepest root, I think, in a set of childhood experiences that I would call, "savage receptivity" or "natural fusion." This aspect of my psychological world came about in the following way:

In the late nineteenth century, as North America industrialized, the air around its big cities, like the New York metropolitan area, became heavily polluted. The impact of this pollution on the health of children was rationalized away through economic necessity, the need for family, and the importance of school. But during the summer, when even Northeast North America gets very hot, the air pollution created a stifling environment, and responsible parents sent their children to summer camps in the dispersed open lands that were still widely available in the United States. Summer camps varied by economic strata and by ethnicity.

By the twentieth century, children's summer camps were established institutions, but they tended to exclude the children of parents who did not have adequate economic means. Private organizations, like corporations and charities, began to provide "fresh air funds" where poorer children could have an outdoor summer away from the city at a subsidized cost.

I went to a semi-private, semi-subsidized fresh air fund camp in the Pocono hills of Pennsylvania not far from my home city of Newark, New Jersey, which was part of metropolitan New York. The camp I went to had almost no infrastructure. Children were sent to the woods to live under primitive shelters made of canvas lashed to wooden poles and sticks. These shelters stopped rain coming down from the sky, but were open on the sides, accessible to wind or damp air, and a magnet for mosquitoes and flies. We lived like savages. This rough immersion in nature was mythologized into the quintessential Native American pioneer, backwoods experience. The more mosquito bites you had on your skin, the truer a boy you were. There was no kitchen, and the only stove was a wood fire.

In this unhoused, barely sheltered, primeval lifestyle I developed over serial summers into a person who had many animal instincts.

We lived by the light of the sun, moon and stars. Birds sang to us from a few feet away. We bathed in streams and rivers. We shared paths with deer. We were antisocially unshowered and ragged. We sat around campfires with flickering light from incandescing carbon scintillating across our retinas. We sang. We revelled in knowledge about trees, wild flowers and ferns.

The central feature of this way of life was its unfiltered receptivity to the living organic whole biospheric atmosphere. We were denizens at the bottom of the great green pyramid and we inhaled its smells, sounds and relationships. The music of thrushes was part of every evening and every morning, and we lost the ability to clearly differentiate ourselves from the other inhabitants of planet Earth.

I felt that there was a life that preexisted before all lives, and that it moved through and within me as it did through and within everything else in the savage state.

This is the background to the stanza of the poem that begins, "The silence found throughout the world..." This is why I believe, "The silence is not an absence, but a presence." In my teenage years, I clearly and repeatedly heard "...the passage of eternity, rustling between the cells of my mind...a presence waiting...a universal language of mortal things...connecting existence with existence."

I don't know whether this way of developing, removed from civilization and immersed in nature, was an experience, a transcendence of experience, an I-thou experience, or a fusion. It made me feel a great and universal love, and an empathic vulnerability. I revel in it, and I suffer from it.

Like Wordsworth, I felt the intensity and frequency of these savage fusions fade but they are still with me and informed this poem.

Michal

"In this unhoused, barely sheltered" environment, with no parents around and no surrounding walls, I can imagine myself, or someone else, become a person with "many animal instincts." Animal or human, such instincts and formations can manifest differently, depending on personal and interpersonal, physical and psychic circumstances, traits and contexts.

I can easily imagine the simple, rough conditions taken in as too harsh impingements (the wind, the damp air, the insect bites, the probably uncomfortable beds; the lack of private room or bathroom, only shared spaces), creating a sense of being unprotected, attacked and hunted, lonely and deserted. And how, facing this continuously, all sorts of second-skin and other protective layers may grow.

But I can as easily imagine the situation taking an entirely different course, leading to different tracks of life and experience. I can see it evolving into what Paul had named "savage receptivity," allowing for and resulting from one's immersion in nature and in the aesthetic experience. I can see it evolving into empathic vulnerability and the capacity for universal love, which in their pure form, I think, spring not from the delusional-denying aspect of fusion, but from deep connection with internal and external reality, from sensing and recognizing and intimately knowing the immanent vulnerability, ephemerality and dependency of all things. I can see it evolving into a capacity to stand, as Wordsworth (1799 I.17–26) put it, naked in a thunder-shower, in a world bronzed with a deep radiance (p. 15), a vibrant being amongst all vibrant beings and things. Perhaps like him, who was "fostered alike by beauty and by fear" (p. 15).

Mitchel

"You can never speak up too often for the love of all things." Two weeks ago the porch to my house was "confiscated." It was made clear to me that I no longer had free reign or freedom of movement on my own porch. And I was caused to even feel a slight but present anxiety if I were to move too freely.

A mother cat had discovered an open closet on the porch with a well-padded shelf to have her babies. I anxiously brought the mother food to eat and water to drink. As I placed the water she leaped at my hand and drew first blood between us. She had a look that my son later explained to me, "She is all mother instinct and no mind function." That look was saying a fight to the death but don't take it personally.

My neighbour complains saying, "the mother cat keeps attacking me every time I open the window to my porch, you have to do something!!" (her porch is attached to mine). I gently open discussion with the mother cat, she is a bit more reasonable than my neighbour. The mother cat tells me she will try, but no promises.

Eventually the porch is freed but not before an overwhelming party of fleas is invited by our gracious mother cat host (apparently a known phenomenon). I sense the fleas invading the pores of my skin. And I angrily forget the beauty of nature.

"You can never speak up too often for the love of all things" suddenly feels different. We need to speak up for the sake of our own hardened hearts. We need not only to remind the world of its natural ease of forgetting love, but to remind our own heart and soul of our own capacity to abandon our inherent love of all things.

As I read Paul's poem, I heard Paul's music. As I read Michal's ruminations, I heard the tides of our being. We are always moving. Moving to unknown and undigested worlds yet to be experienced. And in counter movement, simultaneously seeking known land. I know of grasping, even of desperate grasping. Grasping of possession, of knowledge, of experience, of an other's time place and person. But in between the caretakering of oneself, there is a moment of O – an unfathomable unformulated enigmatic moment that says the milk is honey, the air is sea-salty and the ground is gently solidly singing its love ballads. But because this place and state is unfathomable, it is not experienced as sense or even as experience as we know it. It is in the form of a strange yet intimate truth that has no actual, material, milk sea or song but rather a simple and yet infinite wave of the soul, sweet as honey, vitalizing as sea air and enwrapping as the ground of our being.

Paul

We are indebted to Martin Buber for pointing us towards the clouds of knowing.

This Trialogue reminds me about the final indeterminacy of thinking and writing about our lives. Writing is like trying to stuff clouds into containers. Each person's language contains both recognizable conventions and strangely-shaped mysteries. Other peoples' reports about their psychological world are always simultaneously familiar to our shared categories of human experience, and also unfamiliar, with pulsing and shape shifting commentary.

We need all those firm categories, beliefs, compartmentalizations, I-it experiences in order to negotiate the pragmatics of living as animals, bodies and pack members. But we also always aspire to escape from the static and confined world, because it is not accurate to the continuous morphing that is the essential process of everything in the universe, including our subjective interiority.

So we are constantly bouncing among our psychological balloons, and we are constantly encountering our friends, family and tribe members whose clouds and balloons are bouncing against and mingling with our own.

Most people have favourite and savoured escape hatches that open out into unconfined realities. Communing with nature is one of them. Music is another. But language is the great guiding paradox. It is language that conceptualizes, defines and contains the world inside the cognitions of experiences. But it is also language that creates the woodland trails of subtlety, musicality, intuition, juxtaposition and gnosis that all elevate human life into its thin, high stratosphere. Talking and writing are our prison and our escape, and through the iterations of a lifetime of language we create the banners by which our life waves aloft in the sky.

When I was studying to be a psychiatrist, psychotropic medications were still relatively new and sometimes dangerous, with side effects like dangerous falls of blood pressure. So, very agitated patients who required heavy doses of medication, or repeat doses, were still managed with the ancient tools of the psychiatric profession. Really wildly troubled people were wrapped in cold sheets, an experience that desperately disturbed people would find to be calming and anchoring.

I only recently realized that my obsession with swimming in outdoor ponds and lakes during the short North American summer is a kind of wet blanket treatment for myself. Here the skin, the hypothalamic thermo-regulators and the vasomotor reactions, subsume my human identity, and allow me to submerge into a primeval body-based animal, wrapped in his enveloping media. Last week I swam in a pond that had both a snapping turtle and a snake, and I partly felt them to be frightening enemies, but I also recognized that they were my siblings.

Mitchel

> The its of our being
> Where sense and experience know each other well
> She is mine

The object of my mind
What is me is me
I negotiate what is you
I learn to know you
To see you
To recognize you
An object that is not me
and yet you are my experience
and thus a part of me
my possession
to be as I sense
as I see hear smell and touch
my experience
my other

And yet winds of the sea
musical notes of beating hearts
And the clouds of being
Before narration
Seek no where
No taste
No smell
Until after the O
For if I smell and taste
It is the aftermath of the unfathomable encounter
When face to face
There wrapped in the sky's blanket of infinity
Eyes meet
Undreamed Dreams and untold stories packed in nanoville
Infinite languages in Borges' libraries of Babel
And before a book is selected
Before a knowing is known
a non-experience of two unnamed I-less subjects
Experiencing freedom from experiencing
Already enamored in a touch-less touch
Whisper without a word
"Hineni"[3].

Notes

1 Pāli: sakkāya diṭṭhi.
2 Paul R. Fleischman, 1999. Sweet Pond, Guilford, Vermont, May 31 1999 – Memorial Day. From: Paul R. Fleischman (2005), You Can Never Speak Up Too Often for the Love of All Things, Onalaska, WA: Pariyatti Press.
3 Hebrew for "Here I am."

References

Bion, W.R. (1970). *Attention and Interpretation*. London: Tavistock.
Dhp 212–216.
DN 22.
Fleischman, P.R. (2005). *You Can Never Speak Up Too Often for the Love of All Things*. Onalaska, WA: Pariyatti Press.
MN 138.
Sandler, J. (1993). On Communication from Patient to Analyst: Not Everything Is Projective Identification. *International Journal of Psycho-Analysis* 74: 1097–1107.
SN 12.11.
Ud 8.1.
Ud 8.3.
Winnicott, D.W. (1989). *Psychoanalytic Explorations*. Ed. Clare Winnicott, Ray Shepherd & Madeleine Davis. Cambridge, MA: Harvard University Press.
Wordsworth, W. (1799). *The Prelude or Growth of a Poet's Mind: An Autobiographical Poem*. London: Edward Moxon, 1850.

Epilogue
The Clouds of Knowing

Michal Barnea-Astrog

We're feeling out "the clouds of knowing" (Fleischman, 2023), where the centre is strangely luminated as the fringes grow dark. Or the clouds of unknowing, where it's supposedly the other way around.

Martin Buber's face gazes at me from the cover of The Dialogue on Man and Being (1923), as I pull it out from its local temporal community of texts and thinkers. I have no idea what kind of person he really was, but his brown eyes seem warm and wise. His moustache joins his beard, both slightly overgrown. Somehow, he looks fatherly to me (my father's eyes are brown this way, and when I was a child, he had long, wild moustache and beard of his own). And I think of Buber's ultimate meeting with the tree: the tree which is not inserted into any kind of category, which is being totally taken in, unmediated by imagination, rationalization, desire or memory. I swing from a branch of this tree and feel the weight of my body, the stretch of my arms, the warm air on my face, the swift and light flow of my thoughts. I swing from a branch of this tree and jump into a deep round well of O.

And in this well, I can feel the ghosts of those who preceded me, of those who are there at present and of those who are yet to come. The ghosts of beings who feel lonely and frightened in the unknown, who freeze down there or desperately try to climb the slippery walls. I imagine the letters F, H, L and K (Bion, 1962)[1] being used as stools or as ladders. F flips from side to side, from Faith to Fear, like a fluttering fish gasping for a watery breath outside of his natural habitat. H swirls around its axis like a wind vane, from Hate to Hope, from Hope to Hate, from Hate to Hope. L remains Love, but it has no bars, only a thin base and a tall pole, and it requires dedication and

Learning to climb on. K offers quite a few hinges to cling to, but you could easily slip right down its slides and the climbing is steep and effortful.

Dwelling deep in a round form, a circle, O. Confined in its own perfect, primordial contours or infinite; vast like space or contracted and dense, sucking everything like a black hole. Then the circle of Zen pops into my mind, and the Zen *mudra* (hands meditation position), which forms a round empty zero. And the late Korean Zen master Seung Sahn's teaching, which I briefly encountered over two decades ago, before undertaking the practice of Vipassana, echoes: "Only don't know."

Becoming in O. Suspending the urges to understand and to interpret and to control. Relinquishing memory and desire. Relinquishing any boxed sense of the self and of the other. Clearing some space and maintaining it unsaturated. Shedding adherences to conventional, superficial truths in order to touch deeper ones. Not neglecting the old ones altogether (simply forgetting doesn't work), but changing their status. Seeing the clouds and the light and the vastness and the bright or dark fringes. Following the fringes until they open up into fields of meaning; or until they melt completely and drop us in the midst of nothing, which might contain everything but offers nothing to hold on to.

Knowing deepens when objectification subsides, when the I-It relation turns into I-You. It deepens further when other realms are entered, where the self-and-other constructs become obsolete and wither away too. Then in seeing, there's mere seeing. In hearing, there's mere hearing. In sensing, there's mere sensing. In knowing, there's mere knowing. No self-filters involved (Ud 1.10; DN 22).

I sit in this deep well and feel the ghosts of lonely and frightened beings who desperately try to climb its slippery walls, the ghosts of beings whose F flutters between Faith and Fear and whose H swirls between Hate and Hope. And like a most pleasant, gentle breeze, I also feel the others, who have gone there to enjoy the pure waters of truth, of a knowing that is beyond the knowable. I feel how some of them just sit there, and linger, letting the light breeze touch their arms and faces, hearing the distant birds' song. Until the walls of the well disappear altogether and all points of reference are gone. And there we meet. Eyes open, eyes closed.

***

Note

1 Bion preferred to use single letters to remind the reader that all of the psychoanalytic conceptualizations are forms of representations of emotional experience and not a real thing. The letters "L," "H" and "K" are the three "links." Links are forms of relations between people. People either love (L), hate (H) or know (K) the other. This is close to Freud's three instincts, love, death and epistemophilia in a relationship.

The letters F and O are more complex. F represents "Faith." Faith that a truth exists. Truth is O.

Bion (1970) writes, "I shall use the sign O to denote that which is the ultimate reality represented by terms such as ultimate reality, absolute truth, the godhead, the infinite, the thing-in-itself. O does not fall in the domain of knowledge or learning save incidentally; it can be 'become' but it cannot be 'known'" (p. 26).

References

Bion, W.R. (1962). *Learning from Experience*. London: Tavistock.
Buber, M. (1923). *The Dialogue on Man and Being*.
DN 22.
Ud 1.10.
Fleischman, P.R. (2023). *Third Associative Trialogue: On "No Experience" with All My Heart and Soul* (with Michal Barnea-Astrog & Mitchel Becker). In: M. Barnea-Astrog & M. Becker (Ed.), *Relational Conversations on Meeting and Becoming: The Birth of a True Other*. London: Routledge.

Index

For Product Safety Concerns and Information please contact our EU
representative GPSR@taylorandfrancis.com
Taylor & Francis Verlag GmbH, Kaufingerstraße 24, 80331 München, Germany